D1196364

THEODORA

WOMEN IN ANTIQUITY

Series Editors: Ronnie Ancona and Sarah B. Pomeroy

This book series provides compact and accessible introductions to the life and historical times of women from the ancient world. Approaching ancient history and culture broadly, the series selects figures from the earliest of times to late antiquity.

THEODORA

ACTRESS, EMPRESS, SAINT

David Potter

OXFORD
UNIVERSITY PRESS

Oxford University Press is a department of the University of Oxford. It furthers the
University's objective of excellence in research, scholarship, and education by publishing
worldwide. Oxford is a registered trademark of Oxford University Press in the UK and certain
other countries.

Published in the United States of America by
Oxford University Press
198 Madison Avenue, New York, NY 10016

© Oxford University Press 2015

Cataloging-in-Publication data is on file at the Library of Congress
ISBN 978–0–19–974076–5

1 3 5 7 9 8 6 4 2
Printed in the United States of America
on acid-free paper

Contents

Maps

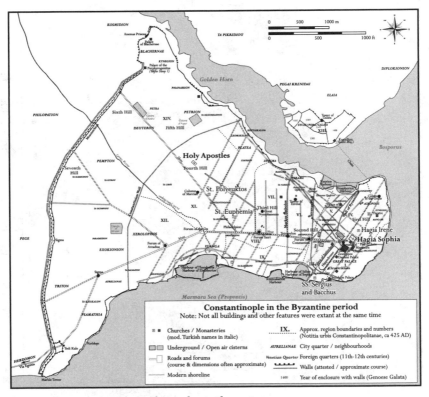

MAP 1. Constantinople in the early sixth century.

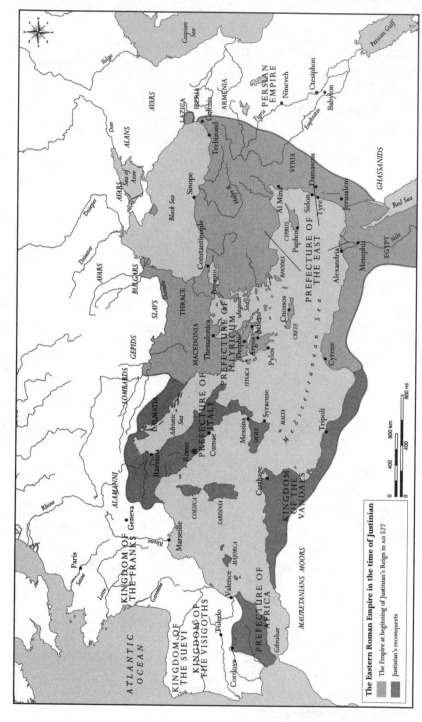

MAP 2. The Eastern Roman Empire in the time of Justinian.

Acknowledgments

I owe many debts in the composition of this book, first to the series editors and Stefan Vranka for suggesting this topic, and again to Stefan for his help in actually finishing the book. Lester Monts, as Senior Vice Provost for Academic Affairs, offered invaluable support for the research at its inception. I also received crucial assistance from scholars who shared with me work that was either forthcoming or difficult to access through Michigan's library, including Geoffrey Greatrex, Henning Böhm, John Scarborough, John Matthews, and Manna Vestrinen—who sent me her unpublished doctoral dissertation on actresses, a splendid work that enabled me to understand Theodora's initial profession. As this book was in its final stages Professor Maria Wyke enabled me to see scenes from Carlucci's *Theodora*, while teaching me, and others, about film's emergence as a medium of expression in her splendid series of Jerome Lectures. I owe an especially great debt to Oxford University Press's anonymous referee, whose generosity has saved me from many errors and caused me to rethink a variety of issues. I could not have undertaken the book without Jason Zurawski, who, with great patience, enabled me to appreciate the wonders of Coakley's Syriac grammar. Matt Newman was an extremely helpful reader of the manuscript at an early stage, as was Laura McCullagh; Kevin Lubrano and Parrish Wright provided important help at a later stage. Pete Oas listened to this story unfold over coffee at the *locus amoenus* provided by the Expresso Royale on Plymouth Road in Ann Arbor, Michigan. Sue Philpott proved again that she is the best copy editor anyone could hope to work with.

Claire, Natalie, and Ellen tolerated the persistent home invasion by yet another ancient person. It is with this in mind that the book is dedicated to the women in my life.

Introduction

On Monday the eleventh of August, AD 559, Emperor Justinian entered Constantinople. Many dignitaries greeted him as he rode through the Charisios Gate on the city's northwest side. Before going any farther, before traversing avenues so crowded that there was barely room for his horse to pass, Justinian stopped. He turned in to the great Church of the Holy Apostles, close by the city gate. There he lit candles in memory of his empress, who had died eleven years earlier. They had had no children together, nor would he have any in the future, nor even remarry. She had been his "gift from God," the great love of his life.

The story of Justinian and his empress Theodora is one of the most remarkable in the long history of the Mediterranean world. She had been an actress—not a respectable profession in sixth-century Constantinople. He was born into a south–central European family of peasants. She had sustained him through two great crises when it seemed that their rule might end. She was tough; she was smart, very smart—even those who hated her would grant her that. She was passionate. She was extremely beautiful. Beauty and passion were two of her qualities that even those who hated her would acknowledge. She championed the downtrodden and protected the weak; she was steadfastly loyal to her friends. Her enemies feared her, and with good reason.

We may still see her in all her splendor in the astonishing mosaics that decorate the Church of San Vitale in Ravenna. We can feel the intensity of her being as we gaze into her eyes. She dominates the scene, far outstripping her husband, who faces her. Outside the church the same is true, even in the twenty-first century: "Ah, Teodora," said the woman running the shop where I stopped to pick up some souvenirs, as if speaking of a dear friend. Theodora's image was everywhere.

Theodora—her name does indeed mean "gift from God"—is today a saint of the Syrian Orthodox Church. To some she was the "beloved queen." To others she was a demon incarnate.

Theodora lived at a time when people felt the hand of God guiding their lives. They believed in a God who would take note of their sins, a God who would protect them in their faith or punish them terribly for their impieties. She lived at a time when people believed it was possible for the lucky or pious to see the angels who gathered around the altar when the priest prepared the communion offering. These same people believed, too, that it was entirely possible to encounter a menacing demon while walking down the street. They knew that some people were closer to God than others, and that such individuals would often voluntarily subject themselves to great privations. Most people hoped that one of these special persons might help with his or her problems, channelling divine force to protect them. One might glimpse the preternaturally pious "Stylites" standing on pillars that reached towards heaven, perhaps dressed in rags; the pious might gather about these pillars, inspecting the feces and observing the exercises of the saintly.

Everyone knew that raids from across the imperial frontier might shatter their lives at any moment; that their empire was not what it once was. They knew that God's vengeance could be even more terrible than the pain caused by their human enemies. Contemporary chroniclers refer to natural disaster as the "wrath of God," and the Roman Empire in the sixth century had more than its share of disasters, in the form of violent earthquakes and all-enveloping tsunamis. It was also a time of war and riot; Constantinople would be wrecked once in Justinian's time by its own citizens, and again by "the wrath of God." And it was in Justinian's and Theodora's time, too, that the bubonic plague first came to Europe and the Mediterranean lands.

Theodora was the product of an age of rapid transition; she was the agent of change. Everyone agreed on these things, even those who disliked her intensely. Of such people there were quite a few in her day, and their spokesman for us today is a man named Procopius.

Procopius was a secretary and advisor to Belisarius, a great general of the period, who wrote about the wars of his and Theodora's lifetime, and about the great building projects of her husband. He also wrote the *Secret History*, a denunciation of Justinian, Theodora, and all their works, unpublished in his own lifetime. The interpretation of the *Secret History*, the answer to the question of whether it should be seen as a profound work of criticism or a nasty partisan pamphlet, is a central problem in trying to understand Theodora's life. We will be returning to the issue again and again in the course of this book, for even if we agree to view Procopius' book as a collection of scandalous misrepresentations (the correct approach in my view), we will see that not all scandalous stories are created equal. Some may be simple inventions, but others may conceal important truths within themselves.

Of those who loved Theodora, their most vociferous spokesman today is John, once bishop in the countryside around Ephesus, the great city of western Turkey (the modern Efes). John of Ephesus was born near Amida (modern Diyarbakir) in eastern Turkey; his parents placed him in a religious community when he was six years old. He rose to greatness through his passionate advocacy of the religious beliefs of his people; his portraits of Theodora come to us through his *Lives of the Eastern Saints*, in which he records the deeds of men and women who, like him, devoted themselves to asserting the correctness of the brand of Christianity that countered the decrees of the Council of Chalcedon of AD 451 and was dominant in the Eastern empire.

The council of Chalcedon had imposed a definition of the relationship between the human and divine aspects of Jesus Christ—the crucial question for understanding the significance of his life and crucifixion—in a way that many regarded as unacceptable, allowing as it did that Jesus had a human as well as a divine nature. It was his human aspect that had suffered on the cross and died. Furthermore, the split between supporters and opponents of Chalcedon's definition of the relationship between the members of the Holy Trinity—Father, Son, and Holy Spirit—was partly theological and partly political, bound up with differing notions of community within the empire. Ultimately, the most serious of these splits proved to be between majorities within groups whose first languages were Greek and Latin as opposed to those within groups who spoke the Coptic tongue of Egypt or the Syriac of Rome's eastern frontier.

The schism at Chalcedon was not the only big split that shaped the world in which Theodora lived. The breakdown of the relationship between the eastern and western halves of the Roman Empire, which took place about forty years before Theodora's birth, fundamentally altered ancient power relationships. Even before the final collapse of the Western empire, a couple of decades before she was born, there had ceased to be a recognizably traditional governing class. Generals born outside the empire vied with officials from rural Anatolia and Thrace. Eunuchs from beyond the frontier played crucial roles in the politics of the new age, and bishops whose command of Latin and Greek—the traditional languages of government—was decidedly secondary to their abilities in Coptic or Syriac vied for power with bishops whose first tongue was Greek or Latin. A peasant raised in a monastery outside Amida, when elevated to the rank of bishop, would be more influential than well-educated urban Greeks who occupied lesser places in the imperial bureaucracy. The question of what gave any person the right to govern, of what qualities might open the path to power and influence, was far more open now than at any time in the earlier Roman Empire. It is quite possible that merit actually mattered more in the sixth century than in the previous eight hundred years of Roman dominance.

The sixth century was not only a time of extraordinary ferment and crisis; it was also an era of extraordinary accomplishment. Every day, we live with the achievements of these years. On a mundane level, we can instance as deriving from this time the belief that Jesus of Nazareth was born during the year Romans knew as the consulship of Gaius Caesar and Lucius Aemilius Paullus, in the 754th year after the foundation of the city of Rome. This is our AD 1—Anno Domini 1. It is also to this era, and to the direction of Justinian, that we owe the codification of Roman law that established the foundation of the European tradition of civil law, and it is to the genius of the emperor's architect, Anthemius, that we owe the glory of the great church of Hagia Sophia, which even today dominates Istanbul's skyline. We may even owe to forces with which Justinian and Theodora had to deal in the Arabian peninsula, the passions that fueled the visions of the prophet Mohammed.

Theodora's story is not easy to tell. We cannot be certain we have a single word she spoke; both her friends and her enemies were prone to put words into her mouth, and the letters attributed to her in the surviving tradition have no great claims to authenticity. Hers is a life known through others. It is, in a sense, a palimpsest, a document that has been erased so that its writing surface can be reused. Often we can uncover what was originally there, since few erasures are ever complete. Thus, as with old written-over manuscripts, or Istanbul itself, we can glean a knowledge of Theodora indirectly, reading sometimes quite literally between the lines, by setting older accounts of what things looked like alongside what we now see before us. We can walk the streets of old Istanbul, feel the air, and, in "Aya Sofya," Theodora's Hagia Sophia, we can stand where she stood overlooking the great church from the "empress's spot," watching the devotions of her husband and of the other men who were allowed to enter the church proper. Or we can stand in the much more intimate space of the Church of Sergius and Bacchus, which survives today as the Küçük Ayasofya Camii, or "Little Hagia Sophia Mosque," down below the Blue Mosque, which stands where the imperial palace once stood.

Most importantly, we can still hear how people spoke to each other, reading their words in their own languages so as to begin to understand what motivated them, what they saw, loved, and feared. We probe the shadows of tradition and interview the phantoms of history, both hostile and friendly, for the truth, which we find in silences as often as in assertions. As we do so, we may find that the questions she faced were questions that we still face. Can a woman do the same job as a man in the same way—or, indeed, should she even attempt to? Are expectations different? Do gendered stereotypes prevent women from holding the same positions as men? Could Theodora be a woman *and* a ruler?

In the end, we may find Theodora by first understanding the contexts within which she acted. Through invective and through adulation, we will discover some patterns that will help us detect *some* truths, at least; and we must admit that there are very basic things about her life that we can never know. The things that we can know reveal to us a person who was in life every bit as remarkable as the image we have of her in San Vitale.

1

Constantinople

This story begins in Constantinople, probably in the area currently occupied by Istanbul University. It most likely started at the foot of the hills that drop down towards the Golden Horn. The tops of those hills, cooled by sea breezes, were for the aristocracy, for the palaces of the great. They were not for circus folk, people like Theodora's parents. Theodora's first home was some way from Constantinople's high-rent districts, and even though modern Istanbul now covers the old city, blotting out most relics of the past, we know something about where she spent her earliest years.

As visitors to Istanbul today, we can begin to imagine Theodora's world if we follow roughly the route of the great ancient avenue, the Mese, that ran west from the imperial palace along the city's spine to the Capitolium, the monumental temple that the Roman emperor Constantine the Great (c. AD 282–337) built when, in 330, he refounded the ancient city of Byzantium to be his new capital. The temple's title, and quite probably its architectural style, evoked the great temple at Rome where triumphal processions ended. At the Capitolium, the avenue divided, so that one branch ran to the northwest and the Church of the Holy Apostles at the spot now occupied by the Fatih Mosque, while the other ran southwest to the Golden Gate, the city's main entrance. In following this route through Istanbul's streets, modern visitors pass by the areas that were once two districts, where the staffs of the rival organizations that ran the great entertainments in the city's chariot-racing arena were housed. The Hippodrome, where the races took place, stood just west of the imperial palace at the east end of the peninsula upon which the city was built.[1]

The rival groups that managed the races in the Hippodrome were called the "circus factions." These factions provided the horses, charioteers, and everything else that was necessary for people to enjoy a day at the races. This form of organization had its origins in old Rome, where there had been four factions, and had been adapted to Constantinople in Constantine's time. For Constantinople's people, the successes and failures of the factions were of immense interest, effectively dividing the people between fans of one group or the other, and likewise divided some of the city's space into sections devoted to specific factions. By the time of Theodora's birth, there were two factions that mattered, the Blues and the Greens. The Blues' district was the first that we would have encountered as we moved west from the palace, towards the portico of Domninus—roughly the area of modern Istanbul's Grand Bazaar. The Greens' quarter was centered on the Diakonissa, where stood a church consecrated to the Mother of God, the Theotokos. It would have been somewhere near here that Theodora was born, but she would have grown up, from the age of five onwards, in the other faction's district. It is up and down the surviving winding roads and alleyways we can now walk along that we feel her presence, if we are so minded. As the shopkeepers, now as then, open up their businesses along the street fronts, and restaurants start to prepare the day's fare, we can sense a little of what her life was like. Then, as now, there would have been spiced meat on the grills, and bread baking, and delicious soups steaming.[2]

We can be pretty sure that her tale begins in Constantinople, despite the raft of claims floated for other birthplaces in later years, because Theodora's father worked with animals in the circus there. We think we know roughly *when* the story begins—AD 495 or thereabouts, maybe a year or so earlier. And since this is a story about a human being, we can be sure it opened with the usual noisy expression of shocked irritation as its protagonist entered this world.[3]

Theodora was a middle child, a few years younger than her sister Comito, and maybe a year or two older than her other sister, Anastasia, who seems to have died young. This was the fate of a great many infants in Theodora's time: nearly half of all children perished before they reached the age of five, victims of poor nutrition and negligible health care. The traditional knowledge of midwives and other wise women who helped children into the world and helped their parents nurse them could only go so far in keeping them safe. Ancient cities were dirty, dangerous places.

FIGURE 1.1. Cheerleaders at the races shown on a device used to determine the starting gates for chariot races. Dating to the years of Theodora's youth, the images of children cheering her may show us one of Theodora's own activities as the daughter of people connected with the circus factions in Constantinople.

© bpk, Berlin / (name of museum) / (name of photographer) / Art Resource, NY

What makes our story different from other stories of children born at this time and place is that Theodora would escape the circumstances of her birth—escape the likelihood that she would give birth to a few children, then die, probably in her forties. When she died, in her early fifties (AD 548), she had outlived most of the women born when she was born, and had born a daughter who had produced three sons.[4]

Theodora's career would be unique; and, unremarkably, the experience of her early years shaped the woman she became. The few facts we can recover about her early life, along with the basic things we know about Byzantine life at the time, are crucial. The two most important pieces of information about Theodora herself are that her father was the bear keeper, or *ursarius*, of the Green Faction, and that she was literate. These two facts are probably connected, and can tell us more about her childhood. We are told many years later that she would read to herself, although she seems to have been nearsighted, so she required her books to be copied out in large writing. Her career before she knew Justinian, which seems to have included preparing confidential reports about factional activities in Antioch, required that she could both read and write without help.

These were not skills that everyone possessed. Even wealthy women whose literacy came at their father's knee would rarely write on their own. The earliest surviving sentence written in a woman's hand, found in northern Britain and dating to AD 100, was scribbled on the back of a dinner invitation that was otherwise prepared by her scribe. Letters from women in Egypt, preserved in their original form and original handwriting on paper fashioned from papyrus leaves, were usually the product of a village scribe. One of the longest and most powerful surviving statements in a woman's hand is the disturbing diary of the martyr Perpetua, a young woman condemned to death by Roman authorities for her obdurate profession of Christianity in AD 203. She kept a record of her dreams while in prison, dreams that persuaded her to abandon her newborn child and reject the pleas of her father who could have arranged her release, preferring to be exposed to the beasts and certain death in the amphitheater at Carthage. The father whose pleas she rejected was a wealthy man who had presumably seen to it that she had the necessary skill to produce this diary.[5]

It is possible that Theodora's mother and father, or their employment, played some role in her education. Her older sister, Comito, was an accomplished singer, and her career would have been greatly facilitated if she could read. The law of the land dictated that children should follow their parents' occupations, which means that Theodora's mother had been an actress and was thus herself likely to have been literate. At the same time, the faction administration had an interest in seeing that the children who were going to take up jobs within it were trained in whatever arts were required for their faction to thrive. All sorts of people were needed to keep the crowd entertained during the intermissions between the chariot races. Within years of Theodora's birth, we hear of singing rope dancers and mimes in Egypt who performed on the track, and we know that in large households with lots of slaves, masters would ensure that their slaves' children were taught basic skills. It is quite possible, then, that the factions took some role in educating the children of their professional staffs.[6]

The structure of the circus factions dictated the way Theodora spent her early years. In addition to the Blues and Greens, there were two more factions, the Reds and the Whites. Although they had been independent in Rome, in Constantinople, the Reds were allied with the Blues, and the Whites with the Greens.[7] While the Whites and Reds had their own charioteers, it appears that, other than the charioteers themselves and their cheerleaders—male and female—they had little or no staff to manage the actual running of a race. Theodora's father was one of only two chief bear trainers employed with a major faction. This tells us something about the way Theodora grew up, and would have some impact on her life as a whole.

Bear trainers were subordinates of the faction dancing master, which put them in a category of circus professionals entitled to receive cash distributions at public events. Such disbursements were graded by status, and the heads of the factions, clearly important people, were rewarded on a par with high-ranking palace officials.[8] The faction leaders' chief deputies received a lot less (one thirty-sixth, to be precise) and their chief lieutenants, senior charioteers, and the like got even less, but one-third more than people who held unique positions within their organization and twice what the cheerleaders got. By way of comparison, junior palace officials—"domestics"—were paid at the same rate as charioteers; the subdeacons at the great basilica Hagia Sophia received the same pay as the unique position-holder, and the constables of the city's patriarch the same as the faction cheerleaders.[9]

Although no animal trainers are mentioned in the tenth-century AD text that outlines these payments, the omission reflects the somewhat impoverished circumstances of the chariot factions of that era. A sixth-century list would probably have had the *ursarius* on a par with the faction poet—both individuals with a clearly defined entertainment remit for which they alone were responsible. Theodora's father thus enjoyed a position of moderate privilege, and from this we can infer what she may have had available to her. Her clothes probably comprised hand-me-downs from Comito, and possibly a new tunic from time to time, though likely to have been homemade.

The food on the table would have been an amalgam of the culinary traditions imported into the city after it became the capital of the Eastern Roman Empire. In terms of quality, it would have been nothing special, or nothing special very often. In addition to bread, the staple of an ancient diet, and seasonal vegetables such as chickpeas and lentils, the people of sixth-century Constantinople ate meat of all sorts (including bear). The young Theodora's diet would have included meat, probably most often in the form of sausage—we can be pretty certain that she would have nibbled on *lucanica*, the predecessor of modern salami—and on good days, possibly a lamb chop. Among the breads that could be found at bakeries might be *boukellaton*, a hard, round loaf that constituted a soldier's basic ration (the bodyguards of important men, known as *bucellarii*, took their name from it), or *paximadi*, thick barley bread, baked until hard and dry. This is said to have sustained a young peasant boy named Justin—Justinian's uncle and adoptive father, whom we shall meet later—when he walked all the way to the capital from his home in Thrace. The same soldiers might have washed their bread down with a vinegary wine called *phouska*. And it is possible, given that her parents were reasonably well off, that she sometimes sipped *konditon*, a wine spiced with pepper, cinnamon, spikenard, and cloves that people of some means would drink as an aperitif. There would have been olive oil too, and fish, probably a lot of it.[10]

The great harbor, on the city's north side, got its name "the Golden Horn" from the bluefin tuna that filled its waters in the three-month fall migration through the Bosporus into the Black Sea. Other fish, too, were to be found in the Bosporus' waters, such as bluefish, bonito, sea bass, and horse mackerel. When they reached the city's markets, the expensive white fish, priced for the city's wealthier inhabitants, was separated from the "dark fish" such as the low-quality tuna and mackerel that swam year round near the city.[11] Theodora probably got to eat more "dark fish" than "white," but she is unlikely to have gone to bed hungry very often, even though the periodic crises and natural disasters that interrupted the flow of foodstuffs to Constantinople might well have restricted choice at the dinner table.

We are told that her father died of some unspecified illness when she was five years old. Her mother found a new partner with a rapidity that might raise questions about the stability of her earlier relationship and the effectiveness of the Church's teaching that widows should not remarry. When she tried to acquire for him her deceased husband's position, she found that Asterius, the faction dancing master, had been bribed to give the job to someone else—which further suggests that the post was a desirable one. Here was a crisis in the making. Theodora's mother probably had not worked since Comito's birth, and her new husband was incapable of providing for the family. Whether or not

FIGURE 1.2. The beast hunts depicted here on a consular diptych for AD 506 show the sorts of activities for which Theodora's father and stepfather would have been responsible (image of bear baiting from the diptych of Areobindus, AD 517).

she had been working, she was certainly not lacking in dramatic flair, and she decided to try to redress the injustice done to her by appealing to the faction's fans when they assembled to watch the races in the Hippodrome. That she could manage to gain access to the Hippodrome's floor in order to make such an appeal suggests that she had some support among the rest of the staff.[12]

The Hippodrome ran along the west edge of the imperial palace, to which it was directly connected at the level of the imperial box in the center of the stands on the east side. It held around 50,000 people, a substantial proportion of the city's population, which may have been something like 300,000 to 400,000. The east side of the great stadium appears to have accommodated persons connected with the imperial administration, while the stands to the west were given over to the supporters of the factions; there were separate seats for each group, beginning with the Blues, closest to the starting gates at the north end, then the Reds, the Whites, and, finally, the Greens. On the appointed day, Theodora's mother brought her three girls—Comito was seven, Theodora may have been five, and Anastasia, three—to face the stands of her own faction, the Greens, where their appeal for the appointment of her new husband was rejected. The Blues, however, whose own *ursarius* had recently died, received her appeal with open arms, wishing to show the world that they were more generous than their rivals. Theodora's stepfather now had a job, and she could look forward to regular meals. At the time, of course, no one could have suspected who she might become, but the event seems nonetheless to have caused something of a stir—enough for Asterius' name to be remembered decades later.[13]

Theodora's Constantinople, in all its magnificence, with the palace at its eastern edge, the great bath house and administrative district running between the massive Bronze Gate on the palace's north edge to the great walls of Theodosius II—whose circuit is still visible today—was, by the standards of other great Mediterranean cities, still in its infancy. Byzantium, Constantinople's predecessor, had occupied the east edge of the peninsula for about a thousand years before Constantine rebuilt it and named it for himself, but it had never been a large city. It was only after Constantine had chosen it as his capital that it became a force to be reckoned with.

Constantine's reasons for making this choice are unknown, unless we believe his story, which is that God told him to make use of the place. His tendency to assert that he was in direct communication with God makes it plausible that he did say something like this, and at the same time reminds us that great figures of the past do not necessarily exemplify contemporary definitions of rationality. On a more mundane

FIGURE 1.3. A chariot race from the southwest side of the base of the obelisk of Theodosius I in Istanbul.

© photo by David Potter

level, the place had the advantage that it could serve as an administrative center for the newly conquered eastern provinces and would not be dominated by the palace and palace staff of his recently defeated rival. Nor was it evocative of the memory of Emperor Diocletian, the titanic figure of Constantine's youth, in whose entourage he had grown up before his improbable rise to power. That rise started on July 25, 306, when Constantine was proclaimed emperor of the empire's westernmost provinces, and culminated in November 324 when he defeated Licinius, his last opponent. Since then, the city had grown rapidly and now equaled in size the older cities that had dominated the Mediterranean for centuries: in the West, Rome was now shrinking in significance, its emperors gone; Carthage, in North Africa, was still a great city, and all the more powerful now that Rome had been humbled. [14]

Rome and Carthage had begun to develop at about the same time during the eighth century BC, while the Mediterranean's other two major cities, Alexandria and Antioch, had both developed as a result of Alexander the Great's conquest of the Persian Empire in the late fourth century BC. Alexandria, in Egypt, was both an intellectual and an economic behemoth, channeling the surplus grain of the Nile valley around the Mediterranean along with the rich produce of its overseas trade with East Asia. Alexander had ordered the city's construction in 333 BC; his successors, the Ptolemies, the last of whom was the famous Cleopatra VII, had complemented its economic strength by building it into a major intellectual center based on two great libraries, both inherited from the Ptolemies—one housed in the Mousaion, a part of the old royal palace, the other in the city's temple of Serapis. Well supplied, also, with endowments to support its academics, Alexandria was home to significant pagan philosophical groups and played a central role in numerous Christian debates over the nature of the Trinity.

Then there was Antioch (now Antakya in southern Turkey), once capital of the Seleucid Empire, the most powerful realm to emerge from the breakup of Alexander's kingdom. Antioch was of crucial significance as the headquarters of the Roman army facing Rome's enemy, the Persian Empire, and also a hub of Christian thought even though in the past its people had not contributed significantly to pagan intellectual life.

Constantine had left an indelible mark on the city he created. His own image of himself was obvious to all who looked upon the great column in the center of the Forum. The column, which stands to this day as the "burnt column" on Istanbul's Yeniçeriler Caddesi, is constructed of nine massive cylindrical blocks of porphyry, surmounted by a statue of the emperor in heroic nudity—it was actually of Apollo, with Constantine's head replacing that of the old pagan god. The column evoked similar ones in Old Rome—Constantinople, in Theodora's day, was often called "the New Rome"—dedicated to the emperors Trajan (AD 96–117) and Marcus Aurelius (AD 161–180), recalling their military triumphs, as well as the monuments of later rulers such as the four columns that once stood in the heart of the Roman Forum honoring Diocletian and his colleagues. Constantine's column was, then, an assertion in a very traditional format of his victorious career as emperor.

Constantinople's two most important churches, the first Holy Wisdom (Hagia Sophia) and the Church of the Holy Apostles, recall his less traditional side, the way that he had melded Christianity with imperial ideology. His Hagia Sophia stood where the modern Hagia Sophia now stands, to the north of the Forum before the palace gates, while the Holy Apostles stood in the city's northeast sector. These three great Constantinian monuments, with Constantine's image standing between the two churches, dominated the city's skyline. Next to the Holy Apostles, Constantine had built a mausoleum for himself, which his son and heir Constantius II had joined to the church. It was here that Constantine lay in a porphyry sarcophagus—rumor had it, in the company of Fausta, the wife from whom he had been bitterly estranged and who had predeceased him by a decade. She was Constantius' mother and, it seems, a woman Constantine had never ceased to love, no matter what had come between them. Just beyond the church were the new walls he had built to defend his city.[15]

The walls, the column, and the Forum of Constantine inspired other emperors. Arcadius (reigned 395–408), Theodosius II (408–450), Marcian (450–457) and Leo I (457–474) had all made significant impacts on the urban landscape such that a child growing up in the city would have come to understand something of it's place in the world. Academic history, composed in convoluted prose for an audience of bureaucrats, was not for those who were only just learning their letters. A person like Theodora would have learned history by wondering about these monuments, asking questions of her elders about what, exactly, she was looking at, what it all meant. We have some sense of what this history might have conveyed from a remarkable eighth-century book, the *Brief Historical Notes*, which identifies the city's monuments and tells stories about them. It is possible Theodora would have heard tales of Emperor Severus, son of Carus, who was associated with a large statue of an elephant (among other things). He seems to have been an interesting chap, embodying all the traditions of the city's pre-Constantinian past, even though he never existed.[16]

If Theodora were to walk back towards the city center from the Golden Gate, its spectacular southwest entrance, she would first encounter the great memorial to the Eastern emperor, Arcadius, in the new Forum he or his senior advisors had built (it is not clear just what Arcadius was able to decide on his own, since he was only twenty-one when he died). The Forum was centered on a column impressively carved with the images of a rebellion by a general named Gainas, who had nearly toppled Arcadius' regime in the year 400. The decorative pattern of the column, begun in AD 402–403 and completed in 421, many years after Arcadius' death, is known to us now through drawings made before the Ottoman authorities destroyed it in the early eighteenth century. A small girl like Theodora—even as an adult she was a slight person—would perhaps not have gotten all that much out of the column's sculpted bands showing how God peacefully removed the Goths from Constantinople, how the fleet prevented them from crossing the strait into what is now Asiatic Turkey, then the final battle where they were destroyed by cavalry. One part of the story, depicted in the upper registers, that she would never have gleaned is that the cavalry who destroyed the Goths was composed of Huns, whom, under their king, Uldin, the imperial government had paid to do the job. Even if she could not see to the top of the column, she would have understood the main narrative shown at its base. The strong Christian symbolism stressed the way God had saved the state and the unity of purpose that bound Arcadius to his brother Honorius, the emperor in the West.[17] What she could not have taken away from these images was that Honorius, who hated the Goths and other Germanic peoples, would so alienate the Gothic king Alaric that the latter would sack Rome itself. His people would then move into southern France and Spain to establish their own kingdom.

In Theodora's world, there may have been a further reflection of the events of AD 400 in an annual performance that took place at the palace three days before Christmas. We learn about this from a source composed well after Theodora died, but we can be sure that it must have related to these earlier events because it gives dramatic force to the ideology presented in Arcadius' column, and because the characters portrayed were plainly meant to be seen as having worked for the Romans. For this "Gothic game," dancers from both major factions would show up at a feast, dressed like Goths and shouting Gothic war cries as well as what appear to have been nonsensical combinations of Gothic, Latin, and other languages. Once they had finished their routine, the dancers would mime a surrender and a chorus would recite acclamations of the emperor's power and assertions of God's benevolent aid in repulsing the barbarians. The message here corresponds with that of Arcadius' column, though perhaps for a young person, all that mattered was that God protected the city and its rulers from such outsiders.[18]

Moving back towards the city after pausing briefly to examine the bronze bull in the next forum, the so-called Forum of the Bull, she would climb to the top of the city's main ridgeline. There she would happen upon the next great public space, the Forum of Theodosius (the First, emperor from AD 379 to 395). Theodosius I, Arcadius' father, was the last man to rule the united Roman Empire, albeit only for a few months after crushing a rebellion in the western part. The rebellion had begun when one of Theodosius' own former generals had forced the last surviving member of the previous dynasty, Valentinian II, to commit suicide, and placed his own man on the throne. This former general of Theodosius', one Arbogast, seems to have felt he could not take the throne for himself because, as a German, it was held that he subscribed to the Arian heresy.

It is not clear, now, what being an "Arian" Christian actually meant. The original Arius had been a priest in Alexandria who had preached the doctrine of the subordination of the Son to the Father in the Trinity: he held, crucially, that Jesus had a distinctly mortal aspect, and was thus of an essence that, though similar to that of the Father, was not the same. His doctrine had been rejected at the Council of Nicaea, which Constantine had convened in AD 325. Given that Arius had later recanted his teachings, not even he was actually an Arian at the time of his death. The "Arianism" of the empire's German soldiers seems to have been an aspect of the tortured polemic that went on in the quarter-century after Constantine's death.

It was during these years that Bishop Athanasius of Alexandria successfully painted his ecclesiastical rivals, many of whom were supported by Constantius II, as Arian recidivists. Indeed, Athanasius, whose career as bishop of Alexandria was routinely punctuated by periods of exile for inciting violence against ecclesiastical rivals or otherwise offending the imperial authorities, was largely responsible for creating the image of a vast Arian conspiracy against the Nicene Creed. As a result, "Arianism" became a sort of catch-all label for people who, although Christian, were somewhat "different." The most important group to be so designated were the Germans entering imperial service from north of the Rhine and Danube—and this, on the grounds that a priest named Ulfilas, who converted the Goths, was active under Constantius II and so must have been an Arian.[19]

The construction of the Germans as "Arian" had serious consequences for Theodora's time. For one thing, it meant that an "orthodoxy test" came to be applied to the imperial succession. For another, it meant that persons born north of the Rhine and Danube rivers, no matter how powerful they might become, could not take the throne for themselves. It also meant that some Germans—the Vandals who now ruled North Africa—actively embraced their "Arian" identity as a way of distinguishing themselves from their Roman subjects.

But in Theodora's lifetime, the "Arian" issue became vastly less significant than a new one sparked by Emperor Theodosius II, Arcadius' son, who had summoned a couple of Church councils at Ephesus in 431 and 449: the decisions of these councils gave rise, albeit gradually, to a new movement, based in the eastern provinces of Syria and Egypt, asserting that God the Father and the Son had one nature (*physis*), and one nature only. This approach to understanding the Almighty, descending from the second council of Ephesus, survives to this day in the Coptic and Syrian Orthodox Churches. At the Council of Chalcedon in 451, however, the dominant faction asserted that Jesus was truly God *and* truly human, and thus had two natures even though his divine nature was of the same "Person," and "Subsistence" as the Father and the Holy Ghost—a solution crafted in the hope of reconciling the two factions.[20]

It did not work, and in the decades after Chalcedon, an increasingly bitter divide split the Church between, on one hand, the mostly Syrian and Egyptian theologians who maintained the single divine nature of Christ—hence their identification as "Miaphysites," or "Monophysites," in much modern scholarship—and supporters of the Council's decisions, who were largely found in Anatolia, Palestine, and the empire's western provinces. The fact that Justinian's uncle, Justin, was a strong supporter of Chalcedonian doctrine helped ensure his selection as emperor, paving the way for Theodora's rise to the throne, even though her own faith would come to have a distinctively anti-Chalcedonian flavor.[21]

The Forum of Theodosius I, who had himself played a significant role settling previous doctrinal disputes, seems to have spoken little of religion and a great deal about the emperor's military genius. There was a column in the middle, depicting his victories over the very Goths who had shattered the strength of the Eastern empire at the battle of Adrianople in 378. These claims were somewhat exaggerated: it was the descendants of those Goths, in some cases the very same, who had followed Alaric into Italy to sack Rome in 410, and it was Alaric's successors who, as already mentioned, had established their new state in eastern Spain and southern France. In addition to the column, there were triumphal arches at either end of the Forum. The column of Marcian, which Theodora would sometimes have visited when she followed the Mese uphill from Theodosius' Forum—indeed, it was a place she must have known well since, in her days with the Blues, she would have been living just to the north of it—also commemorated military actions that were perhaps more impressive when celebrated in stone than they had been in reality.

Marcian had succeeded Theodosius II, who had become emperor when he was seven years old. For much of his reign, as far we can tell, Theodosius had been dominated by his slightly older sister, Pulcheria. In fact, when she was fifteen and he was thirteen, Pulcheria had managed to get herself declared her brother's regent as empress (Augusta). At the same time, she took a vow of virginity, as did her younger sisters, and soon became, despite her youth, a dominant voice in imperial politics. She appears to have been the driving force behind the trumped-up charges of infidelity that led to the removal of one of her most serious rivals, her brother's wife Eudocia, and when Theodosius died after falling from his horse, she determined the succession by marrying Marcian, who swore to respect her virginity. Marcian immediately reversed Theodosius' long-term policy of paying off Attila the Hun—the fact that the king of the Huns had turned his attention west may have been a factor in the new tactic—and, in the very same year, reversed his ecclesiastical policies when he summoned the Council of Chalcedon.[22]

The events surrounding the Council of Chalcedon may have suggested, to supporters, that God looked with favor upon their efforts. The Council had been summoned under the shadow of Attila, "the enemy of God," and immediately afterward, things stopped going so well for the king of the Huns. He lost a big battle in France, his army seems to have gotten sick the next year when he invaded Italy; then the year after that, as he was threatening to invade Marcian's part of the world, he dropped dead at a banquet celebrating his most recent marriage (Attila was polygamous). His empire immediately started falling apart. People who remembered the destruction he had wreaked, especially people from the Balkans, may have seen Attila's death as the reward for coming to their senses about the way to understand God. As Emperor Zeno put it in a document he issued in an effort to bring religious peace to the empire, "the origin and composition, the power and irresistible shield of the empire [are] the sole correct and truthful faith."[23] However people might define the "sole correct and truthful faith"—we will look at how Zeno approached it in Chapter 4—the crucial point was that they could not separate the idea of "correct belief" from their view that the emperor was responsible for their safety. If he believed in false things, that belief would be perceived as threatening their welfare in a very personal way.

Despite Zeno's best efforts to reconcile the two sides, the split between them grew ever more pronounced, a sure sign that the imperial government was anything but all-powerful, relying more often on compromise and the ability to play one side against the other than on overwhelming force to get its way. The weakness of the central government was underscored by a series of domestic crises, culminating in the rebellion of a powerful general by the name of Vitalian, who commanded imperial forces in Thrace. His army attacked the city three times between 513 and 515, and Vitalian remained a very influential man, having made peace with Anastasius and withdrawn from public life after his third attempt to capture Constantinople had ended in bloody failure.[24]

The emperor Anastasius' treaty with Vitalian was only the most recent in a series of compromises that kept the government running—not that a girl learning her trade as an actress would have cared all that much about the details, but the factions had played a major role in defending the emperor in the street fighting that raged in Constantinople during Vitalian's second attack on the city. As she got older, Theodora would have recognized that the factions were crucial to the way the city ran; they represented the people at the many imperial ceremonies held each year, and took it upon themselves to represent "right thinking"—even if one faction's "right thinking" was another's anathema. And violence between supporters of the major factions was a matter of course.

South of the Mese, down towards the harbors on the Sea of Marmara, was the spot from which the great armada assembled for the reconquest of Africa had set off, just over thirty years before Theodora was born. The colossal failure of that fleet would have been remembered by many during her childhood; and she would have come upon the palace where its commander—Basiliscus—had once lived.[25] Basiliscus was the brother of Verina, who was married to Leo I, emperor from 457 to 474. Allegedly, Leo had been made emperor by Aspar, the long-serving commander of the imperial army, because Aspar, being a barbarian and an Arian, could not take the throne for himself. An alternative explanation is that he had no need to become emperor because he had been running things anyway for so long, and could do the job more easily if he was not bogged down by the ceremonial aspects of the imperial office.

How were Leo and Verina remembered? There was more than one statue of Verina that might help us reconstruct part of the memory. One of them stood near the Church of Blachernae overlooking the Golden Horn, and inside that church was the greatest of treasures to come to Constantinople in her time: the very shroud (it was asserted) of the Virgin Mary whose worship was increasingly associated with the well-being of Constantinople itself. People could also see statues put up by General Aspar and his sons—they, too, were leading figures of the empire. There was still a statue of Aspar near the Forum of Taurus in the eighth century, along with the great cistern he had built near the Golden Horn. These monuments preserved memory of the general's prominence, and, as his prominence was remembered, so, too, was his murder at Leo's hands. People soon called Leo not "the Great" but "the Butcher."

Verina, if anything, was worse than her husband. She had tried to install Basiliscus, the incompetent admiral who happened to be her brother, on the throne. To do so, she drove her own daughter Ariadne and Ariadne's not especially beloved husband Zeno (then emperor) into exile. It took two years for Zeno and Ariadne to take the city back. In this they were aided by a general named Illus, whose memory was preserved by the huge basilica he built just north of Hagia Sophia.[26]

Verina survived her brother's fall, and Zeno banished her to a convent in Turkey. A few years later, Illus had a major falling out with the imperial family. Complaining that Verina was being mistreated and that Ariadne was trying to kill him, he led a revolt against Zeno. Whatever was happening with Verina, it was certainly true that Ariadne had attempted to have Illus killed and that the assassin had botched the job, cutting off only part of his ear. Illus was able to draw a great deal of support from Isauria, the mountainous district of southern Anatolia, which was his own home district as well as Zeno's, and it was in the course of this revolt that Verina died—of natural causes, it is said. When people later looked at her statue, they sometimes took her for a witch, one whose spell had depopulated an island in the Sea of Marmara. (Verina would not be the only empress people thought was a witch.) The story may well have been beginning to spread during Theodora's youth.[27]

Theodora would certainly have seen Ariadne, the empress, in the flesh. The greatest woman of her time, Ariadne had survived Zeno (we will hear some tales about just how this happened in the next chapter) and selected Anastasius as both her new husband and her new emperor. In so doing, she ejected her brother-in-law, Longinus, from the line of succession—no small accomplishment, as he was an extremely prominent man and well regarded amongst those who were close to her late husband. She lived until 515. She and Zeno had had one child, Leo, who had died young: he was actually emperor for a time because Leo "the Butcher" had wanted his grandson, not Zeno, as his successor. Ariadne never had another child, but empresses did not need to have children to be powerful. Like Pulcheria before her, Ariadne owed some of her power to the fact that she was not in a position to put one of her own offspring on the throne.[28]

Theodora thus grew up in a city already full of history, perhaps not all of it well remembered, some of it growing a bit odder as time passed, as rumor and innuendo morphed into fact, while those who knew the truth kept it to themselves.

2

Telling Nasty Stories

In the year 532 Justinian sent Priscus, a senior court official, into exile for slandering the empress Theodora. It is not hard to imagine what he had to say about her. One of Theodora's admirers who has already been introduced, John—variously described by himself as "of Ephesus" or the "pagan converter" or "of Asia"—rather innocently tells us that when a man named Stephen went to beg for help for the exiled bishop of Amida in the 520s, he sought out Theodora, "who had come from a *porneion* [a term whose precise meaning is neither obvious nor polite], was then a patrician and would become queen along with king Justinian." Much later, people contemplating a statue of her remembered that she came to wisdom out of a disgraceful past. When Procopius claims that in her youth Theodora was the most active and obliging prostitute in Constantinople, he was saying what other people said, but he was not saying anything that was necessarily true.[1]

Procopius' vivid discussion of Theodora's teenage sex life in his *Secret History*, probably composed as an exaggerated diatribe so that Procopius could distance himself from a regime for which he would otherwise have seemed to have been an advocate, is certainly not among the most accurate things he ever wrote. Nor was it intended to be—the important thing from Procopius' point of view was that he would have it to show people if, as seemed possible, the widowed Justinian should suddenly be overthrown. In his depiction of Theodora, Procopius relied on a mixture of old propaganda (this is usually interesting since it tells us something about her), old gossip, and a lot of prejudice about stage performers. In some cases, given that the *Secret History* was compiled around 550–551, more than thirty years after she had left the stage, we can be certain that Procopius was describing events of which he had no firsthand knowledge. In the course of his vitriolic assault on her character, for instance, he confuses her occupation, attributes to Theodora remarks drawn from books about famous sayings by prostitutes that had been in circulation for years, and generally tells us more about his own predilections and interests than he does about her.

Procopius was, it seems, a bit hung up on sex. He appears to have sexually assaulted young Vandal women in the wake of the successful invasion of North Africa in 533, and then, having intimated his activities to his readers, harangued them at length on the evils of rape. As for Theodora, Procopius believed that she, like Justinian, was a demon who had assumed human form with the aim of destroying humanity. Why, being a demon, she needed to learn by heart various aspects of the art of sorcery is not clear, but Procopius says she did. His main interest is in showing that Justinian and Belisarius, his own boss, were the weakest of men, controlled by wives who lived lives of utter immorality and were responsible for the empire's ruination.[2]

While she was still a child, Procopius assures us (he was not there, of course), Theodora got her start as a prostitute by accompanying her older sister, Comito, when she went out to perform. She would provide services to any who were not Comito's clients, and specialized in offering anal sex (a subject that appears to fascinate Procopius to no end) to slaves and other members of the lower classes. When she reached puberty and could take the stage in her own right, she showed absolutely no talent, apparently, and so was relegated to the chorus. Procopius implies, too, that she was unable to move into the more specialized sexual world of the higher-class courtesans. All the same, she seems to have been wickedly funny and soon to have become a star comic—perhaps we need not take too seriously Procopius' statement about her nonexistent talent.

When she was not on stage, where she would gleefully display her "attributes," she entertained the youth of Constantinople—these particular young men came with servants, which also seems to contradict Procopius' comment about her lack of standing—regretting, he adds, that she had only three orifices with which to provide for their pleasure. This is actually a line borrowed from one of those books on famous prostitutes with which Procopius seems to have familiarized himself. He reports, moreover, that Theodora was highly proactive, always thinking of new ways of pleasing her clients and never waiting for men to approach her.

She was able to keep busy in this pre-contraceptive society by having regular abortions—except, of course, when she did not. Procopius omits to mention that she gave birth to a daughter during these years, though he does invent a son for her, which the father took from her arms at birth, knowing that she would kill him. He raised the boy in the province of Arabia, the historian goes on, whence he would later emerge to visit his mother as empress, then disappear without a trace.[3] Although, according to Procopius' version of her life, she would have been out of business for quite a while with two pregnancies in the five or six years of her professional career, Procopius does not supply us with any dates; but we will discover in the next chapter that this was roughly the time she could have spent on the stage.

Procopius tells us that Theodora was enormously popular, especially when she performed such extraordinary acts as the one that involved a goose. (Never mind that this is a mythological mime routine of the sort, he implies, that she would not actually have performed, given that she was in a different line of work.) Indeed, his vivid description of a spectacle that he could not possibly have seen her perform makes one wonder a bit about how he spent his spare time:

> Often, with everyone watching in the theater, she would strip
> and stand, undressed at the center of attention, wearing only
> cloth covering her breasts and crotch, and she wouldn't have
> been embarrassed to show these off as well, but no one was
> allowed to appear totally naked without covering for their
> private parts. Dressed like this she would lie on her back
> on the stage, and attendants, who'd been hired for the task,
> would sprinkle grain on her crotch, and geese, who'd been
> trained for this purpose, would eat them off of her, one by one.
> When she stood up she was not blushing, but appeared to be
> proud of her performance. She wasn't just shameless, she was
> the particular inventor of shameless acts.[4]

The garments that Procopius is describing here amount to what in our terms would be shorts and a sports bra—such outfits are depicted on various works of contemporary and near-contemporary art.

Once she became empress, to judge from what Procopius is *not* able to say about her, Theodora gave up sex. (He implies that the one man she thought she might be attracted to vanished overnight.) In any event, she seems to have been busy with her new favorite pastime: ruining the empire. She tried, he says, to improve the prospects for prostitutes who wanted to give up their trade; to rearrange the personal lives of those around her as she pleased, often looking to humiliate members of the upper classes; she could be a dangerous enemy, but was all too loyal to the women whom she had brought with her to prominence. Her closest associates were her sister Comito; Antonina, an actress, the daughter of a charioteer from Thessalonica and the wife of General Belisarius; and Chrysomallo, or "Goldilocks" (a name common amongst actresses).

Theodora showed no compunction in disposing of men she could not stand—most notably the hugely powerful praetorian prefect, John the Cappadocian, whom Justinian charged with raising money for his various projects, and Belisarius. John was exiled (we will hear more about him shortly), while Belisarius was removed from his command and his massive estates were confiscated (see Chapter 10). Less fortunate men ended up locked away in the dungeons beneath her palace. One senior general is said to have spent two years there in utter darkness—though how isolated he could really have been in a palace in which thousands of people came to work every day is open to question.[5]

Procopius' torrent of abuse is worth paying some attention to when he offers the names of particular individuals; and while we should take what he has to say with a healthy dose of skepticism, there is often reason to think that beneath his inventions lies some semblance of fact, even if he is merely sneering at official propaganda. Take, for example, Theodora's efforts to help prostitutes find a new life, and the well-advertised halfway house for women leaving the profession that she established across the Bosphorus Strait from Constantinople. Procopius says that the women were kept there against their will and would throw themselves off the walls to escape—that this halfway house existed is a fact, but we have no way of knowing whether, or why, any of the women who entered it were suicidal.

So, too, Procopius tells us that Justinian took no interest in the corrupt practices of his governors, while another source records a law that sought to crack down on precisely this; the same source mentions Justinian's giving aid to cities after earthquakes, while Procopius simply lists those that were ruined as examples of Justinian's special ability to attract the wrath of God. He accuses the emperor of debasing the empire's gold coinage, although no coins, as described, exist; while another source points out that Justinian withdrew his currency-debasing plan after a riot. Procopius also claims he heard to behave heard that Justinian's mother alleged she had conceived after having sex with a demon, and that the emperor's head separated itself from his body so that it could wander the palace at night. Moreover, much later, a monk who came to see the emperor refused to enter the throne room because he said he saw himself confronted by the King of the Demons.[6]

This is not the only improbable account of a meeting between the emperor and a monk. According to John of Ephesus, the monk Zoora once enraged Justinian by lecturing him on the evils of persecuting anti-Chalcedonian communities, but as the emperor was pondering how best to do away with him, God's anger struck. Justinian's head was "smitten," his reason departed, and his body swelled up. Theodora, who according to John was very smart, hid him away so that only two chamberlains and two doctors really knew what was going on. She then sent messengers to Zoora asking him to intercede with God on Justinian's behalf. If he should be cured, she would make sure, she vowed, that Justinian stopped persecuting the enemies of the Council of Chalcedon. It is quite likely that Procopius' source for the monk's demonic vision is a text such as John's biography of Zoora, since the point of the story, for John's audience, was to prove that God was on their side. By contrast, Procopius' version seems to be meant to illustrate the proposition that Justinian was a monster—which is likewise a story that would appeal to a non-Chalcedonian constituency. John's story is of further importance for the purpose of understanding Theodora, showing us as it does that one could be very critical of Justinian while still praising her.[7]

Put simply, Procopius tends not to make things up from scratch, but he embellishes, sometimes grossly, what he knows; or fails to tell the whole story. If someone told him that Theodora had been a whore, he felt free to depict her as the world's most plenteous prostitute; or if he heard that she had been an actress, to call her a stripper. As we know, she *had* been an actress, and she *had* had relationships with men who paid her to sleep with them. Given her family background, it would have been surprising if she had not pursued the career she did. But it would never have occurred to Procopius to suggest that her willingness to help women who did not want to follow the path she had followed might indicate how she now felt about the way she had once earned her living.

Indeed, Procopius is perhaps most interesting for what he does not say about Theodora, and it is interesting to compare the treatment that some of her contemporaries received from writers of approximately the same period. We might start with empress Ariadne (ca. 450–515), because she had been, as Theodora would become, an immensely powerful woman. People did not say that Ariadne "slept around"—in stark contrast to her mother, Verina—but suspected she did not much like her first husband, Emperor Zeno. According to one story, when one day he collapsed after dinner with an epileptic seizure, she had him entombed; another version had it that entombment had once been her response when he had drunk himself into oblivion, and when he woke up, screaming to be let out, she ordered that he be left where he was. Yet another story relates that when Ariadne discovered that Zeno wanted to kill their son Leo so that he could rule as sole emperor, she substituted a child who looked like him and hid the real Leo away in a church, where he became a priest and remained thus into the reign of Justinian. And as already mentioned, Ariadne's anger towards General Illus for refusing to agree to release Verina was said to have driven her to hire an assassin to kill him. From this failed assassination attempt was born Illus' revolt, an event of great importance in the later years of Zeno's reign.

The theme of political assassination would not be absent from Procopius' story of Theodora. He claims in the *Secret History* that she had a hand in the murder of the Gothic queen Amalasuintha, a beautiful woman whom she is said to have feared Justinian would divorce her for. Oddly, though, in his history of the origins of the Gothic War, Procopius suggests no such thing. He says it was Amalasuintha's overly ambitious cousin who killed her. That may be true—she was certainly murdered, and the murder was an official cause of the war. At the time Procopius described the assassination in his *Gothic War*, it looked like the war might be successful; when he wrote the *Secret History*, it was still dragging on, so was just the sort of thing that could be used to blacken Theodora's reputation.[8]

Ariadne's mother, Verina, may already have entered the popular imagination as a witch in her lifetime, but there is no question that she saw herself as the emperor-maker extraordinaire of her time. She had been a good deal younger than her husband Leo I, and she plainly did

FIGURE 2.1. One side of an ivory diptych (two-leaved folding tablet) depicting an empress, believed to be Ariadne (r. 474–515), the most powerful woman of her time. Dressed in richly decorated robes, she sits on her throne under a shell-shaped canopy supported by columns. Her throne is similar to the emperor's throne in the *consistorium*. Holding a cross mounted on a globe in her right hand, her left hand is open in a gesture of blessing.

© Erich Lessing / Art Resource, NY

not think much of Ariadne's husband Zeno. So she decided she would drive him from his throne and replace him with her lover, Patricius. But things did not work out quite as she would have liked, and her brother Basiliscus seized the throne instead. In this he was aided by the aforementioned Illus, until Basiliscus so alienated Illus that the latter went on to play a major role in reinstating Zeno. Theoderic, in the earlier part of a career that would end with the transformation of his wayward Gothic army into the "Ostrogoths," and his becoming king of Italy, was conscious of Verina's continuing reach across the empire years after her exile.[9]

One of the motives behind Leo's attempt to invade Vandal North Africa in 468 was the fact that the widow and daughter of the Roman emperor Valentinian III were being held hostage there, having been captured when the Vandal king Geiseric sacked Rome in AD 455. Geiseric claimed that he had attacked the city because one of these women, Valentinian's widow, Eudoxia, had written asking him to save her after her father had been assassinated the previous year. This story bears a strong resemblance to another, near-contemporary tale in which Eudoxia's sister is said to have asked Attila to invade the Western empire to rescue her from the house arrest into which she had been cast when her lover had been executed.[10]

Whatever the truth of any of these stories, the important point here is what they tell us about what educated people *wanted* to believe about members of the imperial household. They took it as fact that Roman royals would order the murder of those they did not like—both family and non-family—and would not hesitate to put their own interests ahead of the state's. For those educated people, the good empress had to be pious, chaste, and philanthropic, and the bad empress must be a greedy, intemperate, sexually voracious witch (or an ally of demonic forces). The fact that Procopius cannot pin a single lover on Theodora after she and Justinian came together is telling. The allegation that he thinks that she could order the disappearance of individuals she did not like is not inherently implausible. The problem for Procopius is that he cannot actually find real individuals to fit that category—which is interesting, as we shall see, because there is some question about what role Theodora played in the death of a pope whose intransigence had made a great deal of trouble for people close to her. Procopius mentions the incident in the *Secret History*, but makes Belisarius' wife Antonina the villainess of the piece.[11]

As many stories about the women of the Western court suggest, the court at Constantinople was not the only place where people were prone to see evil in the actions of others. The stories emerging from these quarters, even more lurid than stories in Procopius, show us how people who were unhappy with government tended to talk about it. This may not have been a terribly sophisticated discourse, but it was the discourse of the time, and if we are to evaluate Procopius' rant, we have to see it in the context of other rants on similar topics.

Starting in Italy, we find that in 536, Vitiges, then the ruler of the Goths, wrote to Justinian from Italy assuring him that he had restored legitimate rule to his people by marrying Matasuentha, daughter of the recently deceased Amalasuintha, who, Vitiges said, had been murdered by her co-regent Theodahad. Procopius claimed that Vitiges had raped Matasuentha, then that she had later helped betray the Gothic capital of Ravenna to the army of Belisarius because she hated her husband. Procopius was not the only one to suggest this: the author of a contemporary chronicle wrote that Vitiges had "entered Ravenna and joined Matasuentha to himself more by force than affection." The story of sexual violence suited Justinian's purpose, even though the surviving sections of the speech delivered at the couple's wedding imply a bit more formality than is suggested in other accounts (which is not to say that a royal wedding cannot also be a rape).[12]

Stories such as these pale into insignificance when compared to the literature that in the late sixth century engulfed the reputation of Fredegund, queen of the Frankish kingdom centered on Soissons, in Picardy in northern France. She was the (joint-) second wife of King Chilperic I, one of four brothers who, on the death of their father Chlothar in AD 561, split the Frankish kingdom between them. Fredegund, so the story goes, was actually a serving girl who had been Chilperic's mistress. Their marriage appears to have taken place after the death of his first wife and to have continued during his marriage to a Visigothic princess named Galsuintha. It is perhaps unsurprising that Galsuintha did not find marriage to Chilperic especially congenial, and she told her husband she wanted to go home. He, we are told, responded to this request by having her murdered.

At that point—it was the year 575—Fredegund formally took control of the palace and saved her husband from destruction at the hands of one of his brothers by sending assassins with poisoned weapons to kill the brother. Nine years later, Chilperic himself was murdered after a day's hunt. Gregory of Tours, the principal historian of the Franks in these years, who hated Chilperic, maintains that a servant did the deed. According to another version, Chilperic sealed his own fate when he returned early one day from hunting, came up behind Fredegund as she was washing her hair, and patted her backside. She thought it was her lover, Landeric, a senior court official, and thereupon exclaimed, "Landeric, what do you think you're doing?!" Chilperic, who loved her deeply, was upset at the thought that she must be having an affair, and went back out to rejoin the hunt. Fredegund summoned Landeric and told him it was time to get rid of her husband; he then arranged the murder, it seems.[13]

The assassination of her husband was not Fredegund's only evil deed. According to Gregory—not a fan—murder and torture were essential components of her administrative toolbox. Nor was she the only powerful woman Gregory had unpleasant things to say about. He does, for instance, state as a matter of fact that the wife of King Gutran, a brother of Chilperic, poisoned the son he had had by his concubine, and that Charibert, another of Chilperic's brothers, divorced his wife to marry the daughter of a wool-worker. He even introduces his readers to the widow of a bishop who evidently made a habit of slicing off men's penises. As this survey also suggests, it was pretty standard for powerful women's alleged offenses to have a sexual component. Procopius' Theodora is anything but original in this regard.[14]

You did not have to be royal to have enemies, of course. Procopius, for instance, plainly hated Antonina as much as he hated Theodora, and devoted a substantial part of his *Secret History* to detailing her adulteries. He heartily disliked the man Priscus (with whose removal from office this chapter began), and was shocked that the Persians consigned losers in domestic power struggles to perpetual imprisonment in the "Tower of Oblivion." Agathias, a poet and historian of this era, describes the intellectual pretensions of Uranius, a philosopher who regularly put on displays of his philosophical learning in Constantinople. So banal was the man that the only sort of person who would be attracted to his lectures was someone otherwise short on education. His stock-in-trade was a series of platitudes about the nature of the Christian God. Agathias goes on to say that he talked about the nature and essence of the Deity, which at this point must have included some reference to Chalcedon, although it sounds as if he might not have been associated with any specific faction. It is possible that Agathias' decision to compose a lengthy attack on this self-styled savant was connected with the fact that Areobindus, a powerful courtier, was so taken with Uranius that he took him on an embassy to Persia, where he intrigued no less a figure than King Khusro himself. Plainly, there were some who found Uranius more interesting than they did Agathias himself, which rankled.[15]

Agathias also disliked intensely a man from Africa named John. This John was on the staff of a general called Justin, who was a member of the imperial clan, being the son of Justinian's cousin Germanus. It was probably his closeness to Justin that had boosted this John's career, since he seems to have started out on a very low rung of the ladder of imperial preferment, as the personal servant of a member of Justin's bodyguard. Working in Lazica, on the Black Sea coast near the border between Turkey and Georgia, he was by the late 550s a supply officer. He would take a sum of gold from Justin with which to supply his staff with food, promising both to feed the staff and to return the money, with a premium. His method of operating, evidently, was to repeatedly threaten villages with requisitions for valuable commodities until he received a sufficiently hefty bribe to buy elsewhere—and in this way the supply officer would turn a handsome profit. Justin, who was delighted by his efficiency, did nothing to stop him. Agathias does not tell us what became of John, but states firmly that Justin's failure to rein the man in was later punished: Justin was murdered by Justinian's successor (also called Justin). It is likely that the story of Emperor Justin and his wife Sophia, Theodora's niece, kicking the general Justin's head about the palace is another instance of the sort of the gossipy and unfounded nastiness that Procopius and other writers of the period indulged in.[16]

Agathias' portrait of John is not all that dissimilar from the portrait of another imperial official—John of Cappadocia, Justinian's long-serving praetorian prefect—offered by another imperial functionary whose name was also John. This John, known in the modern world as John Lydus or John the Lydian (we will meet him again), was a fairly high-ranking official in the prefect's office, having moved up through the ranks in Emperor Anastasius' time (regnant 491–518). His book *Concerning the Magistracies of the Roman State* presents a long lament on the overall decline in the nobility of the prefecture, which he feels is the result of lax oversight by otherwise well-meaning emperors. His John of Cappadocia is a demonic spirit who rose to his position after climbing from relatively humble beginnings to be a secretary on the staff of the commanding general of the army around Constantinople (*magister militum praesentalis*), in which role he seems to have come to Justinian's attention. Justinian promoted him to praetorian prefect in 531, in which role he served, with a brief hiatus, until 541. As prefect, the Cappadocian delighted in fleecing provincials and torturing the rich, while installing dungeons beneath his own office and employing a wide range of thugs to do his bidding. One of these, yet another John, was evidently a hugely obese individual who governed Lydia, arresting, chaining up, beating, and murdering members of the upper classes for their wealth.[17]

John the Cappadocian's misdemeanors were not limited to his public functions. According to John the Lydian, his namesake was a man of gross immorality who liked to bathe with depilated boys and prostitutes. His profligacy was so great that it was obvious to all in his pallor, says this commentator, and he was seldom encountered without a drink in his hand. The men who carted him about in his litter appear to have been naked, and he did not hesitate to have sex in public with the prostitutes who flocked around him, while eating to such excess that from time to time he would pause to vomit as he went about his daily debauches. Procopius, who also hated John the Cappadocian, offers a rather different picture, suggesting that the crypto-pagan who dressed as an ascetic priest suffered from insomnia and consulted magicians.[18]

Vehemence of expression was not limited in this era to disgruntled officials, but built into the very fabric of government—not all that surprising, perhaps, since John the Lydian and people like him were drafting official documents when not complaining about their bosses. The law that aroused the Lydian's undying hatred for John the Cappadocian—a law drawn up in the latter's office and almost certainly reflecting his own style—decreed that payment for government services must stop because of its insidious effect on the working of the state. "For," says this law, "who cannot rob and steal with impunity when he sees the magistrate sell everything [for his own enrichment]." Thieves know full well that justice can be bought, and thus "arise murders, acts of adultery, thefts, physical assaults, the rape of virgins, disturbances of public assemblies and contempt for laws and magistrates," since everyone thinks that, like the lowest slave, they are subject to barter. John the Cappadocian sees as the fount of all evil the money that supported the salaries of public officials like John the Lydian.[19]

Whatever the degree of truth in these portraits (pretty much everything we have seen needs to be taken with some very large grains of salt), they all have features in common. John the Lydian, Procopius, Gregory, and Agathias were all members of the traditionally educated élite, men who believed that their backgrounds and educational attainments entitled them to positions of importance within the civilian administration. All of them resented people they saw as outsiders coming to the fore: Uranius is found offensive because he lacks the background to talk about the very things he persists in talking about, and John of Cappadocia, quite simply, comes from the wrong side of the tracks.

John the Lydian twice quotes an oracle declaring that the empire would fall when it started issuing decrees in a language other than Latin. This was exactly what John the Cappadocian was doing, and it was in Justinian's time that the age-old practice of issuing laws in Latin came to an end. John of Ephesus, whose shabby Syriac prose suggests that he was not highly literate in his own language, let alone Greek (though he did know the language), most likely exemplifies the sort of person the well educated had no time for. Indeed, this John makes no bones about the fact that he comes from a family of limited literacy and even more limited prosperity, and is similarly open about the fact that his parents placed him in a convent at the age of six. Although he would come to know Theodora personally; become, as bishop, an agent of the imperial government; and possibly be responsible for some outright atrocities, he wrote of the court from the perspective of an outsider. He regarded the people around Justinian, unlike Theodora's acolytes, as largely pro-Chalcedonian and thus heretical; while the way he wrote about some of his heroes, monks like Zoora, shows that he did not regard perfect literacy as essential to the path to salvation.

John of Tella, a leading figure in the anti-Chalcedonian community of Mesopotamia, had instituted the novel practice of testing prospective priests for literacy, which says a great deal about the world he came from—not one in which Procopius or Agathias would have felt at home, for sure. Both in Constantinople and in the West, within government circles and outside of them, the vehemence with which people expressed themselves was a measure of their insecurity and of intense rivalry, as the State competed with the Church for the attention of its subjects, and as individuals from military, civil, and ecclesiastical milieux sought to cement their claims to authoritative positions against people of very different backgrounds. There was no single path to power, and that made the contest all the more ferocious.[20]

We also learn some things about Theodora from what people like Procopius do *not* tell us. Reading between the lines of the *Secret History*, for instance, we see how she dealt with a major crisis that threatened her own grasp on power and her husband's, when the great plague reached Constantinople during 542.[21]

But what strikes us most in all of this is the nature of the debate, the evident antipathy between insiders and outsiders; between those who considered their education as guaranteeing them a place at the top, and those who dismissed this as of little importance, believing that simple piety would cause God to show them the way to the top. In the latter's view, people of compelling piety would have better access to Theodora and Justinian than Procopius or John the Lydian would ever have. We sense in these stories, true or false, the language of a world in flux, a world where people feared for their own status, feared that their values might no longer be relevant. It was a world, after all, in which a comedienne could become empress.

3

Sex and the Stage

In January of 536, Justinian issued rules concerning the six processions that would be held in Constantinople to celebrate a new consul's taking up his office. According to Justinian, the fifth of these processions "goes to the theater, which they say is for the *pornae*, and where, on the stage, there are comedies, tragedies, musical performances, and the theater is open to all spectacles for the eyes and ears." *Pornae* primarily means "prostitutes," but here the word designates a group of actresses, which is why it is possible that when John of Ephesus uses the word *porneion* (brothel in Classical Greek) to describe the place where Theodora came from, he may actually be referring to her past as an actress.

The law of 536 is not the only text in which a life on the stage is equated with sexual immorality. In an earlier law, Justinian had stated that a woman who left the stage, then returned to it, committed the crime of "unchastity" and could not receive the protection of laws allowing her to marry as she chose. The use of such language in documents drawn up years after Justinian had married Theodora, plus another law, issued in 521–522, allowing Justinian and Theodora to wed, reflected the way that people expected girls who, like Theodora, had had professional lives connected with the theater. Uncomfortable and cruel as these assumptions were, they help us begin to understand her complicated teenage years.[1]

There is no reason to doubt that Theodora had been an actress, or even that she had been a "mime"—meaning an actress in what were essentially situation comedies—because those were the only roles open to women. Procopius would have had no reason to say that she was a comic actress and then to concoct the famous act with the goose, if she had not had a stage career. He could have dispensed with all that and stated baldly that she was a prostitute. That Theodora's sister and two close friends were actresses supports the notion that this was the company in which she moved for at least some of the time she was growing up in Constantinople.

That actresses were called prostitutes is emblematic of the same ambivalence that men, including the men who ran the Roman Empire, felt about openly independent women who attracted attention to themselves and who might, through their behavior, arouse the passions of men who looked at them. This male response was nothing new—it had existed for centuries, and the fact that the empire was now Christian had not changed men's fascination, in a status-driven world, with such women.

Women who remained in the home, who nurtured the children and looked after their households, who filled the roles appointed for them by men, were revered for doing their duty. The female being who excited the greatest reverence in the Constantinople of Theodora's lifetime was of course the Virgin Mary. Women could occupy prominent positions as benefactors of the Church, and even in local government. Statues in their honor were displayed in prominent places. Women were honored as saints and martyrs. Helena, mother of Constantine, now a saint, was commemorated by many statues—and in this city where she had barely set foot. One of the most prominent shrines in southern Turkey honored Thecla, a spirited young woman who, inspired by St. Paul, had become a Christian and taken a vow of chastity. According to a legend widely known at the time, Thecla had survived a couple of attempts to execute her and had performed numerous other miracles. The person of the empress was likewise revered. Indeed, Constantinople's political milieu had been shaped both officially and, quite probably, behind the closed doors of the imperial palace, by Ariadne, the reigning empress.[2]

"Respectable" women were those who lived in overtly sex-free environments. The first thing Thecla had done upon becoming a Christian was to break off the marriage her mother had arranged for her. And the exceptionally powerful Pulcheria, sister of Theodosius II mentioned earlier, had publicly declared her virginity; furthermore, many of her most powerful servants were eunuchs, lacking the basic male equipment—similarly, many of the men on whom Theodora would depend in later life had been castrated when they were boys. People were willing to castrate their young sons in the hope that the operation would enable them to obtain positions in the imperial service, thereby becoming far more powerful than they otherwise might. Indeed, this often happened, for, as far as we know, most of the powerful palace eunuchs came from humble backgrounds, and almost all from rural areas on the empire's frontiers, since castration was technically illegal in the empire proper. We have to assume that the parents of these boys were able to deal with the notion that, in effect, being prepared to sell their child's body was the key to his future. In the ideological world of sixth-century Byzantium, respectability required chastity, and power required respectability.

Actresses were the polar opposite of professional virgins. Procopius' description of Theodora's routine with the goose would not have struck an ancient reader as extraordinary on account of its sexual nature, but rather because it was a non-speaking act with animals and involved scantier garb than was usual for a woman (there were male actors who wore a good deal less). Representations and performances of more and less overtly sexual material was commonplace, especially in mime, the genre in which Theodora worked.

For all the bluster and bias of his presentation, Procopius does provide us with some useful information about the way Theodora got her professional start. She began as an assistant to Comito, he tells us, and was part of the chorus before she started getting solo roles—an entirely probable progression for a girl passing from childhood into adolescence. This may also tell us a bit about her parents: they seem to have wanted the girls out of the house and making a living as soon as they could, and presumably they were not too much bothered by the notion that some of this living would come from men who paid to have sex with them. Theodora's home may not have been one where there was a lot of love; she and her sister seem mostly to have had each other for company. Since their mother had had a stage career, she would have known what her daughters could expect: a period of training, some of which she herself might have supplied, possibly an apprenticeship to a dancing instructor, and then the gradual acquisition of other performance skills. It might take five years before a prospective performer was ready for "prime time." Theodora's training probably began when she was about ten; we know from various sources that performers might have had active careers in their later teens.[3]

When she was old enough to take a role on stage, Theodora would have joined a troupe of male and female performers. Their material, which required elaborate costumes and musical accompaniment, ranged from farces that made fun of foreigners or pagan gods, routines involving adultery—a very popular theme—to plays ending in bloody dismemberment, and others that mocked Christian institutions (at one point, holy virgins seem to have been found especially amusing). Variety was important, but so was a basic familiarity with the plots. In large theaters with large audiences, typical of the ancient world, subtle gesture did not feature in an actor's routine, and the audience liked to have some notion, based on past experience, of what to expect when he or she came on stage. The humor could get pretty physical: a near-contemporary of Theodora says that mimes would hit each other with sticks.[4]

Mime troupes could be quite large—one at Rome in the second century AD seems to have involved about sixty people—and Procopius, who is useful on this point, says that players would graduate from less to more significant roles. Theodora started in the chorus and ended up as a soloist, he says, but this may just be guesswork on his part as it was common knowledge that this was the way the acting profession worked. As a chorus member, Theodora might well have played in a dramatized version of the story of Charition, a woman who finds herself stranded on the coast of India. Her brother, who seems to be the main player, accompanied by a clown, comes to her rescue: there is much bumbling about as they make their escape from the temple of the Moon Goddess, where Charition has been living. A chorus of Indian huntresses now comes on stage with bows and arrows and uttering gibberish—clearly meant to represent the local language—then the clown plies the Indian king with wine, and the latter does a drunken dance. The surviving script indicates that music would be belted out as the chorus danced and sang. Charition, like the virtuous upper-class girl that she is, refuses to steal from the temple on her way out. The clown farts loudly and often.[5] We may imagine that Theodora, in her mid-teens, was getting her start in shows like this.

The subject of adultery offered plenty of scope for dramatic interpretation. As early as the late first century BC, a plot involving a dim husband, a clever young man, and the woman he is trying to get into bed was doing the rounds. By the end of the first century AD, a stock scene—one of many—in these plays had been established in which the young lover would hide in a chest from which, fearing suffocation, he would emerge while the husband was still in the room. Meanwhile, minor characters would dash in and out, confusing things, and in some versions of the plot everyone ended up in court. Another of Theodora's contemporaries, writing a defense of mime, suggested that perfectly reasonable people might accuse mimes of promoting adultery. He then said that this was a silly thing to think since the attempted adulteries were always found out. One useful thing a person could learn from seeing such a presentation was how to take a case to court, as well as that people who were caught were condemned.

In one standard "adultery mime," the female lead is the unfaithful wife—she is always much younger than her unwitting husband—whose efforts to deceive him are the centerpiece of the play. In one variation on the theme, she tries to seduce a handsome young slave. In these plays the woman is often portrayed as a pretty dreadful character, sometimes torturing the virtuous slave when he does not succumb to her. In the version of the story that has come down to us, the play opens with a

FIGURE 3.1. Dancers and actresses from the left-hand panel from the consular diptych of Flavius Anastasius, consul in 517; the female figure on the left is a mime actress dressed as Theodora would have dressed when she performed.

slave named Aesop refusing his mistress's advances because of his devotion to another slave, Apollonia. The mistress orders them both killed, only to be told in the next scene that some god has set them both free. Apollonia is recaptured, then Aesop shows up, faking his own death. Enter at this point a new character, a slave who does want to sleep with the mistress, if only she will murder her spouse. The play ends with Apollonia and Aesop showing up safe and sound, and the rescue of the master from his scheming wife.[6]

Christian themes were rather different, and would have been treated rather differently, from the more traditional subjects. Ideally, from the Christian point of view, the plot would involve the sudden conversion of a character who went on to be martyred—a modern version, in fact, of a famous mime attributed to a writer called Catullus (perhaps the famous Latin love poet of the first century BC) about a bandit named Laureolus, whose story ended with his crucifixion. The play had occasioned some bizarre and disgusting twists, including an excess of fake blood on the day Caligula, one of Rome's most vicious emperors, was murdered. The excess blood was later taken as indicative of Caligula's bestial character and as a coincidental forecast of the assassination. Another version, for another emperor, had included a real crucifixion. Presumably, some of these details, though not the most extreme forms of "reality theater," were left in the "improving" Christian version, if martyrdom was to be the story's ending. Other texts suggest that nun roles were sometimes slotted in; a recent discovery has provided us with parts of a mime script from Theodora's time in which we see a character being addressed as a Christian priest, while another is hit with a stick and accused of being a prostitute.[7] Such stories were occasionally forbidden, quite likely after a bishop had complained.

A bishop might get his way if he was protesting about a specific plot or behavior that was especially lewd; we can be pretty sure that the bishop of Constantinople would have had an act such as Theodora's goose mime banned immediately. But mostly, bishops just complained. Emperors were not about to shut down popular entertainments. They saw them as spectacles that made people happy and thus as important in maintaining social order. It would take nothing less than a riot disrupting that order—and they did happen from time to time—to close the theaters.[8]

The largely ineffective priestly rantings that have come down to us are significant today because they give us some idea of what people encountered when they went to the theater. Perhaps the most interesting of these surviving protests comes from a man who may have played an important role in Theodora's life after her acting career had ended, and who owed his survival to her later intervention. This was Bishop Severus of Antioch. At about the time Theodora was on stage in Constantinople, he composed a hymn for his congregation on the evils of dance. They should take heed of the fate of Lot's wife, he railed: if a single glance backwards at Sodom was enough for her to be turned into a pillar of salt, anyone who watched such spectacles as were shown in Constantinople was in dire trouble. Those "who look on the vile gyrations of the dancing madness with their many turns, and in the thought of their heart wander as in deep darkness," should fear lest, as "often happened . . . [they should be] suddenly snatched from this life, when the dread angels come and stand over them." Then they should fear finding themselves before God's judgement seat. Severus also disapproved of games of all sorts because they excited the emotions and distracted people from thinking about God; and worse still was when they cheered at chariot races and invoked pagan divinities such as Fortune. For Severus, the vices of ancient Canaan came to life in the theater's sensuality. "Don't you have anything new to say on the subject?" he once envisioned himself being asked. "No," he tells us he responded; he just wished he could get people to listen.[9]

Severus was not alone in his opinions, and one of his slightly older contemporaries, Jacob, who worked primarily in Edessa (modern Urfa in southeastern Turkey), wrote at some length on the topic. Like Severus, Jacob presented himself as engaging in debate with a theater fan, in this case about one of the "higher" forms of pantomime in which a single male dancer performed in a mythological episode. "So what?" the fan would say. "These are just for fun, and watching them isn't paganism. I'm a Christian and I don't suddenly become a pagan because I watch people dance, I enjoy it and worship God all the same." To this Jacob responded, "Who can bathe in mud without being soiled? . . . Do not love dancing, it is the mother of licentiousness." As for Severus, and for another of Theodora's contemporaries, Choricius of Gaza, the question was whether you become what you watch, or you are what you perform—essentially the same point Procopius made in attacking Theodora.[10]

While Severus and Jacob might have been primarily concerned with the souls of the audiences, it would not have eluded their notice that some people were making a great deal of money from acting on the stage. In 393, the reigning emperor had ordered that actresses not wear gold set with gems, and that they should avoid going around wearing purple, although they could dress in other fine silks and wear plain gold. In other words, they should not swan about looking like the empress. In Antioch, a story circulated about a famous actress named Pelagia whom the bishop is said to have approached one day as she rode by on an ass, decked out in gold, pearls, and precious stones—even on her feet—and with an entourage of boys and girls all wearing golden collars. She is said to have been extremely beautiful, and a prostitute, to boot. When she was passing by the bishop's church a short while later, she overheard him preaching. Suddenly smitten with remorse for her sins, she decided to convert. Lower down the scale, entertainers' contracts that have survived from Egypt show that even traveling performers far from the metropolis, Alexandria, and from the glories of Antioch and Constantinople, earned well above the average income.[11]

Theodora's ability to progress in the troupe, assuming that Procopius is right in stating that she became a well-known mime, bespeaks determination as well as talent. She may have made some good friends during these years—Chrysomallo, for instance, who was certainly her companion in later life—but one can imagine that the world in which she worked was intensely competitive and that success was a zero-sum game, with plainly tangible benefits for the winners. There were no doubt quarrels amongst the actors, fueled by jealousies and dissatisfactions of one sort or another. Later, Theodora showed herself a fierce enemy, one who could hold a grudge.[12]

Theodora's decision, another that she made as a teenager, to supplement her income with money she could make by taking lovers, was most likely not a choice made out of necessity, but rather a move born of opportunity. In the *Secret History*, which Procopius, as we have seen, embellished with borrowings from books on famous prostitutes—for instance, his claim that Theodora wished her nipples had holes large enough to accommodate penises, for she would then have five orifices available—we find there is evidence that is somewhat revealing. He assumes that her clients were well heeled, and maintains that when she exhausted those men of good standing she would, many a night, have sex with their servants: a detail that implies that she had a place of her own, that she was not doing business on the streets, and that it is quite likely she enjoyed a degree of autonomy.[13]

Theodora's situation at this point is not dissimilar from that of other women we have met in other centuries, from antiquity to the present: independent women who made their way in the world, not women who were trafficked or compelled to work in the sex industry, but who chose to do so. In antiquity, young, vivacious professional women would attract admirers happy to supplement their income and provide them with additional comforts and luxuries. Some of these admirers held the highest positions in the state. Emperor Nero may have been notorious for his appalling treatment of women—he murdered his mother and two of his wives, for example—but the person who conducted his funeral arrangements was Acte, a freedwoman who had been his lover since they were in their late teens. (Nero's mother had not improved her relationship with her son by complaining about palace treasures that disappeared into Acte's house.) It was not at this moment in her career that Theodora met Justinian—we can be sure that, had this been the case, it would have been universally remembered. Everyone accepts that they met at a later point in her life—but she had had other lovers from the higher end of Byzantine society.

Although Theodora may not have been forced into her adopted lifestyle, it appears that she suffered, as women forced into prostitution suffer, from a sense of powerlessness and entrapment—she was living an expensive lifestyle that cast her into a cycle of dependency on her lovers. Unlike many victims of the modern sex trade, she was able to move into a permanent relationship that she surely hoped would protect her from the insecurity she had hitherto known—but at the cost of giving up her profession. Much later, she would demonstrate a profound understanding of what it meant to be trapped in the sex trade.[14]

Even if Theodora had not taken on serial lovers, people would have assumed she did anyway, which may have contributed to the trap in which she found herself. Actresses, as the law granting Justinian and Theodora the right to marry makes clear, were generally regarded as promiscuous women whom members of the upper classes could *not* marry. Constantine, emperor from AD 306 to 337, had issued a list of professional women assumed to be promiscuous; then, because poverty could be an honorable condition, the law had been emended by Marcian to exclude women who were simply poor.[15] That Theodora's inclusion in the category of promiscuous persons is not simply the result of scandal-mongering by the likes of Priscus and Procopius may be confirmed by the fact that she ended her acting career to become the concubine of an imperial official. She could, after all, have made other choices; her mother had married another member of the entertainment industry, and, as Choricius of Gaza asserts, actors and actresses often married each other—a point no more surprising in the sixth century than in the twenty-first. Theodora, already hoping to move in different circles, did not want to be like her mother.

There had been many women who, well before Theodora's time, had become very powerful as a result of making the choice that she made. We have met Acte, who did just that. Another, Marcia, in late–second-century Rome, after a series of liaisons with upper-class men, had ended up as mistress of Emperor Commodus, thereby becoming a highly influential person in the Roman state. It was she who arranged Commodus' murder on New Year's Eve of AD 192. Antonia Caenis, the long-term companion of the emperor Vespasian (AD 69–79) after his wife's death, was a freedwoman. In earlier centuries, a woman like Marcia (or Theodora) would have been identified as the love interest of a Latin poet—possessing her own home and her own staff and able to forbid entry to anyone she did not want around.[16]

In Constantinople of the sixth century, we encounter such women in the poetry of writers like Agathias (also a historian—we met him in the last chapter) or Paul Silentiarius, a courtier of some importance. Agathias writes:

> How should one walk upon the path of Love? Should one seek
> it in the streets—beware then the girl's love of gold and luxury
> (for which you're going to pay); stay away from respectable
> girls, though—if you get her into bed you're going to have
> to marry [her]—and stay away from other people's wives.
> Widows are possible, but they're either too free with their
> affections or really not interested in sex. Certainly you need to
> stay away from your slaves—you'll be your servant's servant,
> and if you go for the slave of another, you'll end up in court
> and no good will come of it.

Agathias speaks here for men like himself, men with money who would like a career in government even though, if they made it, they might not have much choice about whom they married. John Lydus, for instance, seems to have been a particular favorite of Zosimus, praetorian prefect in the year 511, who arranged for him to marry the daughter of one of Zosimus' allies. He told Lydus that she was of good character and would bring a good dowry. That was all he had to say about Lydus' prospective wife. [17]

Not every woman was going to stay home at night or wait around at her patron's disposal. As ancient poets advised, to deal with a woman like Theodora, a man had to be willing to give up a bit of control. So what, if you think yourself irresistibly good-looking and lovable? So what, if you think she's bound to be yours?—let her know, and she'll own you. A man yesterday so confident was now his girl's plaything.[18] The poetic language in which these sentiments were couched may be very traditional, and it tells us nothing about the emotional life of any one individual; nonetheless, it can reveal to us the atmosphere of the time, what people thought about women they would meet but never marry.

These men wanted sex primarily, but not exclusively, and they wanted to feel that, pro tem at least, they had won the battle for their girl's affection; and she would know that this was what they wanted to feel. "I have her breasts in my hands, we're mouth to mouth, and I feed in passion around her silver neck, but I don't have the whole girl." She was not going to have sex with him, wrote Paul Silentiarius. Agathias painted us a picture of an actress named Ariadne whose music evoked the Muses, whose beauty was greater even than Aphrodite's, and she was his—or so he said. Paul told us that he now understood the myth of Danaë and Zeus, who turned into a shower of gold to get into her bed.

There you have it: That is what it will take—no need for a lover to pray to the goddess of love: money will do fine. Macedonius, another contemporary of Theodora's, would also declare that gold was the worker bee that would get the love goddess's honey. Sometimes a poet would envisage an encounter at a party or other gathering. Mostly he liked to be alone. The women he sought were in his view free to choose—Galatea slammed the door on me last night, said Paul, and it made him all the keener. He tried to stay away but could not. Then, Laïs loved him, she was weeping. Why? She was afraid he would leave her. That's the way men are.[19]

Paul's Galatea threw him out because he scorned her. We know of few other instances when elements of class slip into his work, or indeed that of his contemporaries. The men are generally looking for love, but the girls remain objects, precious and fun, but not full human beings.

The male gaze is solipsistic—It'll be wonderful when I get her—and of course it will be great for her, too—Why would Parmenis flee me and desire another? Why not?—Will it be great for her? That's not a question. How might she feel? That's also not a question—she's just supposed to be a goddess. . . . Sometimes, though, the "object" breaks. Polemo beats up Rhodanthe. "All-daring hand," writes Paul again, "how could you?! You grabbed her hair and pulled her around. Now, hand, I beat my head with you. She's not letting me back." There may be violence, but one thing there is not, in all of this, is any suggestion of fathering a child.[20]

Contraception was the woman's business, anyway. There were various ways whereby the women of this place and time learned to avoid pregnancy, or to end one. We gain some impression of the measures that Theodora would have had available to her via the works of doctors such as Soranus, who composed his *Gynecology* in the second century AD. Although writing about women's health and incorporating some information from women themselves, Soranus is mostly writing for other male doctors. And his assumptions about sex tell us a fair amount about the assumptions that the men Theodora dealt with brought to her bedroom.

The best way, so Soranus says, to avoid conception, was for the woman to hold her breath when she felt her partner was about to ejaculate so that the semen did not enter her vagina too deeply. Afterwards she ought to get up, sneeze, wipe her vagina and have a cold drink. Before intercourse she should apply old olive oil to her vagina—or honey, cedar resin, or balsam juice, possibly mixed with white lead. Another alternative was a wax salve containing myrtle and white lead. Otherwise, she might insert fine wool, or use a vaginal suppository, for which there were many recipes. One could also take abortifacient cocktails, though Soranus thought these dangerous, as they contained drugs that could cause a good deal of collateral damage, harming the stomach, causing congestion, and inducing sympathetic reactions. He also observed that women might wear amulets to avoid conceiving. If she wanted an abortion—of which Soranus disapproved unless her health was thought to be in danger—he recommended energetic leaping, carrying heavy objects, riding bouncy animals, long baths and draughts that he believed could bring on menstruation. He was aware that abortions could be very hazardous and prevent a woman from conceiving again.[21]

Aëtius of Amida, another doctor, who shows in his writings a more general interest in gynecology, admits to having acquired some of the treatments he advocates from women themselves. A powerful case has been made for his having been Theodora's physician in later life, and for one of the female voices—that of "Aspasia"—in his work being in fact Theodora's. Whether true or not—and it is tempting to imagine that the name of the famous mistress of the fifth-century Athenian politician Pericles, a woman noted for her intelligence, could be used as a pseudonym for Theodora—it is clear that "Aspasia" had much experience of gynecological complaints and knew a good deal about how to prevent or abort pregnancies. Aëtius cites some of her recipes, for treating uterine fibrosis and menstrual cramps, for instance, and recommends the use of fresh horse's or ass's milk (or the same reheated, if not available fresh).

For a woman finding herself pregnant with an unwanted child, Aspasia recommends a course of increasingly severe treatment (similar in theory to what Soranus suggests), beginning thus:

> If the woman should be unwilling or unable to bear the child, during the first thirty days we should do the opposite of those things we said we should do for the care of a pregnant woman. Advise her to shake violently, leap up and down and carry heavy weights. Then it is necessary to heat up the passages that carry the urine, menses and to clear the stomach with harsh infusions. In the bath, rub the area above the abdomen, the pubic area and the lower back, spend a lot of time every day in warm water and rely on a potion made from marshmallow and wormwood mixed with old [olive] oil on its own or with rue juice and honey.

To have access to long hours in a warm bath, Aspasia's patient would not have been from amongst the poorest, and the ingredients for her medicines are complicated. Her first herbal concoction (she gives many others) mingles a poison (wormwood, if taken in large doses) with a substance to ease swallowing (the juice of the marshmallow), plus another with well-attested abortifacient properties (rue juice). Various herbal recipes that Aëtius recommends for vaginal suppositories contain chemical compounds for preventing conception. In one such, the woman is told: "Mix pine bark and tanning fluid in equal parts with wine from pressed grapes, place it in wool before having sex; take it out after two hours and you can have sex." A more complicated recipe states: "[Take] two drachmas of pomegranate flower chalices, two drachmas of oak gall, fashion them into acorn-like vaginal suppositories the size of barley kernels; insert them two days after the end of menstruation, leave them for a day, then you may have sex with a man, if [you wish], but not before. This is the most infallible method."[22]

The information that Soranus and Aëtius offer in their discussions of contraception and abortion is especially interesting because married women were not really expected to engage in either, although Soranus does mention the possibility of a girl wanting an abortion so as to preserve her figure. Most girls tended to get married in their late teens to men some years older than themselves, and could expect to spend most of the next decade pregnant or nursing young children. The average wife might have five, though with the high incidence of infant mortality, it was more than likely that only two or three would live past the age of five—Theodora's family was thus of average size. Women from more aristocratic families married younger—sometimes just after puberty—and they were expected to be sexually active from the start, though doctors noted that early teen pregnancies tended to be difficult and have long-term health consequences for the girls. One argument in favor of early marriage was that pubescent girls were eager for sex; another, according to Aëtius, was that an adolescent girl might suffer from an enlarged clitoris, which would encourage her to enjoy sex. He also had a recipe to treat the effects of "excessive masturbation." Egyptians, he noted, recommended clitoridectomy, and he even provided directions for performing the operation.

One aspect of this marital regime was that young men, especially young men with money, looked for sex wherever they could find it without having to worry about the consequences for their partner. The accent was on excitement. One rabbi wrote that a man could expect to have a wife for children and a lover for sex.[23]

Men did not anticipate their wives' being sexually proactive—that was what they expected of their mistresses. In writing of his dream afternoon with a girlfriend, a Roman poet describes her coming to him in bed wearing a thin shift, which he removes—not that it concealed much in the first place—so that he can run his hands over her breasts, her flat stomach, her shapely thighs. She is young, and this is all we see before he draws a curtain over the scene, then bringing his readers back into the bedroom with the words "Who doesn't know the rest?—tired, we both rested." Note that it was the girl who came to him, which is also the case in an extract, from a Greek novel of the second century AD—and here there was no curtain. The evening opened with drinks, then:

> When we had finally drunk ourselves into a suitable mood
> for the real business of the night, she addressed me sternly as
> follows:
> "Now remember, young man, I'm not called Palaestra for
> nothing [the name means "wrestling ground"]. You're here to
> do some wrestling. Now's the time to show your mettle and
> give a demonstration of your technique." "Don't you worry,"
> I replied. "You won't catch me backing out. I'm quite prepared
> to be put to the test, so let's strip and try a fall right away."
> "Well this is what I suggest," she said. "I'll be the trainer
> and sing out the instructions, and you must be ready to do
> whatever I say."

The subsequent "wrestling" is described in some detail, but the point, again, is that Palaestra takes the lead in this male fantasy, which will soon involve the young man in question being transformed into an ass by Palaestra, in a failed experiment with magic.

The story was retold in Latin by Apuleius, one of the literary geniuses of the Roman world, but with somewhat different detail and dialogue. Here as well we get some idea of what Theodora's partners' expectations might have been, as the two lovers throw off all their clothes and embark on "an orgy for Venus." Apuleius continues: ". . . and when I was exhausted, Photis, with her own generosity, took me in hand, and with our eyes drooping with exhaustion, slumber slipped into them and held us fast until dawn." Procopius, as noted earlier, sees Theodora as sexually creative and proactive. He does not need to have talked with someone who has slept with her to know this—it was what was expected of women in her position.[24]

We know little of Theodora's lovers. We do read that she gave up the stage to become the concubine of a man named Hecebolus, a senior enough official to be appointed as a provincial governor. This suggests that she was then moving in relatively exalted circles. We know that she did not want to live out her life as an actress; and her career might not in any event have been expected to last beyond her early twenties. Facing retirement in the near term, she was quite likely seeking as potentially permanent a relationship as she could hope for—and bearing in mind her official status as "a disreputable person."

Her acting career had certainly ended by 521–522, when the evident stability of her relationship with Justinian prompted Justin to emend the marriage laws, thus allowing her to become Justinian's wife. But it is more than likely that her career had ended four or five years earlier, with the birth of her daughter. The date of that birth is nowhere directly recorded, but the fact that Theodora had a grandson named Anastasius who, by the year 543, she wished to marry to the daughter of her friend Antonina, gives us a rough idea of when the girl was born. Anastasius was probably a child at the time of his betrothal, and around fifteen when he married, slightly before Theodora's death in 548, suggesting that he was born around 533–534—it could not have been earlier, because her father-in-law, a nephew of the deceased emperor Anastasius, was in exile from January 532 to the first part of 533, when the marriage between his son (or grandson) and Theodora's daughter marked an important political rapprochement. The date of the marriage is our most important clue to the daughter's birthdate. Although girls could be betrothed, and even married, in their early teens, the average age for a first marriage seems to have been around fifteen, and doctors recognized the risk sexual activity posed for immature girls. Given what would later be her record in trying to eliminate child prostitution, it is unreasonable to think that Theodora would have been unaware of the potential health risks for her daughter if she married before she reached her mid-teens. The latest the girl could have been born is probably 518, and it is possible she was born a year earlier. [25]

Who was the father of Theodora's daughter, and was she an only child? We can answer both questions with a fair degree of certainty. As mentioned earlier, Procopius claims that Theodora also had a son, whom she would have killed at birth had not the father been present and taken the boy away to Bostra, in what is now Jordan. The child, whose name was John, showed up briefly in Constantinople before Theodora arranged his complete disappearance. The John story can be dated to the early 540s, to a point when she was fighting to keep the throne—and it has all the hallmarks of nasty gossip. A child whom no one saw, whose father no one knew, is likely to have been a child who never existed.[26]

So, yes, the daughter was an only child. Unfortunately, Procopius could not be bothered to give us her name; but then, he was not writing for people who needed to be told, since she had become famous by the time he was slandering her mother. The significance of the girl's birth is simply that, by then, knowing that a child would bring her professional life to an end, Theodora must already have decided to leave the stage behind her. Most likely, her decision to carry on with the pregnancy was motivated by the relationship she was in at the time, and thus the relationship was expected to have some permanency, which in turn would suggest that the father was Hecebolus. We may deduce his paternity both from the chronology of Theodora's life and from the fact that he is the only lover Procopius can actually name. The reason Procopius names him is presumably because there was some good reason for people to remember him at the time Procopius was writing the *Secret History*. The most obvious reason why he was remembered is that he was the father of a now very well-known woman, Theodora's daughter. We may further deduce, from the fact that men did not typically take as concubines women who already had children, that Theodora decided to end her stage career when she was in her early twenties, and before she became pregnant.

As we noted earlier, in later life, the empress took steps to give women who, from economic necessity, were trapped in the sex trade a chance to get out if they wished, and she is said to have been the driving force behind a law aimed at ending child prostitution. Moreover, she seems to have felt a marked antipathy towards rich men of privilege. At least, we might draw this conclusion from a story that Procopius tells of the way, when she was empress, she once humiliated a member of Constantinople's upper class at an audience, not to mention her insistence on court ceremonial involving the prostration of senior officials before herself and her husband. Although she was never a sex worker of the kind to whom she offered assistance, her actions indicate a genuine concern for people whose condition Roman law had ignored for a millennium. Emperors may have deplored the fact that parents would sell their children into slavery, but they took no steps to prevent them from being sold into prostitution by those same impecunious parents. The law of 529 releasing child prostitutes from the pimps who had bought them is unique in Roman history, and our sources attribute this, as well as the later "halfway house" project (see chapters 7 and 10), to Theodora.[27]

Her sympathy for victims of the sex trade may tell us something about her own feelings when she was young. Clearly, she wanted something different from what her mother had had; she wanted, ultimately, to live a life away from the stage, to move in the circles of the rich and famous. Having achieved that, she found that for them she was a fantasy love object, not a person. Her capacity for deep friendships suggests that she would find a life of serial lovers profoundly unsatisfactory. She wanted out, and this is where Hecebolus comes in.

Theodora's relationship with Hecebolus would prove to be a disaster, in the short term. In the long term, it put her in a position to meet Justinian—at which point Hecebolus is never heard of again.

As an actress, Theodora could not marry a man of Hecebolus' rank, but as his concubine she could have certain expectations about how she would be treated, as well as some stability. The status of concubine was recognized as a legal alternative to marriage between people of different ranks. As his concubine, Theodora could expect that Hecebolus would have no other lovers, and that, if there were children, they would be hers in the event of a split. It could have been a relationship, depending on Hecebolus' age and attainments, that she might expect to last for a long time. As a senior official, he was probably a good deal older than she was—possibly in his mid-thirties—and he may well have been married before. Men who had already had children by a previous marriage often chose to live with a concubine so as to avoid the arrival of other legitimate children with a claim on their estate. Children by a concubine could inherit only if their father had no legitimate offspring. For Theodora, the choice to live with Hecebolus meant that, abandoning her stage career, she willingly entered into a relationship whose stability would determine her security. Officially she would have no rights to his property; unofficially, she could look forward to being a person of some power, wherever he ended up.[28]

Hecebolus' assignment was as governor of Pentapolis, the easternmost Roman province, centered on the area around the modern city of Benghazi in Libya. It was a potentially significant appointment, which suggests that Hecebolus was highly regarded. His immediate neighbors were, to the west, the Vandal kingdom, and to the east; Egypt. Hecebolus' title as governor—*comes et dux*—signified his responsibility for the region's civil and military governance, an unusual appointment since military duties were usually separate from civilian ones; but Pentapolis was a long way from Constantinople and at this point under threat from the nomadic desert tribes.

The city from which Hecebolus operated was Sozousa, once known as Apollonia—named for the pagan god Apollo. Its Christian inhabitants had insisted on a name change during the previous century. Sozousa had once been nothing more than the port city for Cyrene, eleven miles to the west, which Greek settlers had founded in the mid–seventh century BC. These settlers, who came from ancient Sparta on the Greek mainland, looked to exploit the great agricultural wealth of the region, and they succeeded in making their new home an important city, the center of a vital agricultural district exporting dates, grapes, olives, apples, and grain. Good horses came from there, and so did silphium. Silphium had once been treasured as a spice with qualities believed to be both curative and aphrodisiac. It no longer exists, the plant having been seriously depleted by the first century AD as a result of poor resource management. Cyrene's decline as a city was possibly connected with silphium's disappearance; by the mid–fifth century, that decline seems to have been complete, and Sozousa had become the region's major city.[29]

When Hecebolus arrived, the new palace complex where he would live had just been finished. Today, we can visualize Theodora spending the night in the one surviving building. The city in which she now lived also had a number of churches, a heterodox bishop—and a host of problems. At some point in Anastasius' reign, the emperor had written to the then–*dux et comes*, Daniel, confirming measures he had put in place to clean up a messy situation in which the soldiers stationed there evidently thought they were being mistreated by the civilian government. Anastasius agreed that the governor's civilian staff should be limited to forty, and that their pay should consist of a single subsistence ration apiece (officials might be given, in addition, allowances for their servants or family members). These same officials should stop charging the soldiers excessive fees for standard services. There also seem to have been problems having to do with an earlier governor who had pitted the soldiers against each other by playing favorites, both within and between units. The soldiers were told that they were not to cause problems for the people in whose houses they were billeted and to exercise

FIGURE 3.2. Palace of the Dux at Apollonia, where Theodora probably lived as Hecebolus' concubine.

© Gilles Mermet / Art Resource, NY

great care to ensure that no one engaged in unauthorized trade with the nomads.[30]

Despite the caution evident in Anastasius' orders, Hecebolus' staff were comparatively well compensated, and he himself must have been able to live in considerable style. His palace consisted of three parts: one for official business; another that housed his attendants, with a gate-house opening through the city wall and guardrooms; and the third was his private quarters. The architects must either have anticipated that the governor would come with a large entourage, or simply have wished the building to look very impressive. It appears to have been modeled on the imperial palace in Constantinople.[31]

Theodora was now in a position, if she was interested, to learn something about the way the empire was run. She would certainly have learned how to live in a palace and to handle a large staff. When she ventured out, she would have seen the large churches on the palace's east and west sides, and she might well have attended the theater just outside the city wall. In Sozousa, the dominant form of the faith was that of the anti-Chalcedonians, who believed, as mentioned earlier, that Jesus Christ as the embodiment of God's word possessed a single, divine, nature rather than divine and human aspects as had been determined by the Council of Chalcedon.[32]

How long she had to absorb these lessons we do not know, but we do know that her relationship with Hecebolus ended badly, possibly when she became pregnant with her daughter, possibly after the child's birth. In any event, he dismissed Theodora. Alone and with a young child, she had to make a new life. She was not going to join the ranks of unmarried women with children, dependent on the kindness of strangers. So she left for Alexandria, then soon left Alexandria for Antioch in Syria, where her life would change yet again.

4

Factions and Networks

Procopius tells us that after Hecebolus threw her out, Theodora made her way around the Mediterranean, sleeping with whoever would pay for her services. Since Procopius appears to be unaware that she had a child with her, and that she would link up in these years with the leaders of the anti-Chalcedonian Church in Syria, there is no reason to believe what he has to say. But, as is often the case with him, there is some gold mixed in with the manure. He tells us that when she was in Antioch, Theodora made the acquaintance of a woman named Macedonia, who, when not selling spells, was an agent for the Blue Faction: the Antiochene branch of the circus faction that had taken Theodora in as a child, and the group most closely linked with the palace. It was at this time, when Macedonia was her confidante, that Theodora first met Justinian. Like Hecebolus, Macedonia is *not* a creature of fiction, or even of slander. The two are linked in a positive tale of Theodora's life in which Macedonia appears as a savior and guide after Hecebolus' emotional and financial abuse, a story that Procopius perverts.[1] Her presence in Theodora's story can help us unravel its greatest mysteries: How did she come to meet Justinian, and how did this young single mother develop the strength and confidence to captivate one of the most powerful men in the world?

To follow her progress at this point, we will stroll with her along the highways and byways of imperial society. Her tale is inextricably connected with the conflicts that erupted on July 10, 518, when it was reported that Emperor Anastasius had died in his sleep. To find Theodora, we move from the Hippodrome of Constantinople to that of Antioch, and into the ambit of one of the great churchmen of her day, Bishop Severus, a man whose influence would become ever more important to her. She would be willing, in the years to come, to defy even her husband in order to protect this man. Perhaps this was just a political ploy on her part—she and the cleric were not always on the best of terms—but that is unlikely. When she married Justinian, Theodora was recognized as a member of a network, including Severus, whom she was unlikely to have met in person, that ran from the empire's eastern border to the imperial palace. Had friends of Bishop Severus given her the support and strength she needed to move ahead?[2]

The Theodora who emerged from her years in Antioch would be a powerful and unique personality. She would be renowned as exceptionally smart, exceptionally beautiful, and exceptionally tough. And it was during this period that she would put her past as actress, courtesan, and concubine behind her for good to become the woman who would rule an empire.

Antioch itself was an extraordinary city, as extraordinary in its way as Alexandria, through which Theodora most likely passed on her journey. Alexandria, at least for the educated, retained the cachet of being an academic center, the sort of place where the children of well-to-do families might go to study—we will meet one of those boys shortly. It had been the home, until recently, of great libraries, and a place where pagan intellectuals could rub shoulders with Christian bishops.[3]

Antioch was different. It was a garish place, enriched by the produce of a huge territory of sixty-two square miles. In the fourth century, one resident praised it for its streetlights, and modern archaeologists working in the city and its environs have found evidence of immensely wealthy houses decorated with splendid mosaics, many of them depicting scenes from the theater, often with mythological themes. It was a city that, perched on the edge of a rough landscape peppered with communities of holy men and solitary ascetics, while proclaiming to the world its devout Christianity, retained something of its ancestral paganism. It infuriated its bishop, Severus, when people cried "Fortune of the city, give victory" at the horse races, because he knew that cheer was an invocation of the city's old pagan goddess. He was none too pleased, either, that the city continued to celebrate the Olympic games—those, too, he was quick to point out, were a feature of pagan worship.[4]

It is possible that Severus was still Bishop of Antioch when Theodora arrived in the city, but if so, the overlap was very short, since he was deposed in the late summer of 518, and Theodora did not go straight to Antioch after the breakup with Hecebolus, in any version of the story. She probably arrived in the city in 519, but she would almost certainly have known a good deal about Severus already, given his prominence in Constantinople while she was growing up and pursuing her stage career. Severus' influence in Antioch, and the empire at large, did not end with his deposition.

It was in 508 that Severus arrived in Constantinople at the head of two hundred monks from Palestine to become the unofficial leader of the anti-Chalcedonian cause in the capital. Theodora might have seen something of the violence that broke out three years later between anti-Chalcedonians and followers of the city's patriarch, Macedonius, who supported the Chalcedonian confession. A few days after the streets were filled with men beating each other over their religious beliefs, Macedonius was expelled from his post (we will be returning to this episode in order to view it from Severus' perspective). The violence that broke out a year later, when a riot in the Hippodrome against enemies of Chalcedon took place, almost cost Anastasius his throne. Theodora may well have been in the crowd when he appeared, without his crown, to beg the crowd's forgiveness for his ham-fisted handling of the protests. These events may well have shaped her response to one of the great crises of her husband's reign, when the rioting in the Hippodrome almost impelled him to flee the city.[5]

The link between the riots of 512 and what happened next might not have been clear to Theodora—it certainly is not clear to us at this point, and there is no reason to think that Anastasius would have broadcast the circumstances of yet another crisis. What she, and anyone else living in Constantinople in 513, could not have failed to realize was that the rebel general Vitalian had thrashed the emperor's army in Thrace and advanced for the second time on the city walls, this time with Anastasius' nephew, Hypatius, as his prisoner—some said he kept the poor young man in a cage. People may have spoken, soon after, of the huge ransom Anastasius paid to set Hypatius free and to persuade Vitalian to leave. The next year there was intense fighting by land and sea, the climax of which was the incineration of Vitalian's fleet in the Golden Horn, which brought his rebellion to an end. Theodora would certainly have known that the circus factions had rallied around Anastasius, and that a charioteer named Porphyrius had played a crucial role in the battle. His monument may already have been erected in the Hippodrome by the time she left town with Hecebolus; and since she mingled with government officials, she may also have known that Severus had been appointed bishop in Antioch.[6]

Severus had lived quite an adventurous life before becoming Bishop of Antioch. Born into a wealthy pagan family at the Pisidian

FIGURE 4.1. There survive, in Istanbul, two of the five monuments that once stood in the Hippodrome honoring Porphyrius, the most famous charioteer of his era. This scene shows us the victorious Porphyrius in his chariot and faction members cheering for him.

© Vanni Archive / Art Resource, NY

city of Sozopolis in what is now western Turkey, he was educated in rhetoric and law at Alexandria and Beirut. Despite the dominance of Christianity in government, there remained many pagans, both amongst the educated classes of the empire and throughout the countryside, some of whom will come into Theodora's story anon.

When Severus arrived in Alexandria, he witnessed the brutal anti-pagan riot sparked by some acquaintances of his who had reported evidence of a continuing pagan cult supposedly involving bloody altars, "heathen images," and a magician. In Beirut, other people he knew, who had formed themselves into a sort of anti-magic patrol, had barely prevented some pagans from beheading an Ethiopian slave in their effort to cast a love spell; Severus then persuaded the pagans to burn their magic books. It was while he was in Beirut that Severus converted to Christianity and took up residence in the monastery run by a leading anti-Chalcedonian theologian near Jerusalem. His actual baptism took place in the Lebanese city of Tripoli in the *martyrium* of Leontius, quite possibly because the Bishop of Beirut was strongly Chalcedonian, and the form of Christianity that had attracted Severus was not in accord with the teachings of Chalcedon.[7]

Shortly after his baptism, Severus parted company with his good friend, fellow student, and future biographer, Zacharias of Mitylene. Zacharias went on to Constantinople to become a lawyer (thereby making his parents happy). Still, the two remained friends, and the link Zacharias provided with the professional classes in the capital probably facilitated Severus' sudden rise to power in the city after fifteen years of living an ascetic lifestyle. In his first years as a monk, Severus had lived in a monastery near Gaza; from there, he went into the desert near Eleutheropolis (now Bayt Jibrin in Israel), where he nearly died. Restored to health in a nearby monastery, Severus founded a monastery of his own outside Gaza and rapidly became one of the most influential teachers of his time, while using family money to support the impoverished. Around 500 he was ordained, and a few years later had a tremendous fight with the Chalcedonian Bishop of Jerusalem, who drove him from his own monastery. So it was that, in 508, at the head of his two hundred monks, Severus arrived at Constantinople.[8]

In the preceding decades, the monasteries of Constantinople, which saw it as their task to succor the poor, had grown increasingly influential. Monks had been arriving from all over the Eastern empire to establish communities, quite often of an extremist theological bent, with a view to making sure their voices would be heard in the center of power. One holy man in particular, Daniel the Stylite, who ordinarily resided on top of a pillar outside the city, had played a major role in quelling Basiliscus' rebellion against Zeno. His career may have showed others the possibilities that lay before them even if their own practices were less eccentric than Daniel's had been. Certainly Severus seems to have spied out the potential of a stay in the capital before he arrived. Through his friend Zacharias, Severus had already acquired contacts in the city, and he seems to have rapidly acquired more within the palace, the most important of whom were a senator, Clementinus, and a eunuch named Eupraxius, a devout believer who valued Severus' theological insights. There survives amongst the fragments of Severus' correspondence a long letter to Eupraxius answering a series of questions Eupraxius had sent him regarding points of doctrine, and setting out talking points for Eupraxius to use in debates with supporters of Chalcedon. There are fragments of two other letters, sent in the same years, to Eupraxius, one of them addressed as well to Phocas, one of Eupraxius' colleagues in the palace. Perhaps with the aid of these men, Severus extended his contacts further to include Theodore, a rich official who consulted him about the possibility of becoming a monk, "telling [Severus] that he thought he saw the light of the divine torch shining in him." Another senior official came and sought marriage counseling for the daughter of a fellow administrator. This Severus declined to provide, pointing out that he was a philosopher, not a magician—though he did allow that there were holy men who would provide this service. It may have been Probus, Anastasius' nephew, who introduced him to the emperor.[9]

Within a few years of being driven from his home in Palestine, Severus had found the patrons who would make him into one of the empire's most powerful men. To accomplish this, he relied on his wits, his undoubted intelligence, and his eloquence. His career shows us what an individual from outside the charmed circle of imperial government, with the right connections and attitudes, could achieve.

It is clear that, while Severus was in Constantinople, Anastasius was not enjoying a healthy relationship with the city's patriarch, Macedonius, who was technically the second–highest-ranking clergyman in the Mediterranean, behind only the Bishop of Rome, thanks to the council of Chalcedon. Macedonius, for his part, was becoming increasingly keen to assert what he regarded as Chalcedonian orthodoxy, while Anastasius was attempting to govern in accord with a document Zeno concocted in 482, the so-called Act of Union, or *Henotikon*. The *Henotikon* was astute to such an extent that it would appear to belie Zeno's reputation as a drunken, incompetent lout. In it, Zeno seeks to bring religious peace to the empire by simply declaring that the Council of Nicaea defined orthodoxy, and that the Council of Constantinople in 381 had confirmed Nicaea (a statement that accorded with a statement by Theodosius I enshrined in the empire's legal code). By saying that "We and the churches everywhere neither have held, nor hold, nor shall hold, nor do we know those who hold a different creed or teaching or definition of faith or faith," from that of Nicaea, Zeno simply refused to acknowledge that either the Second Council of Ephesus or that of Chalcedon had happened. Furthermore, by stating that the Father and Son were consubstantial in both divinity and humanity, he dodged the central issue. He went on to say that people should simply not talk about other councils.[10]

If Zeno was sitting in Constantinople in 476, it was partly because Basiliscus had alienated the population by taking a staunch anti-Chalcedonian line; this led to his humiliation by a mob organized by Daniel the Stylite and convinced General Illus to desert to Zeno's side—the decisive event in this rebellion. At the time he issued the "Act of Union," Zeno had also just escaped another assassination attempt organized by another of his erstwhile relatives (this one was married to Ariadne's younger sister). The Act of Union looks like a reasonable effort to avoid throwing the oil of religious intolerance on a smoldering fire. Anastasius seems to have seen things the same way, and for some time, Macedonius, too, had been of the same opinion.[11]

In the months before the outbreak of the riots that led to his downfall in 511, Macedonius appears to have been under pressure from strongly Chalcedonian quarters to cease his support for the Act of Union. The immediate cause of this particular conflict was the wording of the acclamation known as "the Trisagion," uttered in the liturgy before the recitation of the psalm. The standard wording was (and still is) "Holy God, Holy Strong, Holy Immortal, have mercy upon us." The anti-Chalcedonian view of the crucifixion differed fundamentally from that of the Chalcedonians. The supporters of Chalcedon believed that "the Son of man came down from heaven, when the Son of God assumed the body from the Virgin from whom he was born, and again the Son of God is said to have been crucified and buried, when he endured these things not in the Godhead itself in which he is only-begotten, coeternal, and consubstantial with the Father, but in the weakness of his human nature." By inserting the phrase "who was crucified for us" after "Holy Immortal," the anti-Chalcedonian version of the Trisagion asserted that God was crucified in his divine aspect—which, as we noted earlier, was his only aspect, according to the foes of Chalcedon.[12]

According to Severus, the rioting began at the Church of Hagia Sophia (the predecessor of the great church that now stands on the same site) on July 20, 511. In the course of a service, a group of anti-Chalcedonians chanted their version of the Trisagion. Macedonius, it would seem, was prepared for this demonstration: he had with him a large band of thugs whom he ordered to attack the anti-Chalcedonians. Severus tells us:

> Then, while they were still in the church singing hymns and offering praise in this manner, that son of impiety, Macedonius, inflamed by the fire and madness of impiety, commissioned and hired slaves for money along with other people of their sort, outcasts, who will not refuse to do anything evil, and sent them into the church against the orthodox. These inflicted great blows and other wounds which were difficult to heal upon the brothers who uttered the Trisagion, as they pulled their hair, dragged them, struck them with their hands, kicked them with their feet, poked them in the eyes and plucked off their nails like carnivorous birds.

When the imperial authorities intervened, Macedonius declared that he would assert his faith in the Act of Union. When he subsequently appeared to renege on the deal, Anastasius removed him from office. It was in the immediate aftermath of Macedonius' deposition that Anastasius also deposed Flavian, Bishop of Antioch, and sent Severus to stand for election in his place. Duly elected, Severus immediately set a new tone by closing the kitchens of the bishop's residence, tearing down its private bathhouse, sleeping on the ground, and purchasing the plainest of fare from the market.[13]

By the end of 515, Anastasius had survived war, riot, and insurrection, but he had not survived unscathed. Indeed, by the time of his death on July 9, 518, he appears to have had less power than Ariadne had had when her first husband, Zeno, died in 491. Ariadne had determined the succession—Anastasius was in no position to do so on his own.

Anastasius and Ariadne (who died in 515) had no children, and Anastasius' lack of progeny from an earlier union may have helped qualify him for the office of emperor in the first place. He did, however, have three nephews, all of whom he had promoted to top positions in the army. One nephew, Probus, was in July 518 about two hundred miles from Constantinople, probably keeping an eye on the exiled Vitalian, whose notion of being "in hiding" does not appear to have involved a great deal of secrecy. Hypatius, the second nephew, was in command of the army of the eastern frontier and thus in Antioch. The third, Patricius, commanded the army in the capital.[14]

When Zeno died, the people of Constantinople had been summoned to the Hippodrome. Ariadne entered the imperial box, accompanied by the patriarch and members of the court, to hear from them the qualities they desired in a new emperor. When she appeared, the crowd acclaimed her:

> Ariadne Augusta, may you be victorious!
> Holy Lord, give her long life!
> Lord have mercy!
> Many years for the Augusta!
> An Orthodox emperor for the empire!

By "orthodox," the crowd meant that they wanted an emperor who subscribed to the doctrine of Chalcedon. Ariadne, whose personal theology was strongly Chalcedonian, thanked them for their loyalty, at which point they acclaimed her again, asking for a "Roman" as emperor—which meant no Isaurian relative of Zeno, whose brother Longinus evidently thought he was qualified for the job. Ariadne assured them that the emperor would be both Roman and Christian, and thus that her brother-in-law was out of the running. The crowd then asked that he not be avaricious. After more discussion, which included a demand for a new city prefect (a request Ariadne granted), the empress withdrew to the palace, where she met with the Senate. Some discussion ensued, until the chief chamberlain of the palace recommended that Ariadne be allowed to pick the next ruler. The Senate sent the patriarch to her with this request, and she duly announced that Anastasius, who had been one of her four "silentiaries," or ushers, was to be emperor. Anastasius was then sixty years old. He had achieved considerable prominence a few years before, when his name was being widely touted in debates over who would be Antioch's next patriarch. By inclination he was not especially Chalcedonian (and would become a good deal less so), but his other qualities appear to have won the day. [15]

Some, if not all, of this may have been the product of careful planning and stage-management, but it was at least orderly. The situation on July 9, 518, was very different.

On that day, the silentiaries, presumably all thirty of them, in the absence of the empress (to whom four would otherwise have been assigned), informed the *magister officiorum*, in charge of the palace secretariat, and the count of the *excubitores* (a branch of the palace guard) that the emperor was dead, and they should hold a meeting in the palace forthwith. Celer, *magister* since 508, had played a major role in the exile of Macedonius and thus was so suspect to the Chalcedonians, despite efforts he had made on their behalf in the last few years, that he was in a poor position to claim the throne for himself. Justin, an experienced general who had played a significant part in a couple of important campaigns during the earlier years of Anastasius' reign and had contributed to the defense of the city against Vitalian, was the commander of the *excubitores*. It was he who announced the emperor's death to the assembled officials—which suggests that, despite being over sixty, he was considered a major player.

As the drama unfolded in the palace, the people assembled in the Hippodrome demanding that a general be appointed emperor. Celer, meanwhile, was telling the officials in the palace that they needed to find someone fast; for an orderly succession it was important that the senate and palace officials agreed on a candidate who would then be presented to the army and the people. The more time passed, the more likely it was that something could go wrong, and that either the soldiers or the factions would seize the initiative. Even as he was speaking, the *excubitores* in the Hippodrome proclaimed a man called John, only to be shouted down by the Blues. Inside the palace, another guard unit, the *scholarii*, tried to proclaim Anastasius' nephew, Patricius.[16] But the *excubitores*, who disliked Patricius, were threatening to kill him.

At this point, Justinian, best known at that point as Justin's nephew and as a member of the *candidati* (a guard unit named for its members' bright white tunics), entered the scene. He persuaded Patricius to withdraw to a safe place and to turn down the offer of the throne.

(In any event, the palace eunuchs, who controlled the imperial regalia, were refusing to release it.) Finally, the Senate and other officials spoke, proclaiming Justin. Then, after one of the *scholarii* had punched Justin in the face—the physical assault may actually have hastened the outcome—everyone joined in acclaiming him as emperor, and the eunuchs released the imperial regalia. Properly attired, Justin entered the imperial box, surrounded by officials. There he addressed his people, who lustily cheered his accession, and he promised a substantial "gift" to all the guardsmen.[17]

At this juncture, three significant things happened in very short order. Vitalian was recalled from "hiding" and made commander of the army at the capital; Severus was deposed as Bishop of Antioch—Vitalian hated him so much he wanted to cut out his tongue; and a group of palace eunuchs was charged with trying to assassinate Justin. This story appears to have been invented after a pro-Chalcedonian demonstration at Hagia Sophia named them as heretics who should be eliminated. Another story, which emerged later, was that the chief eunuch, Amantius, wanted to have his bodyguard, Theocritus, made emperor, and that he had given Justin money to have the crowd acclaim his man. In another version, Justin is said to have stolen the money to bribe his own way to the throne; and, in yet another, to have handed the money over and then had himself proclaimed. All of this looks like more nasty gossip concocted well after the event in order to both explain why Amantius, who would have been in control of the imperial regalia on the morning after Anastasius died, was executed, and to denigrate Justin, whom some of the aristocracy regarded as an accidental emperor, seeing him as an illiterate peasant who could not even sign his own name. His wife, Euphemia, they said, was an old whore, at best his concubine.[18]

The circumstances surrounding Justin's ascension to power have one very important thing in common: they all strengthened the position of the pro-Chalcedonian officials against their anti-Chalcedonian counterparts. Justin became emperor, in part because he was not Vitalian, whose earlier career made him unacceptable to many in the capital; in part because he was, like Anastasius, a known quantity; and in part because he was regarded as reliably Chalcedonian. The problem that he faced was how to manage the government in the eastern part of the empire, which was the wealthier half and where the anti-Chalcedonians were in the majority. Religious issues were not, of course, the only stumbling blocks—there were plenty of other tensions, some stemming from the gross inequalities of wealth that were characteristic of the Roman Empire, some from rivalries within cities or between cities, or between cities and the countryside. Indeed, it is fair to say that the politicization of the theological problems that Justin faced was complicated further by the structure of his empire's economy, which played a significant role in determining who should hold important administrative positions, and the way the government would function in the different regions under its sway.

Most money during this age, as in the previous millennia, derived from the land. Land in the Roman Empire was held by peasants farming at near-subsistence levels in villages, or by absentee landlords living in cities, or by institutions; in Justin's time, "institutions" increasingly meant the Church, particularly the ecclesiastical institutions in the east of his empire that were dominated by anti-Chalcedonians. Many absentee landlords were not particularly wealthy; they might own a few estates and rent them to peasants through local agents, while hiring others to work at peak harvest times. Other landholders, a small number who controlled a very high proportion of the empire's wealth, owned numerous estates, which were managed by their own complex bureaucracies and patrolled by what were effectively their own hit men. They mingled their own interests with those of the state, often seeking to compel theoretically independent peasant communities to allow their relationship with the imperial government to be run through those bureaucracies. Their ability to pressure entire communities was facilitated by the fact that many of these people also held high imperial office.

That the richest held a monopoly of such positions was not only resented by peasant communities. John Lydus (or John the Lydian), a moneyed man with aspirations toward a job in government, was particularly eloquent on the topic when complaining about the conduct of Marinus, a praetorian prefect who served Anastasius and who allegedly "treated the cities as nothing less than enemies," for it was his habit to replace local city councils, as the primary tax-collecting agencies, with officials who reported to his office (we will meet Marinus again soon; he was a major player in the era's politics).[19]

The domination of the countryside by large landholders was not a new phenomenon. What *was* new was the fact that provincial magnates were also now becoming high-ranking officials. What was also new was that the Church was increasingly acting as a buffer between the wealthy and the peasant communities, especially in Syria, where the edges of the desert were home to many ascetics. Such people might, like Severus, be highly educated, but unlike Severus, many were of peasant background and had chosen an ascetic life as a way of channeling the power of God to assist their communities—it was their holy power, their miracles, that were thought to keep demons in check. On a more mundane level, they acted to diffuse conflicts both locally and between their neighbors and the forces of the outside world.[20]

The consequence of this system of land ownership was a population, both urban and rural, for whom economic inequality and oppression were a fact of life. Most days and in most places, people simply lived with it. The two groups that could provide the structure within which the common people could stand up to their masters were the Church and the circus factions. Most often, these institutions provided a measure of comfort, both physical and spiritual—it was not ordinarily in the interests of their leaders to cause trouble for the imperial authorities, but they could sometimes find themselves pincered between their relationship with those in authority and with the average man. If mass violence broke out, either the circus factions or the Church, sometimes both, tended to be involved.[21]

From the first century BC until the early fourth century AD, when Constantius II established a new Senate at Constantinople to balance the old one in Rome, disproportionate social and political power had resided with the small group of super-rich landholders who constituted the original Roman Senate. By and large, Roman senators, though they would certainly spend some time in the places from which their families hailed, tended to spend a great deal of their time in Rome, since they saw themselves as imperial rather than local leaders. The Vandal conquest of North Africa, where many Roman senators had significant estates, as well as the occupation of Spain by the Visigoths and the emergence of the Frankish kingdom in Gaul, seriously attenuated the power of this group, which had remained very significant even after the emperors no longer resided at Rome. The Senate at Constantinople was always to remain more closely linked with its provincial bases, which meant that regional cliques could form and exercise a great deal of influence over the palace. There was perhaps no better example of what such a clique could achieve than the accession of Zeno to the Eastern imperial throne, whose family was based in Isauria, a region of south-central Turkey on either side of the Taurus Mountains, north of Syria. And when Justin took the throne, he was detaching himself from his natural position as a subordinate of another regional clique, from his native region (Illyricum), which supported Vitalian. At the same time, he was very aware that he had no natural links with the eastern provinces.[22]

If Justin were to succeed, Syria and Egypt would need to be kept happy. At the same time, he could not lose sight of the forces that had made him emperor. There were officials to be wooed, and Justin needed to bear in mind that monasteries in those eastern regions—monasteries of a strongly anti-Chalcedonian disposition—held large amounts of land. If he were going to last, he had to find a way to be seen at Constantinople as promoting a religious position that was unpopular in a part of the empire where he had no personal connections. In order to succeed, he had to not only work with the officials in these areas and find clergy whom he could deal with; in order to establish connections, he needed, in addition, to be able to work through institutions rooted in Constantinople that also had close links with the major cities. Moreover, he had to be able to ensure the loyalty of the army in an area that had supported three armed movements against Constantinople in the preceding thirty-five years (including the one that had placed Zeno back on the throne). If he could count on the circus factions, he would be able to establish links with the cities of the east that were independent of the Church, the army, and other officials.

In the course of the fourth century, the maintenance of the circus factions had become a civic obligation, one imposed on the town councils, and the factions themselves seem to have taken an ever more active role in the organization of civic space. We can see this in the imperial law codes: here we find, for instance, an order that public storehouses provide fodder for retired chariot horses, and the assertion that it was "necessary, ancient and customary" that people from Campania would obtain horses for their amusement only if they contributed large quantities of beans to each of the factions. In 381, an emperor is seen issuing regulations about how horses should be handled at the games, evidently as a way of preventing price-gouging. Two constitutions of

Theodosius II in 426 attest the existence of an accountant for the theater and another for the chariot horses, and from this time onwards, there is evidence that the factions of the same color from different cities belonged to a centralized network whose members included well-placed individuals.[23] As far as we can tell, although a faction would have its headquarters near a city's race track, it would tend to derive its support from people in specific occupations, since cities were usually divided up into districts where specific crafts were practiced. It is likely as well that families would share a common affiliation, while connections with members of the aristocracy might be partly based on sporting affiliation and partly on other patronage relationships.[24] As factions crossed social boundaries, their activities sometimes represented the interests of different groups within a given faction: hence, while some of the violence associated with the games was "event-based," stemming from what had happened on the field or in the theater, the more serious violence stemmed from very different causes and was planned in advance.[25]

Theodosius II is said to have been so fond of the Greens that he changed the arrangement of the Hippodrome so as to always face them.[26] We do not know when the standard seating arrangement, according to which the imperial guard faced the imperial box, was instituted, but it is not implausible that such features went back as far as Diocletian's establishment of a circus at the same time as the imperial palace in Nicomedia, in the late third to early fourth century. There is no obvious reason to think that Theodosius' alterations to the hippodrome at Constantinople would have resulted in seating changes elsewhere, but the assertion that "he favored the Green faction and took their side in every city" suggests that the impact of his personal allegiance would be felt beyond the capital. Just how far this might extend in practical terms is not obvious, but there is some evidence for imperial micromanagement of faction affairs. An epigram honoring the charioteer Porphyrius claims that the emperor gave him to the Blues as a gift. That arrangement did not last. When at Antioch in 507, the *comes orientis* Basilus "assigned" him to the Greens, whose stable lacked a leader at the time. Porphyrius took the position, was victorious on the track, then led his supporters in violent assaults on the Jewish population; elsewhere we are told that he departed the Blues because of their "idiocy." Back in 486, Zeno had assigned specific dancers to each faction—another sign of direct imperial control—and the fact that they came from out of town demonstrates the reach of the network connecting the court with the provincial centers.[27]

Micromanagement was one thing, but turning a blind eye to murderous conduct was quite another. And yet, evidence of imperial willingness to tolerate—and even encourage—some degree of factional violence alternates with evidence of imperial efforts to curb it. Zeno, who depended heavily on the Greens in ejecting Basiliscus, dismissed one senior official who had tried to keep them from killing Jews.[28] In 507, the Greens demanded that some men who had been arrested for rioting be released. When Anastasius refused, they rushed the imperial box, and the emperor barely escaped being hit by a stone. The riot ended only when a substantial part of the Hippodrome and the city center had been burned down. He then appointed one of the rioters' patrons as city prefect.[29] The Greens also may also have been responsible for the murder of a senior official after that official had killed a member of their faction who had hidden in a church following the anti-Jewish riots inspired by Porphyrius at Antioch. Anastasius had a better idea. He responded to violence on the part of the Greens at Antioch, who had driven out a senior official because he had irritated them, by announcing that he would now favor the Reds. Perhaps this was a slap in the face to both major factions, a demonstration of the emperor's commitment to taking action against any who seriously misbehaved.[30] It was certainly a powerful statement, and it may be that it had something to do with the relative peace and quiet of the next several years—we cannot assume that everything was sweetness and light, but at least we have no report of a major outrage until the mass murder of some Blues in 501.[31]

Justin, when he donned the mantle of emperor, had few natural allies and could not afford a passive approach to the factions. Their networks enabled him to establish his own presence in the empire's major cities, and possibly to break down the hostility towards his ecclesiastical policies. For a person who was both anti-Chalcedonian and a faction member, it is not clear which was the stronger attachment; and anyway, it is unlikely that everyone would rate their allegiances in the same way, some inclining more to the faction, others more to the Church. In Justin's case, working with faction leaders certainly reduced the religious antagonisms. But he was aware that the people he was dealing with were not always reliable. He needed agents in the cities, people who could pass him useful information.[32] This was where a woman like Theodora's friend Macedonia would come in handy, and Theodora, too.

As yet, there were no especially close bonds between Chalcedonians, or their theological opponents, and specific factions. People like Severus of Antioch, who regarded chariot racing as a pagan activity, were unlikely to find themselves close to either party, and he might well have turned a woman like Theodora, in her younger years, away. He disliked the theater, had a lot to say about fornication (none of it positive), regarded Eve as the agent of the Devil, and was passionately interested in doctrines defining the nature of Christ. Some years later, it would become abundantly clear that Theodora did not find Christological discourses as scintillating as Severus may have expected when he recommended them to her attention. So why was it that she emerged from her years at Antioch with a reputation as a woman to whom anti-Chalcedonians in need could appeal? What was there that a man like Severus had to say that could interest her? What evidence is there that the two ever had anything at all to say to each other?

The last of these questions may help us understand the first two. Severus may have been in exile after Justin removed him from his episcopal seat, but his "exile" was a lot like Vitalian's "hiding." Although he moved to Egypt after his expulsion, he remained well known back in Antioch, kept up a wide-ranging correspondence with other well-known people, and was a man whose teaching continued to animate the Church. Theodora, for her part, would become the sort of woman we expect to encounter in Severus' correspondence, but it is unlikely that he had made her acquaintance before the early 520s. His influence in 518 or thereabouts would have been indirect, and it was others, now unknown to us, who brought Theodora into the network of the Syrian Church.

Although Severus' circle of friends cannot be directly associated with Theodora, the surviving snippets of his once-vast correspondence do allow us to glimpse the kind of network that could link a major figure in an important provincial center with the capital. We may extrapolate from the evidence Severus offers information regarding Antioch's and Constantinople's links with the circus factions, which would likewise have facilitated all manner of relationships between the two places. Residing in the provinces at this time did not mean being "provincial." So, given that the surviving correspondence includes two women named Caesaria, one of whom is termed "the really important" and the other merely "the patrician," it is not beyond the bounds of possibility that the first of these is Anastasius' sister. The second Caesaria we know to have been the wife of a powerful official from Cappadocia, in eastern Turkey. She later moved to Egypt, where she endowed the convent in which she lived out her life. In addition to the imperial officials Conon, Eupraxius, and Phocas, whom we know Severus had contact with, we find a eunuch named Misael. This Misael was one of those who had been slow to release the imperial regalia to Justin on the day of his enthronement. He was later accused of participation in Amantius' conspiracy and sent into exile. Later still, he would become one of Theodora's closest servants.[33]

Other letters reveal Severus' association with powerfully placed men in other wings of the administration and in the army. One correspondent is Timostratus, a military commander who was informed by Severus of the importance of priests' sticking strictly to the ecclesiastical rules of conduct. A man named Oecumenius, who received quite a few letters on matters of doctrine, appears to have wanted to become a priest. One of the letters Severus wrote him before assuming the bishop's throne at Antioch provides us with a detailed account of the foundation of his theology, replete with quotations from numerous authorities. After he became bishop, Severus wrote Oecumenius another long letter, quoting different authorities. Oecumenius was deeply interested in his subject, and Severus felt that he was already knowledgeable before their exchange started. We clearly have only a fraction of what passed between the two men. It is interesting that Severus feels the need to apologize in the first letter for his tardy response, claiming pressure of work. The business aspect of their relationship is evident in another letter, in which Severus tells a bishop in Isauria that he has asked Oecumenius to deal with a couple of priests whom he, Severus, has removed for misconduct.

Conon, the imperial official referred to earlier, was known as the "brigand chaser," though his actual title may have been *vicarius*, or assistant, to the commander of the army in the east. Despite Conon's seniority, the bishop was quite sharp with him for what he considered his dilatory handling of matters that Severus thought important. One concerned a woman who held some sort of position in the Church despite having been married three times (her third husband was still alive). Severus was of the opinion that this woman was "possessed of a demon," and was so angry about the situation that he wrote to Conon's commander, Rufinus, to ask him to do something about it. In another letter, Severus asked Celer, the immensely important official we met earlier in this chapter at the time of Justin's accession, to take action against men that he considered heretics; Severus seems also to have gotten on well with the Rufinus, whom Anastasius first sent after Vitalian in 515, and his brother, also a high-ranking military man in the east. (This particular family exemplifies the tendency for important officials to hold office in their home districts.[34])

Closer to home, we see Severus addressing a letter to monks in a monastery in southern Turkey, telling them that he has received a request from some soldiers for a bishop to be assigned to them. He tells the monks that they should send one of their number without delay. He tells the Bishop of Beroia in Syria that he should not unleash violence against the local Jewish community, pointing out that vengeance is best left to God. To Solon, Bishop of Isauria, he writes telling him to get rid of a couple of priests whom Severus finds disagreeable. He tells the Bishop of Tarsus that a projected ordination at a nearby city should not be allowed to go ahead, because coercion by soldiers is involved. A priest named Eustacius is informed that slaves cannot be ordained unless it can be confirmed that their masters have freed them. Within his own district, Severus could pick new bishops from short lists presented to him by the cities petitioning for them, and his power was further enhanced by the fact that, if local magistrates nominated for the priesthood someone he disapproved of, he could forbid it. On one occasion, he was not at all pleased when the people of Apamea, writing him about a new bishop, quoted a pagan author's comment.[35]

Severus built up his power by means of his connections, not only with Constantinople, but also with local institutions. He was devoted to the cults of local martyrs, and traveled tirelessly to other religious sites around his province. One of these cults was that of the martyrs Sergius and Bacchus at Rusafa. The shrine's warrior saints were said to have been executed in the great persecution of the early fourth century; the shrine itself was fast becoming important as a place for the Arab desert tribes to meet with the settled peoples of Syria, and for the transmission of Christianity to their peoples. Throughout the eastern provinces, the cult was believed to offer protection from the ravages of the Persians, who, at this point, were actually keeping the peace they had made with Anastasius. In 524, it would have significance for Theodora.[36]

The links Severus established both locally and with Constantinople while he was bishop of Antioch were not of the sort that would obviously endear him to Justin, for whom his tenure of office was already problematic. For a start, Severus was too well connected with people whom Justin did not fully trust. Severus' eviction from his see was therefore as much a political decision as it was doctrinal. Despite what may have seemed the political necessity, the decision to evict was a bad one and resulted in chaos: Severus' successors attempted to assert their authority with considerable brutality, and failed miserably to do so.

It was most likely at this time that Theodora began to move into powerful anti-Chalcedonian circles; and, if we are to believe the picture John of Ephesus would later paint of her dealings with the holy men of the east who visited her at Constantinople, it is very likely that she learned Syriac—to go along with the Greek that she needed for her career in Constantinople. In her later life, she appears to have been able to deal with the alumni of desert shrines (including John himself) without needing a translator. It was not, however, the anti-Chalcedonian community that would have catapulted her into the company of Justinian—just the opposite would have been more likely. It was the sort of work, whatever that may have been, in which she joined Macedonia that would have established the factional connections enabling her to meet Justinian when she returned to the capital. Procopius is clear—for what any assertion of his may be worth—that they met in Constantinople. What Severus' network reveals to us, as we saw, is just how closely the upper echelons of society in Constantinople and Antioch interlocked with each other via the Church and the factions. If we had the correspondence of Porphyrius the charioteer, we can be sure that it would reveal a network looking a lot like that of Severus.[37]

Theodora's anti-Chalcedonian connections were clearly formed before she returned to Constantinople in 520 or 521, and the fact that she moved in such circles gives us some notion of the woman she was becoming. What would have lured her into this company? Severus and his associates did not like the theater or the circus, and they denounced sex and everything to do with it; the recipients of Severus' letters appear to have had a penchant for theological speculation. None of this sounds likely to attract the Theodora we have met, or indeed will see again during her years in power. Severus' belief that women were subordinate to men because "the deceitfulness of sin came in through the woman" may not have been altogether well received, either—even taking into account his claim that in heaven all was forgiven, so that men and women could exist there on a basis of equality. There was, though, one other very powerful message that Severus preached, which—to judge from the staunch resistance offered by his supporters to Justin's appointees—resonated very powerfully with his people. For he was passionate about the lot of the downtrodden, which was a group with which a single mother, abandoned by her lover, could certainly identify. Might she have found some peace in the Church, some adult conversation, release from the competitive environments in which she had lived for the last few years? And maybe even some help with child care? We are told that she had a particular admiration for Severus, which appears to be confirmed by the comments of an enemy who thought them close. These observations date to the 530s, but there is no reason to think that her interest in his works was not formed at a much earlier date.[38]

Severus could be very hard on the rich. He assailed their profligacy when it came to spending money on themselves, on fancy clothes and lavish accouterments. He suggested that they give some of it away to feed the poor. He regarded the justice system as unfair and was vehement on the subject of debt, believing that the Church should lend without interest and that the subjugation of the poor to bankers was fundamentally wrong. He went as far as to propose a total cancellation of debt. He worked to set up agencies to help the old, the orphaned, and those who were lost. Was it to one of these institutions that Theodora found her way when she reached Antioch? She may not have been utterly down and out, but the implication of the story of her association with Macedonia is that she was in serious need of a job.[39]

For a single mother in a stressful occupation—whatever she and Macedonia were doing when they were "spying" for the Blues placed them in an environment from which violence was never distant—the Church could have been a refuge. When she became empress, she would take up the cause of the poor and oppressed as well as that of the anti-Chalcedonians. Severus' theology was not always easy to stomach. Faced with the question of whether a former poet could become a priest, for instance, he said no—unless the poet had forsworn completely his previous occupation; afterward Severus was "delighted" by evidence that this particular individual had repented his earlier ways. He preached the redemption of humanity, that people were not bound inexorably to their past. This was a message that Theodora seems to have wanted to hear, and one she took to heart. [40]

The woman who would assume the imperial persona seems in these years to have grown up. Most importantly, she had gained a bird's-eye view of the agencies of imperial power. She would later use this new knowledge to her advantage.

5

Patrician

One day in June of 520, Vitalian entered the imperial box in the Hippodrome to watch the chariot races he was sponsoring to celebrate his consulship. After the first race, he and two of his senior subordinates went back into the palace. This was their last public appearance.

The Delphax, the palace's great courtyard that Vitalian now entered, took its name from the columns brought from Delphi in Greece to support the courtyard's portico. This elegant space played an important role in many imperial ceremonies, including the proclamation of a new emperor. It was here that Justin had been presented to the palace officials as their new ruler. To its north and east were the palace's outer walls alongside the Hippodrome and the baths of Zeuxippus; to its south was the reception hall, the triclinium of the nineteen couches; to the east, the barracks of the imperial guard. (Most of the area now lies under Istanbul's Blue Mosque.) As well as being a place of ceremony, it was also the site of a number of assassination attempts, not all of them successful. This one was.

A striking feature of that day's event was that the assassins were never named. Procopius says Justinian was the culprit, but this is deeply improbable. The fact that Vitalian's sons and nephew held senior commands throughout much of Justinian's reign suggests that they did not hold him responsible for Vitalian's murder. The most likely explanation is that Justin had simply had enough of the man to whom he had granted nearly imperial status, and may have been pushing for ever greater control. Justin's decision to execute Amantius and his companions a few years earlier shows that he was prepared to take drastic action against people he perceived as threats. An official statement said merely that Vitalian had paid the price for his rebellions against the state.[1]

Although not responsible for Vitalian's death, Justinian was certainly a major beneficiary of it. First, Justin promoted him to Vitalian's former post as commander of the army in the capital district—a sure step, Justinian may have thought, towards a position from which he might ascend to the throne upon his uncle's death.

Like Justin, Justinian had been born to a peasant family in Illyricum. At the time of his birth in 482 he was known as Peter Sabbatius. His hometown was Tauresium, now Caričin Grad near modern Skopje in the Republic of Macedonia, part of the former Yugoslavia. Justin, whose sister was Justinian's mother, had been born about thirty years earlier near the ruined city of Naissus, modern Niš in Serbia. Formerly famous as the birthplace of Emperor Constantine, Naissus had been destroyed a few years before Justin's birth by Attila the Hun. We do not know when Justin adopted his nephew Justinian, but it was certainly at some point before he became emperor, perhaps as it became clear that Justin and his wife Euphemia would never have children of their own.[2]

Justin's detractors, amongst whom Procopius is numbered, suggest that he was an ignorant peasant, completely under Justinian's sway. This is deeply misleading. To rise through the ranks as he did, Justin must have done some pretty remarkable things—and he must have known quite early which side his bread was buttered on. He had presumably supported Zeno during the revolts of Basiliscus and Illus, and made himself useful to Anastasius. Perhaps most importantly, all the evidence suggests that he had been careful always to be on Ariadne's side. By the time he was in his forties, Justin had risen from common soldier to high command. Anastasius employed him, along with one of Ariadne's relatives, Diogenianus, as a general in the campaign to suppress dissent amongst the Isaurian tribes of southern Turkey, and, albeit briefly, during the Persian war that broke out in 502–503. At this point, he was Vitalian's colleague as "count of military affairs" (*comes rei militaris*) under the command of Celer. The campaign was reasonably successful in stemming the Persian invasions.[3]

Another member of the command group was a wealthy Egyptian named Apion, whose job it was to secure the army's supplies. Then, moving ahead more than ten years, we find Justin serving in the fleet that Marinus, Anastasius' praetorian prefect, used to shatter Vitalian's fleet. For this battle in the Golden Horn, which took place before the eyes of all Constantinople, Marinus equipped his ships with "Greek fire," a sulphurous substance concocted by an Athenian scientist named Proclus, with which to incinerate Vitalian's force. The part Justin played seems to have been significant enough to advance his career—and we can only wonder whether Theodora watched the battle, little knowing what an impact Justin's success would have on her own life.[4]

Justin may have been astutely consistent in his choice of which sides to take while on his way to the top, but once he arrived, he was primarily concerned with staying there, even if it cost old friends their jobs. So it was that both Marinus and Celer, important figures in Justin's past and instrumental in his taking of the throne—Marinus celebrated by ordering a mural depicting Justin's life to be installed on a public bath house—would be out of office by the end of 519.

The reasons were probably religious, since both had strong anti-Chalcedonian credentials, and Justin's support for Chalcedon had been a significant factor in his selection as emperor. Even before the end of the year, Justin had not only removed Severus from his Antiochian see, he was also initiating strong action against anti-Chalcedonian communities in the empire's eastern provinces. Men with better Chalcedonian credentials, all of whom had had trouble with Anastasius towards the end of his reign, would now come to the fore. Amongst them was Diogenianus, whom Anastasius had exiled and Justin now appointed commander of the army in the east. Another such was Philoxenus, also exiled by Anastasius towards the end of his reign, who was given a command in Thrace before being elevated to the consulship, a sign of very high favor. And the Egyptian Apion, who had recently converted from anti-Chalcedonian to Chalcedonian, was recalled from exile to be praetorian prefect, the head of the empire's provincial administration.[5]

Theodora at this time was both a "Blue," which placed her on the side of the palace, and anti-Chalcedonian, which put her firmly on the wrong side of the increasingly bitter religious divide. The path that would allow her to ally with both Severus and Justin, as a possessor of huge influence, was taking shape.

Vitalian's death opened up some important space at the top of Justin's administration. In the previous two years, he had been widely considered a virtual heir apparent, so much so that he received letters from Pope Hormisdas in Rome, just as did Justin, Euphemia, and Justinian.

Inclusion in the pope's mailing list was a sign that a person was perceived as being both important and sympathetic to the Chalcedonian perspective. The pope was politically important in Constantinople as an independent conduit to the senatorial aristocracy at Rome—and especially important as relations between the court at Constantinople and the Ostrogothic regime of Theoderic (king from 471 to 526), based in Ravenna, were becoming ever more unstable.[6] Theoderic had a history in the east, being seen during Zeno's reign as a sort of proto-Vitalian. Then Zeno had persuaded him to overthrow the regime of Odovacer, the German general who had brought an end to the Western imperial line in Italy in 476, with the result that various claimants to the Western throne had either been removed or had simply given up hope. Several descendants of people who had claimed the throne in the years before Odovacer's seizure of power as king were still active in Constantinople, while there was still a notion that the Eastern emperor should be considered as having precedence over all others. Such points had been largely academic while Vitalian threatened the stability of the imperial government.

Freed of Vitalian, Justinian appears to have taken an active role in building up his support, via his connections with the Blues, across the cities of the empire. Theodora at this point, as mentioned earlier, may have been a spy for that same faction. Was it now that she first met the future emperor?[7]

Theodora told Macedonia, Procopius says, that while she was in Antioch, she had dreamt of sleeping with the King of the Demons. Allowing that such an encounter with the King of the Demons is unlikely to have figured in any story Theodora herself told (it being a rather predictable Procopian restatement of a well-known tale), the fact that he told it at all may indicate that some element of divine intervention had found its way into the stories commonly relayed about Theodora's rise to power. For our purposes in trying to get to grips with her life, the story does offer evidence for when she came to Justinian's attention: it must have been while she was in Antioch—why, otherwise, would Macedonia figure in the story at all? Given her extraordinary transposition from Antioch to Constantinople, people may indeed have thought that some sort of divine agency had been at work—for instance, it could be that one version of her life story included an encounter with a holy figure who helped her foresee her future. We have plenty of evidence of Procopius' making hay from just this sort of material elsewhere.

Absent divine intervention, we must settle for the notion that Theodora met Justinian via her work as an agent of the Blues. Emperors were aware that their informants tended to edit reports they sent in so as to serve their own interests. An emperor would know that individual communities had a vested interest in making sure he knew only what they wanted him to know, and he would be aware, too, that his own officials were often self-serving and dishonest. To circumvent these limitations, he would employ people like Theodora to check the veracity of what he was being told. From a document surviving from Justin's reign and from close to where Theodora was living, we are fortunate in being able to get some idea of the sorts of problems that might require a special investigator.

The document in question is a report by an imperial agent, or *agens in rebus*, called Thomas, who had been sent to investigate goings-on in the city of Cyrrhus in the province of Euphratensis, which, as its name suggests, abutted the Euphrates river (on its western edge). In this particular case, it was Antioch's chief financial official, or *defensor*, who was raising questions about the behavior of a bishop named Sergius, a recent appointee. The agent, a sort of "internal affairs" officer employed in the praetorian prefect's office, discovered a lot going on in Cyrrhus that was deeply troubling.

It turned out that the citizens were very proud of an earlier bishop, Theodoret, who had written a history of the Church as well as a book on the lives of some local holy men. Both works survive, and it is immediately clear to anyone who reads them that Theodoret's stance with respect to the prevailing doctrinal issues of the day was not entirely orthodox. It was an event related to his dubious theological reputation that seems to have aroused the *defensor*'s suspicions, for at a recent festival, two priests had paraded Theodoret's portrait about town in a chariot, along with those of other local heroes such as Nestorius, the former bishop of Constantinople.

Nestorius is the key here, and at the time he was an even bigger problem than Theodoret, who had been his staunch supporter; for Nestorius had asserted that Mary was the *Christotokos* (Mother of Christ) rather than the *Theotokos* (Mother of God). These views, which were extreme even for a person with Chalcedonian leanings, had been condemned at the Council of Ephesus in 431 at the instigation of Cyril of Alexandria, a man who combined theological brilliance with a good understanding of the ways things worked in the world around him.

His victory at Ephesus was substantially assisted by the court officials whom he had amply bribed, as well as Theodosius II's insistence that Nestorius was just plain obnoxious. Nestorius was consequently exiled to Petra (in modern Jordan) and later to the Great Oasis in Egypt, where he lived out his life in Spartan conditions. Theodoret had remained a loyal supporter of Nestorius even after the declarations of the Council of Ephesus, so it surprised no one that he was sentenced to virtual house arrest; he was then briefly removed from office after the Second Council of Ephesus in 449. He had the Council of Chalcedon, two years later, to thank for his ultimate restoration. Theodoret maintained his heterodox ways until his death, probably in the mid-450s.[8]

Although Nestorius' views were regarded in most parts of the Roman Empire as heretical, there was a powerful Nestorian community in the Persian Empire, just across the river from Euphratensis. Nestorian missionaries were also seeking to convert to their brand of Christianity the Arab tribes that dominated the desert lands between the Roman and Persian Empires with considerable success. As a result of these activities, crypto-Nestorianism was not simply a religious issue; it was a religious issue tinged with dangerous implications for imperial security, since Nestorian Arabs could not be counted on to be well disposed to a regime in Constantinople that regarded them as heretics. Indeed, as long as the Persians, whose leaders were Zoroastrians, refrained from persecuting them, they had no reason at all to favor Constantinople.

In the present case, the inhabitants of Cyrrhus were all too aware that the imperial authorities would not look kindly on their public display of regard for Bishop Theodoret and his mentor. So they lied about it, maintaining that the Nestorius whose image they were carting about was not the heretic, but a martyr of the same name. Justin's investigator looked into this claim and reported that not only was there no such martyr, but Sergius himself had sung a hymn in Nestorius' honor, and soldiers had joined in the celebration. This was particularly offensive because Justin had recently ordered that all military personnel support the Chalcedonian confession, and open defiance of his order raised serious questions about their loyalty in the face of Persian hostility.[9]

"Special agent" Thomas presumably put himself at some risk to gather his information, and the very local nature of the business he was investigating may have made it harder for him, as an outsider. It is most likely that the sort of material that Theodora and Macedonia were gathering was similarly sensitive. Their reports went straight to Justinian, who appears at this point to have taken over the running of the Blues' information network. (We hear of another of his agents impregnating a woman who ran a tavern in central Turkey—their progeny turned out to be a saint.) Justinian's involvement in the network appears to have acquired some importance around the time of Vitalian's murder, possibly in connection with the latter's consular games and the preparation of lavish games to celebrate Justinian's own consulship in 521.[10]

Who was Justinian, and what was he like? While already a powerful figure at the time he and Theodora began their relationship, he was possibly quite lonely. As far as we can tell, he had led a somewhat ascetic life up to that point. His failure to marry, although he was now in his thirties, was probably attributable to the unwillingness of members of the aristocracy to hand over their daughters to the son of a peasant—even though he was now a high-ranking general—but also to a lack of social confidence on his part. We know of no prior relationships, and there is reason to think that this was because he had had very few; we know of no illegitimate children, and not even Procopius, who hated him, suggests that he spent his time chasing ladies around the palace. Rather, he is presented as a deeply solitary person who suffered from insomnia and who ate very little, while being given to intense theological reflection. We know from one of the earliest of his documents to survive, a letter to Pope Hormisdas at Rome in 520, that he could quote Augustine's theological works and was interested in encouraging a compromise between strict Chalcedonianism and its theologically more moderate opponents who followed the tradition of Severus. To this end, Justinian was deeply attracted to a doctrine known as Theopaschitism, or the belief that God suffered, which was first promulgated by four monks, including a relative of Vitalian's, who traveled from Constantinople to Rome in 519 to discuss the issue. The attraction of this approach was that it allowed that Christ had only a divine nature, the crucial point to anti-Chalcedonians, but could still suffer as a human would suffer, a crucial point to Chalcedonians. Hormisdas repudiated the doctrine after considerable debate, but failed to curb Justinian's interest in the notion. [11]

FIGURE 5.1. Justinian as he appears on a mosaic commemorating the dedication of one of his greatest monuments, the Church of Hagia Sophia, which he is presenting here to the image of the city of Constantinople.

© Album / Art Resource, NY

One aspect of Justinian's character, very pronounced throughout his life, was his deep personal loyalty, a quality he showed in some instances to a fault. Possibly as a consequence of this loyalty, he seems to have been able to delegate business to his subordinates. At times, perhaps, he could be indecisive, especially when these subordinates disagreed with each other. He seems to have been even-tempered, and to have possessed a strong sense of duty. He may have been something of a romantic—he certainly dreamed big dreams—and enjoyed history as well as theology. The friends he had, men who rose under him to positions of authority—Belisarius and Sittas, both bodyguards of his who became generals; Tribonian, a successful lawyer; and John the Cappadocian, who would become his finance minister—all came from outside the traditional aristocracy. Did he feel more comfortable with people he thought resembled himself? Amongst the characters just mentioned, one of them, Tribonian, was an ambivalent soul—people would even claim that he was a pagan, possibly because his interests were more philosophical than theological. What this may tell us is that, deeply as he held his own religious views, there was no theological litmus test for becoming a member of his inner circle. If there had been, Theodora would never have been allowed in.[12]

Somehow, Theodora came to Justinian's notice. Was she especially good as an agent for the Blues? Was there a certain spark of intelligence or wit in her reports that set her apart from others? We cannot know, but we do know that Justinian fell very rapidly, and head over heels, in love with her. Our ability to reconstruct what happened is facilitated marginally by Procopius who, as noted earlier, says that they married only after Justinian in 521 or 522 forced Justin—after the death of his wife Euphemia who, Procopius also says, detested Theodora—to make a law legalizing marriages between former actresses and men of high status. We get a good deal more help from the text of the law itself, whose date of passage we know because it is preserved in the law code that Justinian had compiled in the 530s. And John of Ephesus' *Lives of the Eastern Saints* reveals that the wedding must have taken place by the end of 522 or the beginning of 523.

Justin addressed the law in question to the praetorian prefect Demosthenes, in office from June 521 to July 522, who probably drafted it himself. John Lydus describes Demosthenes as a man who took a very narrow view of his authority, which was not to John's liking; Justinian, though, would reappoint him to the same post in 529, quite possibly as a reward for his support for the new law. The text of this document is in some places extraordinarily person-specific, describing someone who sounds very much like Theodora, a fact that allows us a useful insight into Theodora's position at the time and a rare glimpse of the forces that drove her. Indeed, this law may be one of the most important pieces of evidence we have for attempting to solve the mystery of who the real Theodora was.

The marriage law opens with a long preamble in which the emperor states that it is appropriate to imperial beneficence to take account of the welfare of the empire's people, and that, in his view, "the errors of women, through which they may elect the unworthy [and] turn from honor through the weakness of their sex, may be corrected through proper moderation and . . . they should in no way be deprived of the hope of a better condition." Indeed, it behooves an emperor to imitate the beneficence of God, who, every day, forgives mortals their sins in "His exceptional mercy." The first substantive clause states that it would be unfair if slaves could be freed and granted, by imperial dispensation, the status of freeborn persons, "while women who joined themselves to the entertainments of the stage, and then, spurning their evil condition, moved to a better opinion and fled the dishonorable profession, would have no hope of imperial beneficence, which might place them back into that state in which, if there had been no error, they would have been able to stay." Justin therefore ordered that women who "left their evil and dishonorable choice behind and, embracing a better life," gave "themselves to respectability," be able to petition the emperor for the right of legitimate marriage. Those who married actresses should not fear that their marriages would be voided by the rulings of earlier laws; and that "no disreputable title" would cling to former actresses. They would have the same status as women "who had never sinned."

The second clause states that children born after the marriage of a man to a former actress would be legitimate and have the same rights as any children of her husband by a prior marriage. The third envisages a situation in which women who have successfully petitioned for the right to marry, have elected to postpone that marriage. Even though unmarried at this point, they should still be considered women of good reputation. (This would not happen in Theodora's case, but it might have seemed plausible at the time.) Clause 4 reinforces the third, saying that the situation of women now permitted to marry will be similar to that of "women who have obtained a position of dignity from the emperor as a voluntary gift before marriage, even if they did not request it, by virtue of which position every other stain, through which women are prohibited from marrying certain men, will be wiped clean from their dignity." Clause 5 lays down that girls born after their mothers renounced the stage should "not be seen to be subjected to the laws . . . that prohibit the daughter of a former actress from marrying certain men"; and that girls born before their mother gave up her career could petition for the right to marry—it would not "be forbidden . . . to join with those people who are now forbidden to marry the daughters of actresses because of their rank or some other reason."

The sixth clause looks to women whose mothers have died in the course of their acting careers. These women, too, are allowed to petition the emperor for the right to marry as they wish. The next clause states that rules in other laws that ban marriages between persons of unequal status should not apply to actresses, at the same time declaring imperial hostility towards incest and other "nefarious" unions. Finally, the new law was to be retroactive to the beginning of Justin's reign.[13]

Could whoever drafted this law have had Theodora in mind? Clause 3 describes exactly the situation in which she could have found herself if, for instance, the patriarch of Constantinople had objected to a marriage between someone associated with the anti-Chalcedonian community, and a potential heir to the throne. Then, clause 4 would eliminate any obstacle to marriage arising from Theodora's earlier status as Hecebolus' concubine. The provision that a daughter—it is interesting that the law specifies *filia* ("daughter") here, rather than *liber* ("child")—born while a woman was performing on the stage could likewise expect to petition successfully for the right to marry looks very much like a dispensation designed for Theodora's own daughter.[14]

Finally, the date of the law, the year 521–522, helps us understand the significance of a story that comes down to us through John of Ephesus, in which he attests Theodora's importance to the anti-Chalcedonian cause. It is from John that we learn that in that same year, Justin expelled the anti-Chalcedonian leadership from monasteries around Amida, a crucial city on the border with Persia. The leaders of the community were sent into exile under harsh conditions near the city of Petra.

Our ability to reconstruct what happened next depends upon the history of a hole in the ground. This hole was two miles outside of Mendes, a town in Egypt, and it is significant because another Thomas, not the special agent we met a few pages ago, occupied it for six years after the exiles, through Theodora's intercession with Justinian, had been moved from Petra. Thomas chose to dwell in this pit, previously the residence of another holy man, because the luxurious lifestyle that prevailed locally appalled him. When he had lived there for six years—that is, in 529, the eighth year after the exile from Amida—we are told that Amida's former bishop, Mare, died. The embassy that petitioned Theodora to use her influence to get the community relocated to Egypt must therefore have arrived in Constantinople no later than 523. They noted that Justinian was "then general and patrician and nephew of the king." Theodora is referred to as "from the *porneion* [the actress community], but at that time a patrician and later queen when Justinian was king." It was in 523 that they both acquired the rank of patrician, a status designation to which we will return shortly. The same text also states that Justinian "was then her husband." All of this tallies with what we know about Justinian's career. And the reference to Theodora fits with what we glean about her situation from the new marriage law.[15]

The men who had approached Theodora for help were not disappointed. Justinian took up her request that something be done for them, although he would not be able to restore them to their former homes. About the same time, according to another tradition, the son of a deacon who had been murdered in Alexandria by the strongly Chalcedonian Bishop Paul, is said to have brought Paul's brutality to imperial attention via Theodora. Paul was removed within the year. Although this story comes to us through a later Syriac source and refers to Theodora as already empress, it may have some basis in fact: Paul did last only a year, and the picture this story gives about the flow of information from the provinces to Constantinople does not appear to be influenced by the story about the exiled monks of Amida.[16]

People watched the palace very carefully, to see who was "in" and who was on the way out; so it would not be surprising if, as soon as news broke of this most unusual marriage, people brought Theodora their problems in hopes that she could intercede. Furthermore, she might quite quickly have let it be known that she was willing to listen to them. She would certainly have been quite a different proposition from Euphemia, who was vehemently pro-Chalcedonian. Indeed, if there is truth in what Procopius says about Empress Euphemia's having died before the marriage, it would suggest that she died very early in her husband's reign, and that the fact that we have no evidence for her continued existence after 520 need not be attributed to a blip in the record. She is said to have been laid to rest in a monastery she had founded in Constantinople, and it is a sign of his great devotion to his former partner that Justin ordered that their bodies be placed in the same sarcophagus when he died. Any hostility that Euphemia manifested towards Theodora was plainly (and quite literally) short-lived; that Procopius was keen to allege otherwise is yet another instance of his propensity for twisting and enhancing the significance of any rumor or innuendo that came his way.[17]

Justinian's decision to assist the exiles from Amida might not have been the best career move, given the strongly Chalcedonian atmosphere elsewhere in the palace; but then neither was his taking up with Theodora in the first place. And he plainly felt the need to do anything he could to keep her happy—which is hardly typical of relationships that begin with a massive power imbalance. We see ever more clearly the resounding impact that Theodora made upon him.

The marriage law and the tale of the Amidene embassy demonstrate not only that Justinian was passionately in love with Theodora by the time of his consulship, but also that their relationship blossomed very rapidly. The text of the marriage law suggests that Theodora remained profoundly concerned with her daughter's welfare. She may also have been looking out for her sister Comito, who would marry Sittas—Justinian's bodyguard, then general—a young man said to be good-looking as well as very able. As noted earlier, the general Belisarius, too, would marry an actress—Antonina, the daughter of a famous charioteer from Thessalonica. While it cannot be proved that the language of redemption in the marriage law, which resonates with the writings of Severus, was inspired by any one person in particular, the stress on the bad choices a woman may make cannot fail to intrigue us: the terms the law is couched in make the woman the active party in determining her future.

Was this the way Theodora saw herself? There are sure signs that it was. Although it was not politically wise, she remained true to her anti-Chalcedonian beliefs—she would not abandon her faith even to secure Justinian's hand in marriage. The Theodora who emerges on the public stage of Byzantium does so as a deeply devout and determined woman, abidingly loyal to her friends. She was both a patrician *and* a former actress, and had lived life at the sharp end; she would not walk away from the person she had been even as she approached the pinnacle of power.

Theodora's past was not the only feature that made her something of a novelty on the Constantinopolitan scene. Beautiful young blonde women had not been omnipresent in the corridors of power during the last few decades.[18] Since the death of Theodosius II in the year 450, authority in the Roman state had largely alternated between matriarchy and gerontocracy. Only one emperor during the seventy years after Theodosius died, at the age of forty-nine, had been as young at the time of his accession as Theodosius had been at his death—and that was Zeno, who was forty-nine or fifty when he took the throne. Marcian and Leo had been in their mid- to late fifties, Anastasius was over sixty, and Justin around seventy. Ariadne had been a dominant force for years, as had Pulcheria, sister of Theodosius II. And Verina had been no shrinking violet.

At this point Justinian, still under forty, and overshadowed by Vitalian in the last couple of years, was not seen by everyone as Justin's obvious successor. To judge from the surviving correspondence between Pope Hormisdas and the imperial court, his holiness had envisaged Vitalian as virtually co-emperor with the latter.

Procopius maintains that Justinian dominated Justin. On the two key points that he uses to support this assertion; namely, the significance of any antipathy that Euphemia felt towards Theodora, and Justinian's responsibility for Vitalian's death, either he got his facts wrong—demonstrably—or he twisted them. There is really no point in thinking that what he has to say about Justinian's domination of Justin is true, either. There is some evidence to suggest that in 523 Justinian nearly lost his place in the line of succession. According to this account, which, it has to be admitted, materialized years after the event—at least we do not have to take just Procopius' word for it—there was serious rioting by the Blue faction in Constantinople and in the other cities of the empire. Justin, furious, appointed an official named Theodotus to bring order to the streets, which the latter was in the process of doing when he made the mistake of arresting one Theodosius, a court official, then executing him without trial. This was too much for Justin, who fired Theodotus on the spot.

That is one version. In another, Justinian is identified as the mastermind behind the violence shown by the Blues; and Theodotus, after executing Theodosius, announced that he was going to arrest "Justinian the patrician," who promptly fell seriously ill. According to this same version, it was only at this point that Justin became angry and fired Theodotus, who went off to live in Jerusalem. In Procopius' tale, Justinian fell ill after having inspired the Blues to acts of murder, including one in Hagia Sophia itself, and it was this that led to Theodotus' appointment. Recovering suddenly to find Theodotus closing in on him, Justinian tortured numerous people in order to extract evidence against Theodotus so that he could shut down his investigation. Although one man spoke up to declare that Theodotus was being framed, Justin still exiled the latter—to Jerusalem.

Our second report, which appears in a late Egyptian chronicle, may simply represent an effort by someone to graft Procopius' story onto that of our first source (Malalas' chronicle). This might be a plausible proposition were it not that we have no evidence that Procopius' *Secret History* was being read by anyone at the time, and certainly no other evidence from the Egyptian chronicle that its author knew the work at all. What we have in our second source and in Procopius are certainly two versions of the same story, which they both will have read since both were writing well after the events in question—and the very existence of that story in written form suggests that there were people circulating some very unpleasant tales about Justinian at this point in Justin's reign. That, at least, is thoroughly believable.[19]

Whatever was going on with Theodotus, Justinian survived, and in 523 was elevated to the rank of patrician, in which status Theodora joined him. There was nothing simple about becoming a patrician in sixth-century Constantinople. For both Justinian and Theodora, the event would have been marked with massive publicity, and widely celebrated both at court and in the city. The title "patrician," originally held by the aristocratic families of the earliest Roman Republic, had become under Constantine a mark of personal distinction awarded by the emperor to a favored individual. As with the award of any senior position, it was a dramatic moment. Though we cannot know exactly what was entailed in Theodora's case—all our records of ceremonies having to do with the creation of a new patrician are of a later date and involve happenings in parts of the palace that did not yet exist—we can be reasonably certain that she was introduced first to the senate and members of the court, then to the ordinary people, a series of encounters that mirrored the top-down structure of imperial government.

The ceremony most likely began with senior officials' being led into whichever imperial audience hall was then used for such events. Theodora would have waited outside, attended by a *silentiarius* and the master of ceremonies. Brought before the assembled dignitaries, she would have knelt before Justin. An official would hand her the tablets confirming her appointment, and after prayers had been said for Justin's welfare, the assembled company would leave the hall. Then, surrounded by ranks of senators, other patricians, and court officials for further prayers, she would be led to another part of the palace to be introduced to the representatives of the two main factions (first the Blues, then the Greens), who would shout the acclamation "*Theodora eise Patrikios!*"—"Theodora, be a patrician!" She would then leave the palace for Hagia Sophia, where, in the narthex, she would don the ritual clothing of a patrician. From there she may have gone, as later patricians did, to the Church of the Holy Apostles, where she would have again been introduced to the people's leaders and the factions.[20] We can only imagine what it must have been like for Theodora to stand there in her new finery, applauded by those who had once seen her dancing on the stage, or had despised her, or had lusted after her, or, quite possibly, had been her lovers.

Her home now was the imperial palace. It was not a single building; rather, not unlike its more visible descendant, Istanbul's Topkapi Palace, it was an administrative district with many different buildings. Justinian and Theodora probably moved at this point into a building then known as the Palace of Hormisdas within the same complex, which took its name, not from the current pope, but from the Persian prince who had lived there in the fourth century. Justinian's decision to locate himself and Theodora here was something of a departure from custom; the area where imperial power had traditionally been on view was at the ceremonial heart of the Great Palace, the bureaucratic hub of imperial society. The main parts of the complex, insofar as we can reconstruct them at this point—and much will remain uncertain in light of the impracticality of excavating underneath a major religious shrine and city district—were towards the south of the great ceremonial gate, the Chalke, which faced due west, opening on to the Mese as it passed between the massive baths of Zeuxippus and the Augustaion, the forum in front of the Constantinian Church of Hagia Sophia.[21]

The Great Palace itself was like Mount Olympus, the home of the ancient gods—or so one of its denizens assures us. It was bright and airy, an establishment where all knew their place. Within this complex, the crucial areas were the guards' barracks: first, that of the scholarian guards, which abutted the Zeuxippon; then those of the *candidati* (Justinian's old unit) and *excubitores* ("sentinels"), the latter abutting the Delphax's east colonnade; then the Delphax itself; and finally, opposite it to the east, the *consistorium*, a space that took its name from the imperial council—meaning literally "those who stood around" the emperor (from the Latin verb *constare*). South of the *consistorium* was the *onopodion*, a space whose name, "ass's foot," in Greek indicates that it was probably a horseshoe-shaped courtyard. Proceeding westward, one would pass through the portico of the nineteen couches, and then, turning to the south, into the great dining hall, or *triclinium*, of the

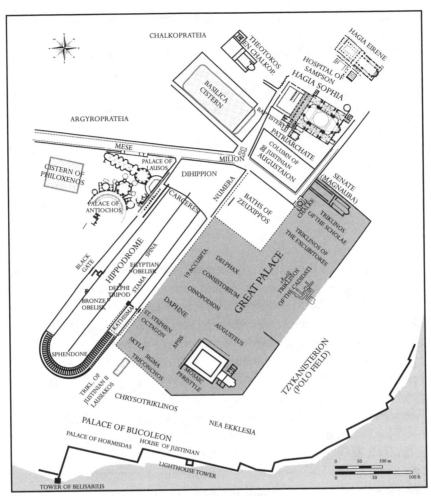

MAP 5.1. The plan of the Great Palace.

same name. Leaving the triclinium on its south side and turning east-ward, the visitor would pass the building known as the Octagon, and from there the Church of St. Stephen and another audience hall, the *Augusteus*. The imperial apartments were south of St. Stephen's.[22]

Of these spaces, the consistorium was perhaps the most important, for it was here that the emperor would meet his senior officials and receive important embassies. It was, we are told, "a lofty hall," distinguished by the presence of the imperial throne which, draped in purple and decorated with gold and jewels, was surrounded by "four marvelous columns" supporting a canopy that shone "like liquid gold." The canopy sported two winged Victories holding between them a laurel leaf, while, barring the great doors, guards kept the "unworthy" at bay. Theodora at this time would have been categorized amongst the "unworthy," since women were not allowed to enter while a meeting was in progress. (That would change.) The triclinium of the nineteen couches was where major public banquets were held, while the Augusteus was where the emperor received embassies from his own subjects as well as from foreign peoples. It is likely that, as Justinian's consort and an important person in her own right, Theodora would often have been seen in both of these rooms. In the smaller Hormisdas palace that she shared with Justinian, it is quite likely she had her own reception area, and that it was here that she met with those seeking her aid.[23]

Justinian's survival and promotion may be connected with horrific events taking place at a great distance from Constantinople—events that called for a change of approach on Justin's part. This is something he was unlikely to have been able to do without help, as this change in direction involved the anti-Chalcedonian community, a continuing area of great delicacy given his staunch Chalcedonian credentials. The reason we think that someone new was involved is that in 523, the security of the frontier in Syria came under sudden threat, and that threat was averted only because the imperial government suddenly showed itself capable of dealing convincingly with its religious opponents. Was it through Theodora's connections that a situation that was getting rapidly out of control was stabilized? In any event, catastrophe was avoided precisely because there were those in Constantinople who knew how to deal with non-Chalcedonians on and beyond the empire's eastern fringe, and this group included people we know were connected with Theodora in later years. Their relationship with the empress, which probably began around 524, helped solidify Justinian's position as heir apparent. The situation that arose in 523–524 concerned the relationship between Constantinople and various Arab peoples, their relations with each other, with the Persians, and with the people of Axum (now Ethiopia).

The story that links Constantinople with the Horn of Africa, complicated and gruesome as it is, begins at the southern end of the Arabian peninsula. This region was important both as a source of the spices that were highly prized in the Roman world, and for its position along the great Indian Ocean trade route that took in the main ports of southern India, in particular present-day Mumbai, where the trade networks of East Asia connected with those of the Mediterranean. It was through these networks that came the silks used to make the fine robes of the Constantinopolitan court, along with spices, especially the peppers that played an important role in the haute cuisine of the metropolis. At the route's western end, on the Red Sea coast of Egypt, was the harbor of Berenice, whence the goods would be transshipped across a heavily guarded desert route to Coptos on the Nile, and from there downriver to Alexandria, and from Alexandria to their final destinations. Once there had been another famous route that ended at Basra, leading up the Euphrates and across the Syrian desert to the caravan city of Palmyra; but that route had largely closed, a casualty and cause of the conflict between Rome and Persia, given the nearly constant cash-flow difficulties of the Persian kings.

The Romans had been intrigued by the Red Sea trade route for centuries, despite their own substantial monetary problems—the Romans shipped a lot of gold and silver to India—because in the Roman world, the ability to demonstrate access to exotic products was a sign of influence, and influence was always worth buying. The first Roman emperor, Augustus, appears to have tried to take control of Arabia, but his efforts failed, and he later denied having been engaged in anything more than a bit of heavily armed exploration. We know that in the second century a Roman garrison was planted on the island of Farasan, off Yemen's southern coast. Presumably, then as now, there was concern about piracy around the Horn.[24]

A few years before the crisis of 523 broke, Caleb, *negus* (king) of Axum, a Christian of an anti-Chalcedonian variety, had invaded western Arabia. The invasion was a success, and he took control of the swath of territory running from southern Yemen into western Saudi Arabia known as Himyar. The ruler who was displaced by this expedition, Dhu Nuwas, had ruled a kingdom that had recently converted to Judaism. In the winter of 523, when bad weather closed off the possibility of reinforcements arriving from Axum, Dhu Nuwas struck, defeating the Axumite garrison and massacring the Christian community living in the city of Najran in what is now southwest Saudi Arabia. Hundreds of men, women, and children were crowded into churches that were then set afire; others were brutalized in the presence of the king, who dispatched messengers northward, boasting of his deeds.

Vivid memories of the horrors that Dhu Nuwas inflicted were kept alive for decades, possibly even into the lifetime of the prophet Mohammed, who referred in the Koran's eighty-fifth Sura to the fires of Najran in his condemnation of religious persecution. A grim account of the massacre was given by Simeon *daruso Parsaya*, "the Persian debater"—a man who had already made a long career out of causing international distress by practicing his brand of anti-Chalcedonian Christianity against Nestorians, Jews, and Zoroastrians in the territory ruled by the Persian king. Simeon was a man whom Theodora came to admire, and in 524 he played an important role in keeping the peace on the Roman frontier with Persia, while Caleb prepared an expedition to exact revenge from Dhu Nuwas.[25]

The massacre at Najran was just one instance of the religious upheaval that threatened the stability of the entire Roman settlement vis-à-vis the peoples of the Arabian peninsula. There was some suggestion that Dhu Nuwas might have been in league with Jewish teachers in the area of Tiberias (now in Israel) who had a deeply ambivalent relationship with the imperial government, and he was certainly in contact with al-Mundhir III, king of the Nasrid Arabs, based at Hira, a city slightly to the west of the Euphrates. Part of the trouble may have stemmed from the ousting and replacement in the last few years of well-established religious figures by Justin's men—the community from Amida that Theodora had recently helped was one such—and it is striking that the two people who did most to preserve the peace were anti-Chalcedonians. These were the aforementioned Simeon, and Abraham, an ambassador sent from the court in Constantinople whose job was also to negotiate the release of two senior officials whom al-Mundhir was holding hostage.[26]

Dhu Nuwas' proposal to al-Mundhir was that he should join him in persecuting the Christians—a request that is interesting in that Dhu Nuwas appears to have seen religious extremism, independent of both Roman and Persian authority, as a possible alternative to persistent Roman and Persian interventions. It is no wonder, then, that al-Mundhir had time to listen to him. A century later, very similar forces, forces that could remember the events at Najran—albeit unfavorably—would once again move outward from western Arabia seeking to draw the tribes of northern Arabia into an alliance informed by faith. This time, prominent leaders would listen, and with consequences that we feel to this day. This time, there would be no possibility of intervention from Roman allies in Ethiopia, and the prophet would be Mohammed.

The possibility that a Jewish-influenced religious movement in southern Arabia might wreck the balance of power on the Roman frontiers in 524 lay behind the meeting at Ramla that al-Mundhir summoned that year. On the Roman side, in addition to Abraham and Simeon, who appeared along with Sergius, the Bishop of Rusafa—the Romans called the place "Sergiopolis"—a city on the desert's edge that served as an important meeting point for the region's sedentary and nomadic peoples, were three representatives of the Nestorian Church in the Persian Empire and al-Mundhir's leading general, who, fortunately for pretty much all parties, was himself a Christian. The meeting's upshot, after a vigorous debate between al-Mundhir and his chief general, was that there would be no new persecution of the Christians, and the hostages would be released.[27]

The outcome at Ramla was important. It meant that peace would be preserved and, given that Justin was in no position to put on a convincing show of sympathy for people he had been harassing, that Theodora had proved her value to his regime. The capital's extraordinarily polarized and polarizing religious politics could not be exported wholesale into the empire without some dire consequences for relationships that were helping to keep the peace. Justinian, and especially Theodora, may well have provided the necessary link to those who could handle al-Mundhir. There was a reason why Abraham's son, Nonnosus, would be employed again by Justinian, and that Theodora would ask that Simeon's remains, some years later, be sent to her at Constantinople. Similarly, Theodora would later bring about the appointment of a new bishop for Axum. And despite their own quite profound differences, the Nestorians of Persia had shown that they would join with their archrival anti-Chalcedonians when disaster threatened.

By the end of 524, Caleb of Axum had stamped out the last embers of the fire Dhu Nuwas had set. Dhu Nuwas vanished, and a new Axumite protectorate was set up in southern Arabia. All of this was a substantial success. But can we be sure that it was actually the work of Justinian and Theodora?

One reason for thinking that it was is quite simply that the right people were chosen and the desired results obtained. The personal connections that we know they had with both major actors—Abraham and Simeon—are an important clue, as is the fact that Abraham is said to have been sent directly from Constantinople. Almost immediately after the conclusion of this business, Justinian and Theodora would build a church in honor of Saints Sergius and Bacchus next to their own residence in the palace of Hormisdas. Rusafa was the center of the cult for these martyrs, so all three of the principal actors at Ramla—Simeon, Sergius, and Abraham—would have some link with them later. Finally, there is the possibility that, if not Justinian and Theodora themselves, the likely agent to have coordinated the imperial response was Hypatius. Hypatius was technically in charge as commanding general (*magister militum*) in the east from 520 onwards, but he tended to foul up nearly everything he touched: the two senior officials al-Mundhir was holding had been captured on Hypatius' watch, and within the year he was said to be on such bad terms with Justinian that people claimed he was plotting with the Persians to topple him. This does not suggest someone who could have successfully managed a delicate situation such as this one—though it does sound like someone whose own very patrician nose may have been badly out of joint.[28]

The year 524 was an important one for Justinian, for he survived whatever threat Theodotus might still be posing, in a stronger position than before. The next year, he would take a crucial step towards succeeding Justin, for in 525, his adoptive father finally named him "Caesar," or heir apparent. There could no longer be any doubt that he was the preferred candidate for the succession. He was not, however, the only candidate, and his promotion may have stemmed from further complexities arising in relations between Rome and Persia. The stresses both in that relationship and within the governing class that had threatened Justinian in 523 would not go away; and would continue to shape his life, and Theodora's, in the years to come.

6

The Succession

While Dhu Nuwas was pursuing his murderous career in Arabia, curious events were taking place at the opposite end of the Roman border with Persia. King Tzath of Lazica—roughly the area of modern Georgia, on the Black Sea—decided to become a Christian. As he was formally a Persian client, it was a moment of considerable drama for him to renounce his allegiance to Persia. Emperor Justin was delighted, and arranged for him to be given a splendid white and gold robe, symbolic of his position, as well as a Christian wife drawn from the Constantinopolitan nobility. The Persian king Kavadh, for his part, was initially furious, but after some complicated negotiations, the upshot of which was that he killed the ruler of the Hun kingdom to his north (this kingdom, a long-standing irritant to the Persians and occasional Roman ally, was no relation to the Hunnic empire assembled by Attila in the fifth century), he felt he was ready to open fresh discussions with Justin.[1]

There is a striking symmetry in the situations that the two rulers found themselves in. Succession issues were uppermost in the mind of Kavadh, too. He was seventy, and desperately keen that his own son, Khusro, succeed, but was worried that he would be unable to secure this in the face of opposition from court cabals and from a powerful heretical sect that was presently a thorn in his side. Many years before, it was believed, the emperor Arcadius, realizing that he was dying, had asked the Persian king, Yazdgerd, to be guardian to his son, the future Theodosius II, who was still an infant. Yazdgerd agreed. All of our evidence for this remarkable turn of events comes from writers of Justinian's time or later, even though there is no very good reason to believe that it actually happened. These writers' conviction that it did is based on the fact that Kavadh was using the story as a precedent when he asked Justin to adopt Khusro and thereby protect him from potential assassins at home. Justin seemed inclined to accept the proposition until, when it was under discussion at a meeting of the Senate, Proculus, his chief lawyer—then in the post of *quaestor sacri palatii*, quaestor of the sacred palace—pointed out that if the emperor complied, Khusro would also have a claim to the Roman throne. So the request was rejected, some senators commenting that it was time Justin did more to stabilize his own succession. King Kavadh was angry, not least because he had been assured by Hypatius that his proposal would be welcome.[2]

The bad blood the incident produced led both sides to begin preparations for war. And it was bruited that Hypatius was plotting with the Persians to get rid of Justinian. In the end, the upshot was that Justin at last agreed to take more formal action to secure Justinian's place as his successor. It was a long time since an emperor had taken the step he was about to take, and it is quite possible that he had been waiting for an incentive such as Proculus had provided to do so. He now conferred upon Justinian the title of Caesar, official heir apparent.

We can imagine the scene. On the appointed day, officials and guardsmen gather in the Delphax; those of patrician rank are admitted to the triclinium of the nineteen couches, where Justin is seated with Justinian. When all is ready, Constantinople's patriarch joins the patricians in escorting the two principals from the triclinium to the tribunal, or platform, in the Delphax, where the insignia of office are laid out on an altar. Here, after a brief prayer, grooms come forward to dress the new Caesar in his imperial garb, and the crowd acclaim him with the words "Most fortunate of all!" followed by the chant of "Many years for the emperors Justin and Justinian, many years for the great emperors, divinely appointed emperors!" Another prayer, and the rulers return to the triclinium where their subjects are waiting, in order of rank, to greet them.[3]

There is Theodora, standing with the patricians. We imagine her emotions as she watches her husband don his fine new regalia, as the praises ring out around her. She now knows that she will be empress, the next Augusta, when the time comes—that is, as long as nothing untoward happens. The son of a peasant and the daughter of a bear keeper, they are only too aware how incongruous a couple they must seem to the assembled patricians. They have to give people time to get used to the idea that they are their new rulers: they must practice their roles. And they need friends they can trust.

Theodora and Justinian will continue to live in the palace of Hormisdas; and it appears to be at this point that they begin, as befits imperial personages, to plan the new Church of Saints Sergius and Bacchus (the church would be finished in 527)—which, as mentioned earlier, survives today as the "Little Hagia Sophia Mosque." The location that he chose was close to his palace and abutted the Church of Peter and Paul, which Justinian had earlier patronized. This part of the palace complex was thus intended to reflect the official heir's own religious concerns. Both churches, facing out over the Sea of Marmara, would be invisible to passersby. The people permitted to see the new church and to worship there, then, were not the ordinary folk, but the select few who were regularly admitted to the palace.

Sergius and Bacchus were well chosen, as saints representing the idea of service. According to the legend that surrounds their death, they were close friends, both soldiers, who had been tortured and killed on the orders of Emperor Maximianus in the early fourth century. The story of their deaths was composed over a hundred years later, and as we have seen, their cult was extremely important at Rusafa, whose bishop had participated in the conference at Ramla. Bishop Severus had

FIGURE 6.1. The church of Sergius and Bacchus, built by Justinian and Theodora near the Palace of Hormisdas in the mid-520s, shows their interest in experimental architecture, and stands in stark contrast to the gigantic Church of St. Polyeuktos along the Mese in Constantinople.

© photo by David Potter

preached on the subject of the martyrs in 514. And it was in the 520s that Justinian may have contributed to the improvement of the city's walls.[4]

The new church was very different from the Church of Peter and Paul, which followed the then-standard basilica style and comprised a long chamber, or nave, facing the altar at the front. The Church of Sergius and Bacchus, by way of contrast, consisted of two main elements: a domed octagon set within a rectangular exterior. The octagon, whose floor space is roughly two hundred and fifty square feet, is surrounded by a two-story colonnade that rises to a height of just over thirty feet and provides support for the dome above. According to one witness, the interior, well lit through windows below the dome, was once filled with mosaics, as well as gold and other decoration. Taking pride of place would have been a relic of Sergius himself (a toe), which had been brought from Rusafa.

The celebration of Sergius and Bacchus served to drive home a point not merely about the imperial couple's architectural creativity, but also about their connections with Syria, a claim ever so slightly tinged with the contemporary anti-Chalcedonianism. The Church of Peter and Paul spoke of Rome. Was the message conveyed by this juxtaposition simply that the disputes of the past were to be left in the past, and that in the new world order, diverse groups must learn to coexist? Many of the palace insiders were less concerned with religious controversy than the rest of the city's population. This might be a message they were interested in hearing, even if it proved impossible to realize in the long term.

Another message conveyed by the building of the Church of Sergius and Bacchus was that the imperial couple had no intention of being pushed around by those who thought they were the wrong people to be moving into the Great Palace. The small church was an architectural response, in novel style, to a church built about twenty years earlier along the Mese—the main avenue leading from the palace to the Church of the Holy Apostles—by Anicia Juliana, daughter of the emperor Olybrius, staunch Chalcedonian, and at the time one of the world's wealthiest women. It is not going too far to read a reference to her church—at that point Constantinople's last great ecclesiastical construction—into the inscription carved in the nave of Sergius and Bacchus, there for all those entering to see. The inscription's message is this: While other rulers may have honored people who led useless lives, Justinian, who fosters piety, dedicates this church to St. Sergius, who was persuaded by neither fire nor sword nor unjust trial to abandon his faith, his death permitting him to enter into Heaven. "God-crowned Theodora, whose mind shines with piety," is ever active in her efforts to aid the downtrodden.[5]

Anicia's tone had been very different—though equally provocative. Her Church of St. Polyeuktos (also a martyr, though of an earlier persecution) replaced a previous one built by a member of her family. She had also given over her nearby family palace to serve as a convent, thereby creating an Anician religious zone in the very heart of the city. St. Polyeuktos, which was huge, was itself something of an experiment: the walls of the nave supported a large dome, and a series of bays along the central nave were all inscribed with verses celebrating Anicia. Setting the scene, they announce: "On either side of the aisle, pillars standing on strong pillars lift up the rays of the golden dome; the bays poured into arches on each side catch the eternal light of the moon." These lines give us some sense of the grandeur of her space, which she saw as surpassing the Temple of Solomon. She carried the analogy so far that the architects she employed for this building used the biblical cubit as the unit of measurement throughout.[6]

FIGURE 6.2. A reconstruction of Anicia Juliana's church of St. Polyeuktos, built using biblical units of measurement and advertising Juliana's imperial ancestors.

We know less about the second of Anicia's religious foundations—the one that used to be her home—but we get an idea of what it was like from a variety of sources. Our first clue comes from the name, St. Euphemia. St. Euphemia was a young woman, allegedly martyred during the persecution that had seen the deaths of Sergius and Bacchus. She died at Chalcedon (Sergius and Bacchus had died in Syria). In fact, she was so important to the community at Chalcedon that the great basilica there, where the famous council had taken place, was named for her. A shrine to St. Euphemia was thus an advertisement for Chalcedonianism. The verses inscribed there proclaimed that Anicia had scraped off the former palace's aged coat to give the place a new bloom, and that in its new form its beauty rivaled the stars.[7]

The dedicatory poems, conveying in no uncertain terms the impact Anicia hoped her buildings would have, did not stop with their architectural splendor. A massive building such as this, in the heart of the capital, is by definition both a theological and a political statement. Anicia was well known for her devotion to Chalcedon, but the inscriptions made it clear that her concerns went well beyond the proper way to worship. In so doing, these same texts enable us to feel the intensity of the theological issues bedeviling both Justin and his successors-designate, and the passions against which Theodora now had to contend. Quite simply, these poems give voice to the emotions of very powerful individuals who felt they had as good a claim, or better, to the throne.[8]

In her church for St. Euphemia, Anicia would write that three generations had built this former family palace and dedicated it to the Trinity. Eudocia, wife of Theodosius II (we will forget for now that she died in exile), represents the first generation. Her niece Placidia, who had been taken captive by the Vandals when they sacked Rome in 455, represents the second. Released after years in captivity, she married Anicius Olybrius, who was emperor in the West, briefly, in 472 (as Leo's candidate). Since her father was the Western emperor Valentinian III, Placidia was directly descended from Theodosius I, who died in 395 as the last man to rule the united Roman Empire. Finally, of course, comes Anicia herself. Her husband, Areobindus, was a high-flying general who had directed most of the Roman operations against the Persians during the war that took place under Anastasius. In 512, when Areobindus had already left town, a Constantinopolitan mob had tried to proclaim him emperor. In the event, Areobindus rejected the proposition. Their son Anicius Olybrius could reasonably feel that he had a claim to the job his father had turned down. Those ambitions come out clearly in the poems decorating St. Polyeuktos. They open:

> Eudocia, then empress, wishing to honor God, built the first temple for Polyeuktos, the servant of God; but she did not build it as splendidly as she might . . . because, her prophetic soul told her, she left it for a descendant who knew better how to adorn it. Thus [Anicia] Juliana, glory of her blessed parents, having imperial blood from them in the fourth generation, did not defeat the intentions of the glorious queen, but she built it up from a small temple to its present size, increasing the honor of her many-sceptered ancestors; all that she did she made more splendid than did they, having the proper faith of a Christ-loving mind.[9]

Anicia's claims to virtually imperial status in the dedicatory inscriptions of both her churches reveal just how unstable Justin's grip on power—and thus even more so that of Justinian and Theodora—actually was. Anicia was presenting herself here not just as the descendant of empresses, but as the modern embodiment of Constantine's mother, the great Helena herself.[10] Anyone inscribing something like this in an earlier age would have been executed for treason. In the present era, however, the verses' author continued to be an influential member of society and could expect the emperor to attend one of her churches at least once a year.

Anicius Olybrius was not Justinian's only rival for the throne. For a start, we can add to Olybrius sundry relatives of Anastasius, men whose main official disqualification from office seems to have been their suspect religious credentials, plus people claiming connections with various earlier imperial families. One of these was Anthemius. His father, also named Anthemius, had been emperor in Italy—with Leo's support—from 467 to 472. Despite the fact that the younger Anthemius had participated in a failed coup against Zeno, which resulted in his rapid flight to join the Goths in the Balkans—whom he accompanied in their takeover of Italy in the 480s—he was now back in Constantinople and an individual with status. Ariadne had asked Anastasius to make him praetorian prefect—the emperor refused on the grounds that he had insufficient experience, but then made him consul. Anthemius had impeccable Chalcedonian credentials and, like other old men who had recently held imperial office, had never cavorted with anti-Chalcedonian ex-actresses.[11]

Anicia's decision to set up a religious institution was very much in line with contemporary forms of religious patronage: and in a major city, of course, it would be bound to have political implications. There were now several important monasteries in the capital that were bastions of Chalcedonian orthodoxy. The political power of religious foundations had become especially apparent when Daniel the Stylite played a significant role in destabilizing the anti-Chalcedonian regime of Basiliscus, facilitating Zeno's return to the throne.

Around the time of the Council of Chalcedon, the monastic community of the Akoimitai, the "sleepless ones," so-called because communal prayers were being offered twenty-four hours a day, seven days a week, had actively promoted the Chalcedonian cause. The Akoimitai were doctrinally aligned with other monasteries in the city, especially those of Dalmatius, Bassianou, Auxentiou, Matrones, and Stoudios. Some of the bigger monasteries—the Akoimitai and Stoudios in particular—had extensive connections in the provinces, especially in Palestine: the Jerusalem area was a heavily Chalcedonian heartland and had extensive links with the West as well as with Constantinople. At Constantinople, insofar as they were aligned with the patriarch, these monasteries could provide him with the muscle necessary for asserting his authority. Together with the factions, religious foundations offered a vehicle through which the wealthiest in the capital could influence opinion both within and beyond the city's walls.[12]

The perceived threat from monks and factions, at least from the perspective of a highly educated member of the imperial élite, emerges plainly in a fascinating dialogue on ideal government, written at some point during Justinian's reign. The anonymous writer rails against people who join monasteries, who, he says, would have done humanity a great favor by staying home to farm; neither has he anything better to say about the factions. If it were up to him, both would simply be banished. The impracticality of both of these suggestions, however, is made amply clear by ceremonies such as those having to do with the proclamation of a patrician. Such ceremonies were intended to focus the attention of all classes on the emperor's beneficence, because the imperial government needed the support of everyone. And there was indeed a continual threat from the factions and from monks—hence, in recognition of their importance and in the hope of averting dissent, their incorporation into the rituals.

On the other hand, whatever precautions were taken, riots were always a possibility, for whatever reason. While without the factions one might have to deal with fewer riots, one would at the same time have no effective way of communicating with the citizenry or of rallying them in defense of the regime against a renegade like Vitalian. The same crowd that could riot against an emperor one day might well have acclaimed him the day before. The fact was that the factions and the monasteries provided the downtrodden with an institutional response to the well-entrenched and persistent inequality that was rife in imperial society. An emperor could change none of this, but if he was well equipped and forever on the alert, he could manage it.[13]

The management of everything began in the palace, which was a law unto itself: an elaborate set of rituals governed the lives of its inhabitants. For several years now, Theodora would have been learning how to deal with all sorts of people, ranging from imperial bureaucrats to courtiers and special advisors. The change in her status as soon as she became Justinian's companion would have affected her life in many ways, from the clothes she wore—now lots of silk and jewelry—to her food and her sex life. She was now a very wealthy woman, with estates of her own to provide her with a substantial income.[14]

To begin with what she ate: her food would have been better and different from what she was used to, and certainly a lot spicier, as élite cuisine featured "mixtures," a sign of sophistication. The new regime would have been accompanied by lots of advice on the best ways to eat healthily, since contemporary medicine was still based on the four humors, deriving from the theories of the great Greek doctor Hippocrates—author of the Hippocratic oath—of the early fifth century BC. According to Hippocrates, a healthy body was one in which the humors—blood, phlegm, yellow bile, and black bile—were kept in balance by means of diet and lifestyle choices. The work of a popular intellectual named Herophilus, who probably flourished a few years after her death, gives us an idea of the kind of advice Theodora would have been receptive to.

In his dietary calendar, designed to introduce people to a healthy gastronomic regime, Herophilus recommends that in January, for instance, one should worry about phlegm. To counteract the sluggishness that this humor causes, each day should begin with three doses of fine aromatic wine, drunk slowly. Meats should include roast lamb and suckling pig, accompanied by gravies of spiced pepper, spikenard, and cinnamon; amongst other spices, seasonings should include eastern caraway; and pork should be basted in honeyed wine before roasting. Small birds are also a good idea, as is rare and imported fish such as sea bream, fried in a spicy sauce and accompanied by vegetables like cabbage, turnips, leeks, and carrots.

Regular bathing is also *de rigueur*—one suspects that a patrician would bathe a bit more often than the four times a month that Herophilus suggests. In February, the wise person avoids beets and wild vegetables, but might add shellfish to the diet, along with plenty of sex. In March, one might turn to sweet flavors (always remembering to avoid excess). In May, one had to watch out for black blood and therefore avoid anything dry, shift to lamb and poultry, and expand the range of fish, at the same time moderating one's sexual activity. In June, one did what one could to avoid hot blood: sex was most definitely off the menu. July and August were months in which both forms of bile were to be controlled; when bathing, one should use a lotion that contained clay brought in from the Aegean island of Kimolos. September, November, and December were also months during which sex was highly recommended—though finding herself under courtiers' and others' beady eyes, it is quite likely that Theodora's relationship with Justinian became very much less physical than those we have envisioned, with the aid of contemporary poets, for her earlier years (Chapter 3). But that too, as we have seen, would accord with contemporary ideas of married life.[15]

As for the officials, the closest to her would have been her personal servants, both women and eunuchs, who would have assisted her with her wardrobe and basic needs. She must have had a personal secretary through whom her correspondence would pass, and she probably had bodyguards as well. It would have been imperative, if she was going to function in government circles, that she acquire a command of Latin—still the language in which government did business. Even if she had a smattering before she entered the palace, it no doubt took some effort to reach the level necessary to function easily in the convoluted style of the court. Her experience on the stage, and with lovers from various strata of society, would have introduced her to the different registers of Greek ranging from the language of the street to the somewhat artificial, archaic style of imperial government, but here, too, she probably needed some practice if she were to play her new part as well as possible.

A remarkable papyrus from Egypt gives us some idea of how she might have gone about doing this. The text consists of a glossary of Greek terms in one column, and Latin, written in Greek characters, on the other. Words are grouped by category. Thus the section "Concerning stars" is headed *peri astrôn* on the Greek side and *de seiderivous* (an incorrect form) on the Latin, and below are listed the names of stars and other celestial phenomena such as "iris" or "rainbow." Or she might have had a book laid out much like a modern grammar book in which Greek verbs were conjugated opposite their Latin equivalents, all in the singular so she could remember that *hupêretô* meant *ministro*, or "I serve."[16] Theodora was a traveler making her way in a foreign land.

Insofar as Theodora needed to be able to deal with the great bureaus of government, we have already gotten some sense of just how acidic those people could be. So what were they actually like? What made them tick? What occupied them when they were not spreading nasty stories? For these were the people with whom Theodora would be dealing daily, and her ultimate success or failure would be determined by how well she could reach across the vast experiential gap that presently existed between her life and theirs.

Given that the palace was an alien world where deep chasms might open up before her, negotiating the perils along her path demanded a delicate balancing act. If she was, as Procopius suggests, an isolated figure with just a few female friends, dependent for her authority on the "demonic" influence she exercised over her husband, she would indeed be more of a mythical creature than an empress. But as the coming years would reveal, she was anything but the solitary figure he depicts, and was remarkably successful in building a broad-based band of supporters all over the empire. But to do so, she had first to win acceptance within the palace itself.

In order to appreciate what she was up against, let us now meet a few members of this group. It makes most sense to start with John

Lydus (our John the Lydian), because in revealing a good deal about himself, he allows us some insight, more generally, into the way such officials had themselves come up in the world.

John was probably born in 490, a couple of years before Theodora. He was well educated in his home city of Tmolus in Lydia, a region on present-day Turkey's west coast. He probably would have learned Latin there, and it bespeaks the availability of an excellent local education that John had no qualms about moving from Tmolus to Constantinople when he turned twenty-one: roughly the same age as Severus of Antioch when he elected to continue his education in Alexandria and Beirut. John said that he came to Constantinople "in the consulship of Secundinus"—a simple phrase that speaks volumes about his outlook. Flavius Secundinus was Anastasius' brother-in-law, the father of Hypatius and Pompeius (whom we have not yet met); he shared the consulship that year with a noble-man from Gaul, a nominee of Theoderic's, named Felix. For John Lydus, people like Felix were non-persons—to accept his existence would be to accept the legitimacy of Theoderic's regime in Italy. Since legitimate imperial government had, as a result of the actions of Odovacer and Theoderic, ended forever by the time John wrote his book on Roman magistrates, there was no point in mentioning a western official. John shared with others in the imperial service a deep sense of tradition.

Another person with whom John's path most likely crossed was Procopius, probably about ten years his junior, who had also trained as a lawyer, though we may well wonder how much they would have had to say to each other. John thought Theodora's ascension to power was a very good thing, and would later value her interventions in court politics. Another person who would cross John's path, though John does not mention him, would have been Tribonian, rumored to have been a pagan.

False though it might be in Tribonian's case, the charge of pagan-ism is an interesting one. Procopius, for instance, claimed that John the Cappadocian, whom John the Lydian detested too, muttered pagan prayers, although he was actually a devout Christian. Severus, as we have seen, was suspected of paganism (probably with good reason) before he began his clerical career. Indeed, the world of higher educa-tion generally was tinged with traditional belief. Even if one was not a practicing pagan, there was a feeling abroad that an individual with a really good classical education might not be thoroughly reliable when it came to issues of religious orthodoxy.

For such people, pagan or Christian, the real passion was for the past. Devotion to the classics shaped their sense of self. John of Lydia, for instance, went so far as to celebrate the fact that the principal guard unit, the *excubitores*, which Justin had once commanded and in which Justinian had served, were uniformed in bronze helmets with chain mail, carried a short broadsword on their left, two broad-bladed javelins on the right, and wore woven black greaves and traditional footwear—this, he tells us, was once standard gear for all Roman soldiers, and the very attire in which Aeneas had arrived in Italy to found Rome. The *excubitores* were now the only troops to retain the traditional gear—as "these days" Roman soldiers and barbarians had become virtually indistinguishable. Romulus had formed this unit; Tiberius, Rome's second emperor, had reformed it. In making the point, John cites several Latin works as a demonstration of the range of his learning. He seems unbothered by the fact that the unit in question had actually been founded by Leo "the Butcher." It is likely, though, that this sort of "history" was told even at the time the unit was assembled.[17]

John Lydus, and men like him, were proud of the way their learning set them apart. He himself had moved directly into the imperial service, and after just one year had been promoted into the praetorian prefect's office by Zoticus, who would himself hold the office and in whose year of tenure John profited to the tune of one thousand gold pieces. It is perhaps not surprising, then, that John wrote a poem (in Greek) in Zoticus' honor; nor, perhaps, that Zoticus ordered that he be paid at the rate of one gold piece per line; nor that Zoticus arranged John's marriage to a wealthy woman. While this sort of patronage might give today's "human resources officer" pause, for John it was nothing to be ashamed of—he was in fact very proud of it, and proud, too, that at a very young age he was one of the group that would propose new regulations before the senate. In his words:

> I set about writing *suggestiones*, which are as follows. In the beginning all the assistants in the secretariat to what was once the first of offices used to be outstanding in learning, and they worked hard to excel in Latin, which was very important to them. When a legal case subject to appeal would be brought, and was put before the senate for adjudication, the most senior

of the assistants would draw up the so-called *suggestio*, or "clarification," for the assistance of the senate so well as to leave the quaestor of the senate, as well as those once called *antecensores*, now called copyists, astounded.

The impact of these *suggestiones* can still be seen in many of the texts preserved in the fifth-century law code promulgated by Theodosius II in 438, and in the great code that Tribonian would soon compile for Justinian. Emperors and their most senior officials, lacking specific knowledge, would depend on people like John for the minutiae of the matters they would legislate upon.[18]

John did his job so well that he was promoted further; he reminds his readers that in those days, he and his colleagues would expect to be paid by those using their services. This was not a new practice—a remarkable text from mid–fourth-century North Africa records the payments (in grain) that officials would expect from merchants and others for doing the jobs that the government already paid them to do—and it was clearly not regarded as corrupt. Furthermore, imperial officials expected to pay a fee for the offices they obtained, and to be paid by their successors upon leaving office. As John puts it, "All-wise Justice, comforting men in just pursuits, made me respectable in the eyes of officials and not undeserving of honor from the rulers."[19]

Men like John Lydus, Zoticus, and Herophilus were people whom Theodora would now deal with every day. She had gained entrée to their world, but in doing so she had lost her privacy. It is no surprise that into the cliquish ambience of the palace she would bring her own clique, and that those who could expect her favor would resemble, not her erstwhile lover Hecebolus, one-time governor of Cyrenaica, but people who, like her, had come up the hard way. Justinian, son of peasants, had once been one such; and that, too, no doubt drew them to each other.

By the year 527, Justinian and Theodora were well established at court. But background and experience still mattered, and just as the last two regime changes had brought in emperors who were not obvious choices, so, too, did Justinian and Theodora have to protect themselves against the influence of men whom the hyper-educated palace staff would find more compatible.

It was that same year that Justin solved the potential problem. On April 1 (probably), he summoned a meeting of the patricians in the consistorium, and announced that he was making Justinian "Augustus." The assembled officials then moved into the Delphax, where they were joined by the rest of the palace officialdom and the guard. The patriarch, Epiphanius, said a prayer, then crowned Justinian. The ceremony was modeled on the one that took place when the young Leo II was proclaimed Augustus in 474, except that this time the palace was the venue, whereas Leo's acclamation had taken place in the Hippodrome. Perhaps the reason for this was that Justin, who was unwell, might not have been able to face the crowd. Three days later, there would be a second ceremony.[20]

Theodora's proclamation as "Augusta" would also probably have taken place within the palace, starting off in the Augusteus. Let us once more picture the scene. Theodora enters, veiled, accompanied by Justinian. She approaches the patriarch. The patriarch prays. Then her veil is removed, and her imperial robe is draped over her. She is now dressed just as we see her in the mosaic at San Vitale. The patriarch prays over her crown and hands it to Justinian, who places it on her head. The ceremony complete, Theodora replaces her veil and then, with Justinian by her side, joins a procession of women, assembled according to rank, who then escort the couple into the triclinium of the nineteen couches.

There she receives the acclamations of the Senate, possibly of the representatives of the people, and the guards. She removes her veil again, and the audience acclaims her with the Sanctus, "Holy, Holy, Holy, Glory to God in the highest and peace on earth." She may now light a candle and place it before a fragment of the True Cross—wood from the cross upon which it is believed Christ died. The crowd acclaims her again; then, finally, she retraces her steps back through the Augusteus.[21]

The parts of the palace used for her ceremony are different from those in which Justinian's take place, which symbolizes the different spaces they will occupy in the grand scheme of things. After generations of dominant imperial females, the empress will not be a mere extension of her husband. She is a ruler in her own right. Theodora understands exactly what this means.[22]

7

Augusta

The First Five Years

Justin survived the coronations of Justinian and Theodora by about four months, dying towards the end of August of 527. In the course of the next year, the imperial couple set in motion a series of changes offering their subjects a new image of imperial power, and what was, in effect, a new government. The main tenets of this government are set out by Procopius in his book, *Concerning Buildings*, on Justinian's building program, a work in which he acts as a mirror for imperial propaganda. Justinian, he says, undertook three great tasks when he became sole emperor. The first was to control the barbarians; the second, to ensure the proper worship of God, setting the empire on the foundation of correct worship and ridding it of all improper versions; and the third, to bring order to the empire's legal code. Many laws, Procopius rightly adds, were obscure, so Justinian began ironing out the discrepancies and "cleansing" the codes of verbal trickery.[1]

As the new emperor set about his tasks, anyone casting a fresh eye over the palace would have been struck by a number of changes. Justinian's inner circle was younger than Justin's, and had little time for anyone with a traditional administrative background—except, that is, for Tribonian. Tribonian was the legal genius charged on February 13, 528, with creating a new collection of laws; his influence as *quaestor sacri palatii*, "quaestor of the sacred palace," which we may still appreciate via the numerous laws he wrote in Justinian's name, was the most obvious of any of the emperor's ministers. Aside from Tribonian and his assistant Constantine, there was no other figure who stood head and shoulders above the rest; praetorian prefects, controlling fiscal matters, passed regularly through the revolving doors, and the best of the soldiers were all quite young. Belisarius, who would become one of the empire's dominant figures, was only just beginning his first major command; and there were others who would later be important—John of Cappadocia, for instance, and Germanus, Justinian's cousin, prominent under Justin but now, suddenly, invisible.

Theodora herself was one of the few obviously significant and stable members of a rather fluid inner circle. Even if she would not be able to prevent the ascendance of one particular person that she clearly disliked (John the Cappadocian), she was known to have good relations with her brother-in-law Sittas—who would move from an important provincial command to the critical post of *magister militum praesentalis* in 530 (in which post he remained until his death in 538–539)—and two of the praetorian prefects of these early years were known to get on well with her. Her great wealth added to her rapidly growing power and prominence. Just how powerful she now was became immediately evident as she began to attend meetings of the imperial consistory, her husband's council of ministers, which no empress had hitherto done.[2]

What impact did such power have upon Theodora? The essential toughness that enabled her to survive both her life as an actress and the failure of her relationship with Hecebolus empowered her to hold her own in the highly competitive milieu of the imperial court. She was living in a world where the passive perished, and she would prove herself to be a dangerous enemy. There is every reason to think that while she was contemptuous of the traditionally wealthy, she felt a deep compassion for the poor, the deserted, and the destitute.

The broader themes that dominated the first five years of her reign with Justinian were an ongoing effort to establish the legitimacy of the regime, frenetic administrative change, plus a pronounced desire to put the religious quarrels of the immediate past behind them, and to secure a stable relationship with God. The latter was not unrelated to the struggle for legitimacy, for a series of natural disasters that struck the eastern Mediterranean from 526 onwards, the date of a destructive earthquake at Antioch, were interpreted as the visible manifestation of God's anger. Such events were not convincing advertisements for the validity of Justinian's claim that he was God's agent on earth. The issue was all the more serious because, according to the author of a contemporary work of political theory, the emperor had been created in imitation of God, a view that was foundational to Justinian's view of imperial power. Justinian did not see himself as answering to the people, who in legal texts of the period were for the first time referred to as *subiecti*, "subjects." He saw the people both collectively and individually as potential beneficiaries of his "divine" benevolence.[3]

The quest for legitimacy entailed a degree of imperial proactivity that had not yet been seen in the lifetime of anyone in sixth-century Constantinople. While in theory united—government was supposed to be more efficient, less corrupt, and better aligned with the will of the Almighty—the reality sometimes fell short of the mark. Moments of innovation were followed by bursts of reaction; the ramifications of local scandals, the unintended consequences of imperial intolerance, spread across the empire; magnanimity clashed with brutality; the regime failed to offer a coherent vision of the new future. All of this was the consequence of trying too hard, but latent opposition, or the fear of bureaucratic sabotage, necessitated the effort. Moreover, Justinian had to acknowledge that the empire no longer had the power to dominate its immediate neighbors. Toward the end of Justin's reign, when the military situation was not being resolved in Constantinople's favor, there had been trouble with the Ostrogothic kingdom of Italy where its territories abutted those of the empire. And there was the threat of trouble with Persia. The Persian emperor, Kavadh, was always on the lookout for chinks in the Roman Empire's armor. He was again angry about the loss of his client kingdom Lazica to Christianity; and he needed money to keep his neighbors on the steppes at bay, regarding the empire as a potential bank, if and when his resources permitted him to raise a sufficient army to raid it.

The first five years stand apart from the rest of Theodora's reign because of the necessary concentration on internal affairs, and because the Nika Revolt, which threatened to topple her husband's regime in January 532, would set in motion some major changes, both in Constantinople (see Chapter 8), whose political center would have to be rebuilt, and across the empire. And before the end of that year, Justinian would begin his attempt at retaking the Western empire, a massive task that would dominate much of the rest of his reign. The end of the Nika Revolt would establish once and for all that he and Theodora no longer felt the need to justify their position—there could be no doubt, when that moment came, that they were on the throne to stay.

Some of Theodora's official activities in these first years fell within the parameters set by earlier empresses, such as giving expensive gifts to cities or communicating in her own right with foreign dignitaries; other actions would reflect her own life experiences and interests. In other words, some things she would do simply because she was who she was, and as empress it was possible for her to do them. Some believed that one of her first tasks was to murder Amalasuintha, queen of the Goths in Italy, so Justinian would not marry her instead of Theodora. This is probably untrue, but nonetheless reveals what people thought her capable of. Likelier deeds, and better attested, are to do with the empress's roles vis-à-vis the Church and within the palace, where she would promote men she liked and, from time to time, persuade her husband to get rid of those she did not. Procopius alleges that Theodora could act pretty much as she liked in order to dispose of people she found threatening, which implies that she had a large and loyal staff (quite likely running to over a thousand). As one who could, and did, provide significant endowments for the institutions she patronized, she plainly had discretion as to how she would spend her money; and she was expected to function as a public face of the imperial regime.[4]

She would begin her day, Procopius says, in her quarters—the empress had her own space in the palace and her own bedchamber—with a long bath followed by breakfast. He claims she would then sleep most of the day, getting up to consume an ample lunch, then an equally large dinner—we may well doubt the truth of this last, given that he also says that she was slight of figure. What he leaves out is the time she spent reading. This emerges from a letter Severus wrote to the eunuch Misael, one of those who had been exiled for complicity in Amantius' alleged plot against Justin in 518. Now restored to a position of trust as one of Theodora's personal eunuchs, one of his jobs seems to have been to keep track of books that were sent to her. Severus mentions that he copied out books for her in large letters—large letters, presumably, on the assumption that she would read them herself and because, certainly by sometime in the next decade, she was getting shortsighted. As mentioned earlier, reading to oneself was not typical amongst the upper classes, and it is a sure sign of her genuine desire to participate in the empire's governance and culture.[5]

It was important for Theodora to look the part of empress, too. The famous San Vitale mosaic at Ravenna gives us one impression of her, flanked by her court (figure 7.2). She is carrying a large gold vessel,

FIGURE 7.1. Consular diptych of Justin, the last man to hold the consulship, dates to AD 540. The portrait of Theodora on the top left of each panel is the only lifetime portrait of the empress.

© Museum für Byzantinische Kunst, photo by Sailko

wears a white *chlamys*, or underdress, over which is a purple robe with an image of the three Wise Men embroidered across the bottom and gold embroidery along the hem. The Wise Men (Magi), who represent Persian client kings in the process of abandoning their original allegiance, also symbolize her role as the representative of the Virgin Mary, "Mother of God." Around her shoulders is a wide, jeweled necklace; she wears long gold earrings, and on her head is a gold crown set with jewels. To her right is a pair of male attendants; on her left are seven women of her retinue. In the one certain lifetime portrait of Theodora that survives (the San Vitale mosaics were completed after her death) we likewise see her wearing an elaborate crown, though the rather miniaturized version of the empress on this object—a diptych of 540 celebrating the consulship of the last man ever to hold that office—makes it hard to detect any greater detail (figure 7.1).

FIGURE 7.2. Theodora and her court from the Church of San Vitale in Ravenna: although the most famous portrait, it was completed after Theodora's death.

© Alfredo Dagli Orti / Art Resource, NY

Other surviving statues and portrait busts plainly representing empresses are difficult to identify with a specific ruler because they project strikingly similar stylized images from the fourth through the sixth century. In Paris, there is a full-length statue of such a woman, and a bust, sometimes identified as Ariadne; at Niš in Serbia there is a bronze "empress" head, and in Milan a bust claimed to be Theodora herself (figure 7.3). The painting of the Theotokos, dressed as an empress and holding the Christ child, in the crypt of Rome's Church of San Clemente, is influenced by contemporary representations of empresses (figure 7.4). The Theotokos and all the empresses wear jeweled diadems, and their faces radiate serenity—prosperity and calm are their crucial attributes. Most of the empresses depicted are also slim, a hint perhaps of personal asceticism. These are portraits, not of individuals, but of the perception of an empress's power. A contemporary poet tells us that public portraits obscured Theodora's blonde hair.[6]

The administrative space that became Theodora's had been carved out by empresses of earlier times. The first was Helena (c. AD 270–328),

FIGURE 7.3. Bust of a Byzantine empress, thought to be Theodora, found at Milan.

© Scala / Art Resource, NY

mother of Constantine, who had promoted pilgrimage to the Holy Land by constructing churches on two sites of Christian significance and had had her mausoleum built next to the Church of Saints Marcellinus and Peter on Rome's Via Casilina. According to legend, she had discovered the fragment of the True Cross when she was in Jerusalem. Later, in the fourth century, speeches in praise of empresses stress their wisdom, kindness, openness, generosity, and overall care for the family. Pulcheria, sister of Theodosius II, as noted earlier, had further emphasized the religious role of imperial women, declaring herself a perpetual virgin and persuading her sisters to live with her as nuns in the imperial palace.

Throughout Constantinople were to be seen statues representing imperial women, often in the company of their spouses. Individual images helped reinforce the notion that an empress was a powerful figure in her own right. It was in the course of the fifth century that veneration of the Virgin Mary was on the increase. The cult of Mary had to do with the First Council of Ephesus in 431, then was reinforced twenty years later by the Council of Chalcedon. According to Chalcedonian doctrine, Mary was the *Theotokos*, and as such the ideal intermediary between God and mortals; by Theodora's lifetime, the image of the Theotokos had come to replace the old pagan image of the city goddess.

As Mary's cult grew, so, too, did the importance of the empress as a person who could intercede with the emperor: indeed, her role was the earthly equivalent of Mary's.[7] Given Theodora's background, this was especially hard for some to swallow. Even more difficult for them was the change in court ceremonial whereby

> ... everyone, including those of patrician rank, had to make their entrance by falling straight on the ground, flat on their faces; then, stretching their arms and legs out as far as they would go, they had to touch with their lips, one foot of each of the two.[8]

The not-so-subtle message was that the old days are now over, and this empress is on an entirely level peg with her husband. Furthermore, the two are now to be addressed as "Master" and "Mistress." A further

FIGURE 7.4. The image of the Virgin Mary from the Church of San Clemente in Rome, with her jeweled crown, takes on aspects of the image of an empress in the age of Theodora.

© photo by David Potter

factor here might be that, although Justinian had been very much part of the scene during Justin's last years, this was the first time in half a century that a son had succeeded his father.[9]

While the new symbolism stressed distance and imperial superiority, making no bones about who was in charge, Justinian and Theodora realized that this was not enough. Both went to some pains to reinforce the message, and it is the law code that Tribonian was in the process of compiling that reveals the tenor of the new era in considerable detail.

In announcing the first edition of the Code on April 7, 529, Justinian proclaimed:

> The greatest protection of the state rests on two things: arms and law, and, ensuring its own power through these two things, the fortunate race of the Romans has been placed above all nations and has been made to rule them all in past times as, with the assistance of a propitious God, it will in the future; arms and laws both have always flourished with the assistance of each other, for just as military affairs are protected by laws so are laws guarded by the protection of arms.

Much of what survives of the Code takes the form of what were essentially administrative memoranda exchanged between Tribonian and senior officials, especially the praetorian prefects. Tribonian's texts assert, amongst other things, that the confusion typical of past legislation is hereby being set straight; that the emperor has genuine concern for his subjects; and that he has the highest expectations of those engaged in public life, both in the imperial service and in the Church.

About this time, when the state was expressing a particularly strong interest in maintaining the moral order of society, the Patriarch of Constantinople was involved in a vigorous correspondence with other churchmen concerning the way the clergy should behave.[10] In keeping with these themes, it is striking that two early measures that attracted the attention of a contemporary chronicler addressed the factions on one hand and heresy on the other.

The law on heresy, an uncompromising statement on divergent beliefs, had been issued sometime before Justin's death, while the law restraining the factions dated to shortly after it. The first of these measures excluded Jews, Manichaeans, and Samaritans—the last of which was a Jewish sect that held that Mount Gezirim rather than Jerusalem was the chosen place to worship the God of Israel—from participation in the imperial government. (In some cases, the intention of the legislation may have been more symbolic than real.) The Manichaeans followed the revelations of the third-century AD prophet Mani, whose faith combined aspects of Christianity, Judaism, and Zoroastrianism with the products of his own fertile imagination. There were not a lot of Manichaeans to be found in the Roman Empire, and those that there were seem to have been concentrated on its fringes, in places such as the monastery at Kellis in the Egyptian desert. As for the Samaritans, they were considered to have changed their faith if they changed their names (and without anyone asking too closely about their confessional choices). The legislation against them, which led to a bloody revolt in which local Christians attacked members of the Samaritan community, was thought to have been moderated because a Samaritan who had changed his name to Silvanus held an official position in the region. Christian heretics were defined as those not adhering to the "Universal Church" and the emperor's "holy, orthodox faith." The only exception allowed under this law concerned Gothic soldiers, who were felt by definition to be Arians.

The main point of this law was that one should always act in such a way that "the safety, honor, and the good name of the adherents of the holy faith be increased." No contemporary would have failed to notice that anti-Chalcedonian preaching was not covered by the decree—indeed, was not mentioned. It was as if to say that "right belief" could accommodate both sides of the Chalcedonian debate, just as did the imperial palace, where the ever-so-orthodox Justinian lived side by side with the ever-so-suspiciously unorthodox Theodora. If the empire was to succeed in meeting the challenges it faced from abroad, it had best be at peace with itself.[11]

The measure dealing with the factions, by banning factional violence throughout the empire, may have been intended to cast a veil over Justinian's notable early partisanship of the Blues. But the practical effect of such a decree was going to be negligible, so what was Justinian actually thinking when he approved it? It might be that he was simply being foolish—never something that can be discounted in any time or place. There had been times in the past, and there would be times in the future, when his judgement would be suspect; but at this moment, his message to the factions may just have been that they, no less than any other groups, would be subject to the new code of civil laws that Tribonian was working so hard on. Justinian was determined to put a new face on the empire; or, to use the language of the heresy law, to "restore and thereby strengthen" the system. As well as reforming the administrative structure of the empire, his plans extended to the material fabric, too—he was engaged in some major building projects in Constantinople and out in the provinces. The symbolic importance for a new ruler of a decree asking his subjects to look forward to a new era of domestic peace was incontrovertible. The proposed new way forward, however, would be cast by some as a return to an earlier era, when Rome had ruled the whole of the Mediterranean basin.

Claiming that, by seeking to restore past glories, one was moving forward was hardly new. Nor was there just one way of defining what those former glories had been. Men like John Lydus and Procopius would define them as belonging to the time when people like themselves ran the empire. Hypatius, for instance, would regard the glorious past as one *not* involving the son of a peasant and a former actress occupying the throne; for Severus, now living in Egypt, a good past was one in which the Council of Chalcedon had never happened; for the patriarch in Constantinople, it was one without Severus. The challenge for Justinian and Theodora was to present a vision of the past in which the competing aspirations of their contemporaries could be subsumed with the least possible conflict. Or, if not with the least conflict, then with the least possible scope for resistance. In practical terms, this meant that Justinian's new legislation would pursue a vigorous course. One half of its remit would be to restore whichever of its physical assets could be restored, improve those that could be improved; and to forge ahead with a significant building program to restore places threatened by his neighbors or recently ruined by natural disasters.[12]

Leaving the domestic front, there was more urgent business calling for attention: war was threatening in Lazica on the Black Sea, where the Persians were still smoldering over the Lazican king Tzath's conversion to Christianity. At the same time, negotiations continued with various peoples, ranging from the tribes around the Black Sea to the Ostrogoths in Italy. Appearing before the world as her husband's partner and equal, Theodora had her own connections with foreign courts, her own sources of information. Simeon "the Persian debater," who spent most of his ecclesiastical career in the Persian Empire, got her to write on his behalf to the "senior Queen of Persia"; Kavadh's son Khusro would make fun of the Eastern Romans because they had "allowed" Theodora to write to a senior Persian official on imperial business (or so Procopius claims). Sudanese tribes would later ask her to send them a bishop (which she did).[13] In the present situation, though, any diplomatic initiative that Theodora might wish to launch would take place in the context of the worsening relations with Persia.

The advantage at first lay with Justinian, who struck a significant blow by making an alliance with one of the rulers of the Sabir Huns, who lived around the Caspian Sea, at the beginning of 528. This king promptly attacked other Huns who had shown an inclination to support the Persians. The resulting chaos on Persia's northern border gave the Eastern Romans time to improve their defenses further south, in Mesopotamia.

Clearly, there was more work to be done, and Justinian now set about strengthening the imperial presence on the eastern frontier, rebuilding the walls of the ancient city of Martyropolis and renaming it "Justinianopolis" for himself. The attention he was paying to Martyropolis, which was not far from the anti-Chalcedonian center at Amida, suggests that he was trying to establish links of patronage with a region where affection for the central government was in short supply, as well as creating a more easily defensible frontier at a time when there was a high probability of an armed confrontation with Persia.

Another of Justinian's projects was to rebuild Palmyra, which had been one of the Eastern empire's greatest cities until its ruler, Queen Zenobia, quarreled with the imperial government at Rome—a conflict that resulted in her city's destruction in AD 273. The new Palmyra would not evoke the renowned caravan city of the past, grown rich on trade with India (now largely redirected to the Red Sea). Instead, it would be accorded a biblical heritage as the spot where David defeated Goliath. Solomon had then built it into a magnificent city, the Bible tells us, much as Justinian was now doing, in honor of his father. That Justinian should embrace this story is especially interesting in light of Anicia Juliana's claim that she had intended her own church, St. Polyeuktos in Constantinople, to rival the Temple of Solomon. Was Justinian, like Anicia but on a larger scale, trying to reclaim for himself the full heritage of the great biblical monarch? On a more practical level, al-Mundhir III, king of the Nasrid Arabs, had recovered from the bout of lethargy that had set in about the time of the conference at Ramla in 525, and was raiding the Roman frontier. Palmyra, which controlled a large oasis, was a useful base for operations, both against pests like al-Mundhir and in support of Rome's Arab allies, the Jafnids.[14]

The work at Martyropolis reveals something about Justinian's approach to Persia. A new circuit wall was constructed within the old one, and the gap between the two was filled with rubble, creating a wall now twenty feet high and twelve feet thick. The decision to build the massive new structure at this particular spot reflected the Roman conviction that the best way to confound a Persian invasion was to delay the enemy's advance with heavily fortified sites located in the traditional region of conflict between the two powers. This contrasted with Justinian's approach to the usual northern conflict points in the Armenian highlands and in the lands bordering the Black Sea, where he was willing to be considerably more aggressive. Was he hoping to distract the Persians away from where they could do the most damage? These were areas that were in the process of recovery from the devastation inflicted by the earthquake of 526. With a couple of spectacular exceptions, Justinian was reasonably successful in doing just that. What was perhaps just as significant from Theodora's point of view was that, when the command structure of the eastern frontier was given a shake-up in preparation for the Persian war, a senior position went to her brother-in-law Sittas, and Belisarius, husband of her friend Antonina, was in line for a high command as soon as any of the existing staff had to be replaced—which would happen before the end of the next year. At the same time, operations were somewhat hampered by the fact that Antioch, the main base for Roman administration in the region, had been wrecked by the recent earthquake.[15]

A surviving description of the earthquake of 526 suggests it was of massive proportions. A second quake would strike two years later, again killing thousands, and led to renaming Antioch, Theopolis, "City of God." As a way of contributing to its reconstruction, Justinian and Theodora each donated a church in their name. Justinian built a new Church of the Virgin Mary just inside the new city wall, while Theodora chose to repair the Church of St. Michael the Archangel. Such undertakings were in keeping with the projects characteristic of an empress, which might also involve the construction or patronage of monasteries, poorhouses, and hospitals. We may well see such good works as symbolizing women's interest in family, stability, and order. But in an age when questions of community identity were bound up with confessional allegiances, it is not possible to draw a line between the political and the cultural, or the specifically male and female. Public buildings were statements of public importance, features of what one scholar has aptly described as a "public culture of sovereignty."[16]

In the case of Antioch, Justinian's and Theodora's foundations are significant in different ways. In choosing to honor Mary, Justinian was supporting his new bishop, Ephrem, whose less than diplomatic dealings with the anti-Chalcedonian majority were rendering him deeply unpopular. For Theodora, the aspect of St. Michael that may have been most significant was his role as a healer, which is exactly what many in Antioch were in need of at this moment. At the same time as she was repairing St. Michael's, she rebuilt the basilica of Anatolius in the city center, transporting the columns all the way from Constantinople, while also sending an expensive cross, set with jewels, to Jerusalem.[17]

Although friends and foes alike would tend to present Theodora as a creature of faction, her actions in the year 528 suggest that she was trying to rise above factionalism. The gifts she gave to the city that had seen her life change beyond recognition, and those she had given to leaders who did not share her confessional outlook, suggest that what she wanted to convey was that, like Justinian, she was there to be a ruler for all Romans, no matter what their religious convictions. As with the decree banning factional violence, both empress and emperor were asking their subjects to turn away from the divisions of the past towards a new future. In the same vein, further east, two groups of monks that had been expelled from their monasteries at Edessa and Amida in 521 were allowed to go home. Was this a recognition of the fact that the heavy-handed pro-Chalcedonian policies of Justin had done little to reinforce loyalty in the crucial border region? In any event, it is certainly a sign of Theodora's influence, since she had connections with both groups, having arranged for the removal of the Amidan monks from their harsh exile at Petra to Egypt; and she is explicitly said to have obtained the order for the return of the Edessan community, which was entrusted to Belisarius.[18]

Her efforts to promote reconciliation were more idealistic than practical, but Theodora felt she had changed—and radically: furthermore, the stress on repentance in the marriage law was not just rhetoric; and for political reasons, she never lost the need to be seen as different from the actress her enemies liked to remind people she had been. For her, being empress was not an act: she was continually striving to be worthy of her new role in life. And if *she* could achieve such a transformation, she hoped to be able to show others the way to a new future.

Two measures, against heretics and dealing with "religious deviants," show us a quite different aspect of imperial government from the top-down/center-periphery model we have so far seen. Both seem to have sprung from isolated cases that caused Justinian to take more wide-ranging action. The first dealt with men engaging in same-sex relations, the other with pagans in the context of ongoing natural disasters, or signs of the "wrath of God." In 528, this was exemplified by a massive earthquake at Soloi Pompeiopolis (in what is now the southern Turkish province of Mersin), said to have swallowed up half the city, as well as the earthquake that hit Antioch in the same year. The report of a city suddenly half submerged beneath the earth may be rhetorical exaggeration, but it reflects the sort of thing people believed possible when the Almighty was in a bad mood. Allusions to a link between what was seen as sexual deviance and God's anger refer to incidents that took place in 529 involving two bishops (and there were comparable cases subsequently).[19]

The action against men engaging in homosexual relations had some background in earlier Roman laws banning what was seen as openly transgressive sexual conduct. In this case, two bishops, one from Rhodes, the other from Thrace, were brought to Constantinople from their respective sees and tried before the city prefect, who tortured one of them, then sent him into exile. He castrated the other and had him displayed in a litter. Justinian then ordered a more comprehensive round-up of people engaging in pederasty. John Malalas, the author of a contemporary chronicle and our most important source for these carryings-on, says that great fear fell upon those "afflicted with lust towards men." The penalties for conviction on charges of "religious deviance" included public humiliation, flogging, and castration—sometimes inflicted with such brutality that the victims died.

Procopius alleges that Theodora took advantage of this law to deal with a man named Basianus, described as a wealthy supporter of the

Greens, who was slandering her. According to Procopius, she had him dragged out of a church and tried. In his case, as in that of the Bishop of Rhodes, he was tortured during the trial and castrated upon conviction. The brutality inherent in these proceedings, especially against people of high status, suggests that Justinian, like others, associated same-sex relationships with pagan practice, and that this was the first phase in a concerted effort to eliminate what he regarded as deviant religious behavior. When issuing another edict against same-sex practices in 559, he says that he is acting out of fear of God's wrath, though here he states that those who confess their sins before the Patriarch of Constantinople and receive a "cure" from him will not be punished. Magistrates will take action against those who do not do as required in order to conciliate God, who is "justly angry with us."[20] It is unlikely that his thinking on the issue had expanded much in the thirty years that separated whatever prompted this statement and the decisions he had made in 528.

The next year, a series of not-dissimilar events resulted in the closure of the philosophical school at Athens where that particular teaching tradition, which had links with the origins of rational European thought, could be traced back for more than a millennium. This school, long in the academic doldrums, had recently returned to prominence thanks to a new head named Damascius who taught a particularly "edgy" form of Neoplatonism that included the concept of wisdom gained through direct divine revelation.

As with the incidents just described, this one opens with action being taken against some prominent individuals in Constantinople—later broadening out to deal with comparable happenings in the provinces—accused in this case of engaging in astrology. Our knowledge of what happened at this point is limited to the odd brief line in chronicles of the period dependent on the work of John Malalas. In any event, it appears that local enemies of Damascius took advantage of an edict aimed at certain pagan practices—in particular, the consultation of an oracle that involved the casting of dice or knuckle-bones, a practice already Christianized in some areas—to shut the school down. A couple of years later, in 531, faced with more comprehensive anti-pagan legislation, Damascius and his colleagues packed up and moved to Persia. The transition from local to imperial incident was a natural result of the *suggestio*, or responsive, process that John Lydus has described for us, in that a *suggestio* arose from a local request that the emperor could choose, whether in the long or short run, to make the basis of an empire-wide ruling.[21]

Legislation against heresy and religious deviance was but one feature of these years. Extremely active in many areas, Justinian attempted amongst other things to limit corruption in government and in the administration of the Church. In 529, Tribonian produced the first draft of his new law code, the systematization of precedent in Roman law that is now known as the *Codex Justinianus*, one of the foundational documents in the Western legal tradition.

In it, we glimpse Theodora active alongside her husband in cases of domestic disputes, which relates to the role that the empress had come to occupy in keeping a stern eye on the domestic arrangements of the aristocracy. Procopius claims that her interventions were often capricious and cruel—she "forced" the daughters of a deceased patrician to marry below their station, he says. Theodora's version might have been that she was looking to protect the weak from the strong. In one case, a man named Eulalios, who had died deep in debt, had made Justinian his heir—heirs were responsible for paying the debts of estates they inherited. Justinian announced that he was accepting the estate because caring for Eulalios' distressed daughters was a pious act, and he promptly placed all three of them in Theodora's care so she could bring them up in the imperial apartments. Acting in her own right, but also in the interests of ill-treated children, it was Theodora who brought about the passage of a law dealing with child prostitution—a prime example of the care for the downtrodden advertised in the inscription on the Church of Sergius and Bacchus. John Lydus refers to her vigilance and concern for victims of injustice. He is in this case referring to himself, amongst others, but his mention of Theodora reflects her public persona.[22]

John Malalas, again our prime source, reflects in his own text the public language of Justinian's time, giving us a sense of the way Theodora was perceived: he opens his account with the statement that the "pious Theodora did this in addition to her other good works." The problem she wished to solve in this instance was that pimps were routinely offering impoverished parents money for their children, promising that no evil would come to them. But once free of the parents, they would force the children into prostitution. Theodora ordered the arrest of all the pimps, along with their victims. When they came before her—we should envisage her in the Augusteus—she ordered the pimps to declare under oath how much they had paid the parents. When they replied that they paid a few gold pieces (*nomismata*) each, Theodora gave each one five *nomismata* per girl, then ordered the girls' release. The pimps were forbidden to go back into business, while the girls were given fresh clothing and one silver coin, and sent home.

The event appears to have been highly stage-managed, but the solution was genuinely original in treating the prostitutes as victims and the issue as social rather than moral. The Roman state had long taken an interest in preserving families, while recognizing that in times of hardship the poor were likely to abandon their children. From Constantine's time onwards, the state had made an effort to discourage this practice, but with minimal success, given that it could not or would not address the root causes of social inequality. Here, Theodora was helping people who had no other recourse, but it remains an open question how well the children she rescued were welcomed home. The fact that she would take a very different approach to the issue of prostitution generally might suggest she had discovered that a one-time act of benevolence on her part in respect of a deeply rooted social ill made for better theater than policy. The fact that she was treating child prostitution as a social issue rather than a moral one presents an interesting contrast to the official handling of same-sex relationships in 529.

It is also one of a number of signs that her concern for the weak was evolving into actual policy statements. A law of 531 stating that the slave concubine of a man who had died could not be reduced to slavery by his heirs, but rather, unless her partner had specified her continued slavery in his will, she and her children would be free, would appear to evince a concern to protect otherwise powerless women. Laws of this sort reinforce the impression that she was counting Tribonian amongst her palace allies.[23]

Towards the end of 530, Theodora did something she had not done before and would not do again—at least, with anything like the publicity she garnered at this point. She made an elaborate imperial procession across the Bosphorus to the so-called Pythian spring in Bithynia (now the modern resort of Yalova); the place was pleasant, and the expedition gave her a chance to make donations to churches, monasteries, and charitable institutions along the way. Many patricians were among the crowd of some four thousand who made the trip with her, as was

Menas, the praetorian prefect, whose stand against bureaucratic corruption is evident in a number of texts. No explanation of the procession survives, but the presence of Menas and the stress on upper-class participation suggest that she may have envisioned the expedition as a moment for bonding with a group of people with whom she had often hitherto had frosty relations.[24]

For all her efforts to be seen as a source of assistance to the unfortunate, incidents like that concerning Basianus, and the exile during these same years of Priscus, who had been accused of slandering her, did nothing to reinforce the desired image. People would allege all manner of things. After having claimed, rightly, that Amalasuintha's royal consort Theodahad had been responsible for her murder, Procopius then came up with the story that Theodora was afraid that Justinian would dump her in order to take up with the recently widowed, and allegedly quite beautiful, queen of the Ostrogoths, thereby implying that Theodora had had something to do with the murder herself. Certainly, it is clear that Theodora was in contact with senior officials in the West. There survive two letters from Cassiodorus, the powerful Roman senator who played an important role in managing relations between the Gothic court and its Roman subjects. One of the letters suggests that Theodora may have made a rather dubious request of the king: Cassiodorus, writing in the king's name, says "in the case of that person too, about whom a delicate hint has reached me, know that I have ordered what I trust will agree with your intention." The opacity of the reference would indeed suggest that Theodora had asked Theodahad to do something not entirely laudable; and she was, as Procopius asserts, empowered to make independent policy decisions. It would not be reading too much into this letter to infer from it that even very important people thought it a good idea to do her bidding.[25]

Within the palace itself, Theodora was not about to stand aside and cede influence to John the Cappadocian, appointed praetorian prefect in 531 and someone she seriously disliked. She had assembled a list of grievances against him that she had presented to Justinian, and John Lydus makes it plain that she was the one individual willing to speak out publicly against him. Procopius claims that she and Justinian were often at odds on matters of public policy—and where religion was concerned, this would have been significant. In this case, there is some corroboration of what Procopius says, even if the person confirming his claim was predisposed to favor Theodora's taking the stand she did.[26]

Theodora was growing into her position. She was every day more confident in her abilities—her whole life shows that she was willing to take risks and could be a fierce adversary, and that she did not suffer fools gladly. But she was more than that. She was consistent in taking an interest in women she thought had been dealt a bad hand, and equally consistent in reminding the imperial aristocracy that her position required them to treat her with respect. One thing that we have not so far learned is whether she wanted more children, but this she surely did—perhaps she believed, as did Tribonian (revealed in a law issued on February 20, 531), that Nature created women to have children and that this was their greatest desire. At about the same time, another law was promulgated stating that a child born of a love affair that ended in marriage and in which more children followed would be as legitimate as these later children (such, of course, as Theodora's own daughter).[27]

Our best information on Theodora's interest in having more children comes actually from a hostile source, Cyril of Scythopolis' *Life of Sabas*. In 530, Sabas, the head of a monastery in the Judean desert, learned that Justinian and Theodora were annoyed with the Christians of Palestine in the wake of the previous year's violent Samaritan uprising. He went to the capital to discuss the issue with the emperor. Justinian greeted Sabas with enthusiasm—running up with tears of joy to kiss his head, we are told (evidently prostration was not required of high-ranking holy men), and invited him to visit Theodora. The empress greeted him warmly and asked, "Pray for me, Father, that God grant me fruit of the womb." Sabas responded, "God the master of all will guard your empire." She repeated her request: "Pray, Father, that God will give me a child." He assured her that the God of glory would maintain the empire in piety and victory. At this point Theodora gave up, though she seems to have been visibly upset that he would not grant her request. When asked later why he did not pray as the empress had asked, Sabas said that "fruit will never come from that womb, lest it suck in the doctrines of Severus and cause worse upheaval to the Church than Anastasius."[28]

For Theodora to be so public in her desire for a child, she must have been desperate to become pregnant. Public admission of failure would not strengthen her position in the world at large; having been married to Justinian for a decade and still finding herself childless by him, it is more than likely that at this moment, for once, we hear Theodora's own voice.

By January of 532, the eve of the revolution that would threaten both their positions, Theodora was an independent woman willing to disagree with her husband in public, and able to exercise considerable influence around the Mediterranean. So, to some degree, the Theodora of Procopius is real. But this is only part of the story, for while she wished to make it clear to the aristocracy that she was in charge and let it be known that she was none too impressed with their claims to hereditary importance, she cared deeply for people she saw as victims of abuse. She was willing to allow a man like Sabas a good deal more leeway and respect than Procopius, and able to win the admiration of men of the caliber of John Lydus.

8

Revolution

The outbreak of war with Persia in the year 530 altered the speed of domestic change and challenged Justinian's own security on the throne. If the slew of natural disasters that had struck one after the other since his accession were not enough to raise questions about the emperor's fitness to rule, the Samaritan revolt, followed by lackluster success in the field by generals selected by Justinian himself, would raise others. War and misfortune during the period from April of 527 to December 531 form the backdrop to the catastrophe that would occur in the first half of January 532. This catastrophe, beginning with relatively minor riots in the Hippodrome, was one of two events in the next decade where Theodora's personal intervention is well attested as having changed the course of her husband's reign, saving him from deposition.

As with all things to do with Theodora, disentangling fact, opinion, and outright fiction depends upon our ability to isolate clues in our various sources, be they inconsistencies between the documentary record and later narratives, or between narrative accounts and factors that we can establish as typical of the period's political culture. What we may see in what is quite simply one of the most remarkable interventions by a woman in the political life of the Roman world, described in this chapter, is an extraordinary strength of character, devotion to family and friends, and a ruthlessness of action when she deemed it necessary. Theodora wished to be seen as the friend of the downtrodden, but this friendship existed within boundaries she herself set. To preserve her position, she was willing to countenance the extraordinarily brutal repression of the very people whose nurturance she had taken upon herself. [1]

One factor that most likely played into the weakening of Justinian's position was beyond his control: a run of natural catastrophes. We have already noted the two major earthquakes at Antioch in 526 and 528, which also caused extensive destruction elsewhere; then the one at Pompeiopolis, also in 528. In September of 530, a comet appeared in the western sky for several weeks, which was taken as a sign of impending catastrophe, allegedly sparking widespread violence.[2] In addition to the trouble with Persia, there had been a sudden raid by the Sabir Huns, a people who, as John of Ephesus put it, had never before crossed the Euphrates; and then came the Samaritan revolt. The war with Persia, which exploded along the central front of Mesopotamia, opened with a major Roman victory outside the city of Dara, just inside the Roman frontier; then the redesigned Martyropolis withstood a heavy Persian assault. But a debilitating Roman loss outside of Callinicum on the Euphrates in 531, partially due to poor communication between the Roman commanders, led Justinian to overhaul the command of the eastern army, recalling Belisarius to Constantinople. He then opened peace negotiations with Kavadh, who promptly delivered a demand for a great deal of money.[3]

If the cost in money and prestige could be kept within reason, peace with Persia made a great deal of sense. The Roman army was not strong enough to undertake the sort of offensive action that could yield a major change in the status quo. Heavily fortified cities on both sides of the frontier made it difficult for either party to launch serious threats into the other's territory, and the two armies were well matched from a tactical perspective. Justinian was right to want to get out of a war that he could not win quickly, but one more obvious failure would not strengthen his hand as God's putative representative on earth—and if negotiations were to be opened with the enemy, the arrival of a Persian embassy in the capital would hardly pass without notice.

Moreover, every natural disaster, Hun raid, or encounter between the Roman and Persian armies cost money. After five years of intense activity, the significant surplus that Anastasius had left in the treasury and that Justin had managed to retain was dissipating at an alarming rate. It is against this background that Justinian decided to appoint Theodora's *bête noire*, John the Cappadocian, to the praetorian prefecture in the spring of 531, possibly in the hope of some fresh thinking.

Procopius and John the Lydian offer us a litany of complaints about this John's actions, making them out as revolutionary, destructive—even positively demonic. Some of this seems a bit of an overstatement, and indeed, the information from Tribonian that has survived in the *Codex Justinianus* suggests that there was a great deal more continuity with previous prefects than might be deduced from such carping. But this should not surprise us, since important decisions were made by the imperial consistory, then implemented by Tribonian's staff. The major administrative reforms John the Cappadocian was responsible for seem not to have been enacted until his second term as praetorian prefect, between October of 532 and May 541. The fact that John Lydus states that the most significant of these reforms—the creation of an unfair and coercive tax system—occurred before January 532, and then later places it in the years following (which is correct), makes it hard to accept his view that John's activities were a direct cause of the Nika Revolt, the rebellion that broke out in Constantinople during that month.[4]

When it comes to John of Cappadocia, John Lydus' expostulations warrant the same skepticism as many of the things that Procopius has to say about Theodora or Justinian—such as Procopius's assertion that the emperor's head separated itself from his body and roamed the palace at night. What is interesting is that John Lydus was not the only person to blame the Cappadocian for the catastrophe that unfolded in January 532. Pseudo-Zachariah of Mitylene, whose Syriac chronicle for this period is based on the work of John of Ephesus, said much the same thing about the Cappadocian—namely, that in the period leading up to the revolt, there were constant complaints about him. The other John, though, we know, was not then in Constantinople. He arrived at about the time Theodora finally put a stop to John of Cappadocia's career, which makes it likely that later chroniclers found it convenient to blame the Cappadocian for what was still remembered as one of the great crises of the regime—and this in itself indicates just how significant the events of 532 were. To test this view, it is worth looking at John of Cappadocia's role as it appears in the documentary record for the period before the riots broke out.[5]

What we see of his activity suggests that John, like the prefects before him, was dominated by Tribonian's legislative agenda. This lawyer's method of working meant that a large number of measures were sent to the praetorian prefects for action; sometimes months apart, sometimes only a few weeks apart. For example, we find that on November 1, 531, John received instructions on the following matters: inheritance and arbitration procedures; the rights of women in marriage agreements;

financial transactions; adoption; and the abolition of "Latin rights," a status of quasi–Roman citizenship more than a millennium old.[6]

John Lydus' and Zachariah of Mitylene's explanations for the riot do not withstand scrutiny, and neither do either of Procopius' accounts. In his *History of the Wars*, the latter alleges that the power of the factions was a recent development and that it was the madness of their members that led to it:

> The people in each city had long since been divided into Blues and Greens, but recently, on account of these names and the seats that they occupy at the games, they spend their money and expose their bodies to great pain and they do not think that it is useless to die disgraceful deaths.

Faction members fought with each other, Procopius continues, heedless of the peril and knowing that if they took their fight into the streets, they might end up in jail. It was this that triggered in them a profound hatred for the human race, caring nothing for things either human or divine, so long as they could outdo their rivals.

This take on the factions, which we have already seen to be incorrect, nonetheless finds an interesting parallel in the anonymous *Dialogue on Political Science* that survives from these years. In it, one of the speakers, Thomas, states that "the authorities" need to take the love of faction colors under firm control, because it poses a great danger. It is implied here, as it is by Procopius, that factional strife at this level is a relatively new phenomenon. Elsewhere, Procopius offers two other explanations. Regarding Justinian's building projects, he speaks of how the "rubbish of the city" rose up against the emperor, while in the *Secret History*, he suggests that the emperor encouraged the riot as a loyalty test for the Senate—those who failed the test were disposed of so that, at the cost of incinerating the city center, Justinian could fill his coffers. The real cause of the rebellion, as we shall discover, was actually bloody-minded, stupid incompetence on the part of Justinian and his senior staff.[7]

The best narrative of these devastating riots comes, not from Procopius—something for which we may be deeply thankful—but via the chronicle tradition descending from John Malalas. Since the surviving version of John's text is a summary of the original from which important material was omitted, we have to turn chiefly to later writings, such as the *Easter Chronicle* composed in the early seventh century, and Theophanes' *Chronicle*, written in the ninth. What we learn from these sources is that the trouble began in the Hippodrome on Saturday, January 3, 532, when the Greens rose to protest government oppression and demanded the ouster of certain officials. There may have been a particular problem at this point, in the shape of some major movement of people into the city, and the incomers, who seem to have been drawn to the Greens, had quite likely not yet developed the deeper community connections that would have made faction loyalty less determinative of their behavior.[8]

A record, more or less credible, of the exchange that took place in the Hippodrome that day has come down to us through Theophanes' *Chronicle*.[9] The incident begins with an acclamation from the Greens, presumably coordinated by their cheerleaders, with the half of the Hippodrome facing the imperial box on its feet and following those cheerleaders in shouting (hence the use of the first person in what follows):

> Long may you live, Justinian Augustus! May you be victorious
> [*tu vincas*]. I am wronged, O paragon of virtue, and cannot
> endure it, as God knows. I am afraid to give his name in case
> he prospers the more, and I put myself in danger.

Through his herald, the emperor asks the people who they are complaining about. There follow some further exchanges with the herald in which he professes ignorance and the Greens refuse to give a name, though one senses even through the sparse record that things are getting louder and more threatening as the Greens respond to the herald's claim that no one is causing them harm:

> One man and one man only does me wrong, Mother of God
> [Theotokos], may he not hold his head up high.

Now the faction begins to protest that it stands for justice and orthodoxy, whereas, if he does not heed them, the emperor stands for neither. A dangerous situation has now arisen, one that Justinian handles poorly. Instead of defusing the situation when the crowd finally identifies Calopodios the *spatharius* (captain of the imperial bodyguard) as the object of its rage, he merely tells the people they are wrong. When the Greens retort that Calopodios will suffer the fate of Judas Iscariot, the herald counters that they have come to the Hippodrome simply to insult their rulers, not to watch the races. Then he calls them "Jews," "Manichaeans," and "Samaritans." Nettled, the Greens assert their orthodox credentials, then accuse the emperor of covering up the murders of faction members, finally exclaiming:

> Would that Sabbatius [Justinian's father] had not been born,
> that way he would not have a murderer for a son.

For all his efforts to enhance the dignity of the imperial office, Justinian remains, in the eyes of his subjects (or some of them), the son of a peasant; and, presumably, Theodora is the whore she has not infrequently been accused of being.[10]

After further insults, the dialogue breaks off, and whatever else may have happened on January 3, the Greens decide to take the rest of the day off. The issue of Justinian's actual power is left very much open. To a crowd asserting that *it* represents the truth, the emperor, who claims to be God's

FIGURE 8.1. Base of the column of Theodosius I shows the emperor in the Hippodrome.

© photo by David Potter

agent and the master of law and order, stands for injustice and oppression. Things get no better when, on Sunday the 11th, Eudaimon, prefect of the city, tries to bring seven men to justice on a charge of murder. The seven men are led through the city to the place of execution, on the far side of the Golden Horn. Four are decapitated, and three scheduled to hang. After the first has been hanged, the next two, one from each faction, are brought to the scaffold. The executioner botches the job. The crowd that has gathered to applaud the deaths is horrified when he tries to hang the men again—and again botches it. The people begin to acclaim Justinian, now in their reeling minds the image of justice, as a way of demanding that the men be set free. Monks arrive on the scene from the monastery of St. Conon, and offer the condemned men sanctuary. Eudaimon orders the monastery be put under guard—another big mistake.[11]

Public unrest that had begun with just one faction, the Greens, now expanded to include the Blues, so that the issue of imperial legitimacy was even more firmly on the table. On January 13, races were again scheduled at the Hippodrome. Justinian could have cancelled them, but instead he provided an opportunity for another riot.

This time the Blues and Greens, speaking as one, demand freedom for the two men. Justinian refuses to give in—indeed, he manages to inflame the situation even further. The day's twenty-two races are run, and at the end of the afternoon, the factions' chanting changes—to "Long live the merciful Blues and Greens!" Shouting "Nika!" ("Victory!") as their watchword, they advance on the city prefect's office at the praetorium, on the Mese near the Forum of Constantine. Receiving no satisfaction, they free prisoners from within the building and set it on fire, then move on down to the great square in front of the palace's Bronze Gate, and set more fires. One of the buildings destroyed is the Church of Hagia Sophia. Justinian keeps his guards inside the palace and, possibly at this moment, offers sanctuary to members of the senatorial order, including various of Anastasius' relatives, Hypatius and Pompeius amongst them.[12]

The smell of smoke would have lain heavily over the city on the morning of the 14th, when crowds gathered once more in the Hippodrome. Now, though, they had a greater sense of purpose. Imperial injustice, as those who gathered now saw it, had sparked the riots, while imperial unwillingness to listen had caused them to spread. On this morning, the people made it clear that they wanted to see real change, and demanded that the emperor dismiss Eudaimon, John of Cappadocia, and Tribonian—the three men responsible for order in the city and for Justinian's well-advertised program of legal reform. In the eyes of Constantinople's people, they had failed. Justinian chose not to face the crowd on this occasion, but received news through officials he had sent to listen in. Then at last he responded, announcing the dismissal of the three along with the appointment of a new quaestor and a new praetorian prefect.[13]

The mood of the crowd now turned blacker, and people were wondering whether they might get rid of Justinian as well; a mob now made its way to the house of Anastasius' nephew Probus, to see if he would take the throne. But Probus fled the city, just as Anicia Juliana's husband had done when confronted with a similar offer during Anastasius' reign. The disappointed crowd, now chanting "*Allon Basileia tei polei!*" ("Another emperor for the city!"), burned down his house. By now more than a little perturbed, Justinian sent troops into the streets to fight the rioters—but there were not enough of them, and all they did was inflame the situation. Fighting continued on Friday the 16th, and new fires destroyed more buildings, including the Church of St. Irene and a major hospital, killing those within. Meanwhile, tensions were also mounting inside the palace, and on the 17th, Justinian ordered Hypatius to leave, along with his brother Pompeius. If they were thinking of betraying him—which it appears they were—it was best that they remain as far from the palace guards as possible. Subsequent events suggest that the guards' loyalty was indeed wavering, and it may have been at this moment that people were "remembering" how Justin had "pushed aside" Anastasius' nephews in order to become emperor himself. Justinian depended now most of all on the loyalty of Mundus, a general from Central Europe, and Belisarius.[14]

On the morning of January 18, Justinian made a final effort to resolve the crisis. Word must have been sent beforehand from the palace, most likely through faction officials, telling the crowd that the emperor would appear that morning in the Hippodrome. As it was a Sunday, it was not a day for the races—this was, in fact, to be a special event. For when Justinian appeared, he was holding a codex containing a Gospel. He then spoke to his people directly (though his herald may have repeated what he said so that all could hear), and swore this oath to them:

By this power [he may here have held up the Gospel he had with him], I forgive you this error, and I order that none of you be arrested—but be peaceful; for there is nothing on your head. But rather on mine. For my sins made me deny to you what you asked of me in the Hippodrome.[15]

It was an astonishing piece of theater, so completely out of character that one may wonder if someone in the palace with some dramatic sense put him up to it. And it almost worked. Elements in the crowd picked up the loyalist chant of *"Justiniane Auguste, toubikas!"* ("Justinian Augustus, may you be victorious!") Others, however, roared, *"Epiorkeis sgaudri!"* ("You are a forsworn ass!"). At this, Justinian offered no reply, and withdrew into the palace.

The mixed response to the emperor may not have been entirely coincidental, for it does appear that Hypatius had decided to make a bid for the throne, and had been stage-managing events with considerable care. When Justinian withdrew, the crowd poured out of the Hippodrome, encountering Hypatius and Pompeius as it went. Now the chant that rang out from the entire mob was *"Hypatie Auguste, toubikas!"* as they escorted him to the Forum of Constantine. There stood the great column in the center of the Forum supporting a gigantic statue of Constantine, completed on the day of his inauguration of the city. And it was here that people brought imperial insignia that had been stored in the palace of Flacilla, the first wife of Theodosius I. The fact that the palace was a fair distance from the Forum of Constantine is but one of several clues suggesting that Hypatius had spent the previous evening conspiring to engineer Justinian's ouster. He now appeared with his own band of thugs, recruited from the area around that same palace, which was close to the Church of the Holy Apostles where Constantine's body had been interred. The symbolism is obvious—he is drawing upon the memory of past emperors, "real emperors," including the very founder of the city, with a view to ousting the usurper. He was joined now by Julianus, the praetorian prefect whom John the Cappadocian had replaced, plus his brother, as he made his way to the imperial box in the Hippodrome.[16]

What should he do? Justinian was at a loss. Even as Hypatius was heading for the Hippodrome, rumor spread that Justinian had taken ship to Thrace. Flight was certainly his plan when he summoned his advisors to a meeting. It was then that Theodora intervened. Procopius has her speak to the emperor as follows:

> Whether it is shocking for a woman to speak in the presence of men, or to urge on those who are cringing in fear, I think is not a matter for discussion at the present time, whatever one may think. For those whose affairs have come into the greatest danger, there is no other best choice than to look for what is somehow best. I believe that flight is not in our interest even if it should be possible, as now, for it is not possible for a person who has come forth into life to avoid death, but it is not possible for one who has ruled to become a fugitive. I shall never be separated from this purple, nor shall I live for a single day, if those who encounter me do not call me mistress. If you wish to be saved, my Lord, that is not a problem. We have a great deal of money, the sea is at hand and there are ships. But consider, if it will benefit you when you have been saved or if safety would be exchanged happily for death. For me the old saying is best, that power is a splendid shroud.[17]

Since Procopius certainly was not in the room when Theodora spoke, there is no reason to think that she actually uttered these words. On the other hand, there is very good reason to think that she may have had the impact he attributes to her. It was well known in the aftermath of the riots that people thought Justinian was leaving the city, yet in a very different tradition, we are told that Theodora pressed him to execute Pompeius and Hypatius. Furthermore, unlike the *Secret History*, Procopius' *History of the Wars*, from which this passage comes, was written for public consumption while Theodora was still alive. One of Procopius' major themes in *The Wars* was Belisarius' genius, and we may reasonably conclude, since Belisarius was certainly present when Justinian decided not to take flight, that this representation of Theodora's role was acceptable to him, and to others who actually knew what happened. It may also be significant that this version does not cast the vacillating Justinian in an especially good light. The best that can be said is that while Hypatius is shown to ignore the good advice of both his wife and of a senator named Origen to stay away from the Hippodrome, Justinian took heed.

Another point: in describing John of Cappadocia's dismissal, Procopius delivers himself of a torrent of abuse about John, while observing that both Tribonian and Phocas, who now took over the praetorian prefecture, were decent individuals. This would most likely put the composition of the passage quoted above at some point between 541, when Theodora finally stripped John of his powers, Phocas' prosecution for paganism in 545, and possibly even before Tribonian's death in 542—the point when her political clout had again been demonstrated with extraordinary effect. The theme of advice heard but ignored is also important; and the fact that Theodora's allusion to a burial shroud, as reported by Procopius, is borrowed from a tyrant of the classical past rather than from a king might ring somewhat ambivalently in the ears of some, but she did not mince her words in advocating a tough course of action; and responsibility for the violence that would follow rests as much with her as with anyone. The palace did not regret what happened next, proclaiming it an inevitable, if tragic, consequence of factional violence and disobedience.[18]

Whatever she said, and however she said it, Theodora's intervention changed the course of events. Justinian resolved to end the rebellion by force, and when Hypatius took his place in the imperial box, the emperor was ready to act. Hypatius was more ambivalent, at least at first. He had with him a man named Ephraem, one of Justinian's personal guards, whom he sent into the palace to deliver a message to the emperor: Justinian should be grateful, the message went, that Hypatius had gathered all Justinian's enemies in one place. Inside the palace, Ephraem found only the emperor's doctor, Thomas, who told him to tell Hypatius that Justinian had fled. Now Hypatius appeared convinced that he really was in charge. The message that Ephraem delivered remains one of the great puzzles of the day—did he really fail to spot the mass of troops gathering in the palace? How hard did he look? Was he a double agent? The answer is most likely the latter, for he would survive the massacre that followed his return to the box and in the end would suffer only exile, which in the context seems less like a punishment and more like a way of protecting him.[19]

Once Ephraem returned, a group of heavily armed Greens from the area near the Church of the Holy Apostles arrived and offered to break into the palace for Hypatius—their presence again suggesting that there had been a good deal more advance planning on Hypatius' part than meets the eye. But it was too late. Justinian was about to strike back.

The first thing was to create chaos in the Hippodrome, to which end he sent the eunuch Narses to bribe some members of the Blue faction to begin acclaiming him and Theodora (it is a pity that our sources omit to tell us what the crowd had been yelling before this order was given). Once the Blues began chanting the required acclamation, Justinian's generals Mundus and Belisarius brought their own men into the Hippodrome (the emperor still did not trust the palace guards). As the imperial troops entered the arena from three gates, Belisarius' guard approached Hypatius from behind, grabbed him, and took him into custody. The scene was horrific—the acclamations turned to screams, and the mass of the people, now trapped inside the Hippodrome, struggled to escape the men who had been sent to kill them.

In the official version of what happened, no one is said to have escaped. The total number of casualties for this day alone was ultimately put at thirty thousand. Hypatius and Pompeius were executed the next day, their bodies then thrown into the sea; both later washed ashore. In one tradition, Justinian was tempted to spare them, but Theodora insisted that they be put to death. Eighteen members of the highest imperial aristocracy were exiled and their property confiscated.[20]

What did Theodora think would happen when she convinced Justinian he must stand and fight? It is unlikely that the reaction surprised her. But she knew what would happen if she and her husband fled—they would either be murdered in very short order, or, reaching the Persian frontier where the eastern armies were stationed, as Ariadne and Zeno had once done, they would return and retake the capital. Theodora's brother-in-law Sittas was still the senior commander in the east. But if they brought the army back to Constantinople, the eastern frontier would be left open. The treaty that would end the war with Persia was in the process of finalization when the Nika Revolt broke out. The best that could have been hoped for, if Justinian had been driven from his throne, was that the terms, already none too favorable—they included a heavy cash payment—would get even worse. On balance, the decision to stay in Constantinople probably saved more lives than it cost, though that is a brutal calculus, and anyway it is unlikely that Theodora or anyone else did the math very carefully, if at all.

Still, her instincts were correct. And she knew that Hypatius, as we have seen on many occasions, was something of a fool. If he had taken charge, the empire would not have been better off. Whether or not Theodora said any of the things that Procopius attributes to her in his carefully crafted speech, the image of her as a decisive voice is one with which she and her contemporaries, people who were present when she spoke, were comfortable. Her job was to rule. Any who doubted her resolve to be empress, at any cost, were mistaken.

9

War and Religion

At some point late in the year 534, Belisarius left his house in Constantinople to lead a procession into the Hippodrome. For the general, it was a spectacular reintroduction to the city he had left in June 533 as commander of the fleet sent to wrest control of Africa from the Vandal king Gelimir. Gelimir, too, would appear in the arena that day—as a captive. Justinian and Theodora watched from the imperial box as the spectacle unfolded, culminating with the prostration of Belisarius, then Gelimir. Displaying plunder and captives in the Hippodrome had long been a standard feature of imperial victory ceremonies, in Rome as well as Constantinople. But Belisarius' procession was something new, a mark of high imperial favor, putting to rest rumors that he had been removed from his command on accusations of treason. It might also offer him a chance to repair his relationship with the people, who had surely suffered from his role in the massacre of their friends and relatives that had brought the Nika Revolt to a sudden end. Both Belisarius in his glory and Gelimir in defeat were seen as reflections of the power of God, as channeled through Justinian. It was through God's benevolence, the emperor would claim as he stood there bedecked in the traditional robe of celebrant of a triumph, that he had defeated the Vandals.[1]

The treasures that Belisarius brought back from Africa were extraordinary. The items displayed that day in the Hippodrome included many that the Vandal king Geiseric had looted from Rome's imperial palaces and temples back in 455. There were golden thrones, carriages of Vandal royalty, tableware of gold inset with gems, and a vast quantity of silver. Then there were the treasures that Emperor Titus had looted from Jerusalem when he sacked that city in AD 70. If these were the objects portrayed on his triumphal arch in Rome, they included the great menorah taken from the Temple, and the Ark of the Covenant. This last, when members of the Jewish community pointed out that every city that had housed it had been sacked, was shortly thereafter sent back to Jerusalem. Justinian celebrated, in particular, the fact that it was to himself that the imperial insignia captured from Rome were restored. His mind could not conjure, he said, what thanks and praise should be offered to God in return for the victory.[2]

The procession celebrated the most complete triumph won by a Roman army in centuries. At a stroke, Belisarius had not only obtained vast, much-needed treasure, he had also recovered some of the richest provinces of the old Roman Empire and eliminated a power that had previously shown itself unassailable by Roman arms. The previous effort by the eastern government to capture North Africa from Vandal control, Basiliscus' expedition of 468, was still remembered in Justinian's time both for its exceptional cost and for its utter failure. That memory may, of course, have been prompted partly by the contrast it offered to the extraordinary nature of Justinian's success—but it was also a reminder of the risks that had been run.[3]

At the end of January 532, it may have looked to many reasonable observers as if Justinian's power had been crippled. In the face of the bloody riots, he had barely hung onto his throne; his relationship with the Senate left a lot to be desired; he had been forced to cashier some of his most trusted subordinates; the Persians were demanding huge amounts of cash in exchange for peace, and the capital was in smoldering ruins. Something had to change—and fast.

The peace with Persia was concluded, largely on Persian terms, before the summer was over. Despite that peace costing so much, paying was cheaper than fighting. In addition, vast sums would need to be spent repairing the city. Some of this might have come from the confiscated estates of senators (eighteen in all) who were felt to have chosen the wrong side during the riots. On the other hand, these confiscations may have been intended more for show than for revenue. Probus, all of whose property was taken in January, found himself back in control of his assets within the year—and his son or grandson would later marry Theodora's daughter. Was Probus the only one to have struck a deal with the palace? Unlikely. And neither his restoration nor the marriage was likely to have been all Justinian's doing. Theodora would hardly have been excluded from negotiations that had an impact on her family, and if the picture of the relationship between the two emerging from Procopius' version of the Nika Revolt contains a grain of truth, we may reasonably conclude that she took the initiative in dealing with Probus.[4]

The marriage of Thedora's daughter into Anastasius' family is a sign of Theodora's acceptance at the highest level of society. The anti-Chalcedonian tinge to this wing of Anastasius' clan may also have strengthened Theodora's position with like-minded members of the imperial aristocracy, for, as we will see, she becomes, perhaps more than ever, the leading figure to whom anti-Chalcedonians will look. She also becomes firmly established at the heart of an immensely influential network within the government as a whole. The full implications of her range of connections will become clear when we examine secular crises in the next chapter.

In the next chapter we will see how Theodora's network helped her deal with rivals in government, for, no matter how powerful she became, she would not be the only person whose views carried weight with Justinian. Before the end of 532, John the Cappadocian was restored as praetorian prefect, while Tribonian returned as quaestor. John's policies during the next few years, all intended to boost the empire's finances, suggest that he had been recalled because Justinian was desperate for cash and had confidence in his fiscal creativity. Tribonian was still working on his new code along with the massive compilation of juristic opinions on legal matters that survives as Justinian's *Digest*, the crucial repository of the traditions of Roman jurisprudence. The *Digest*, even more than the law code, would consolidate Tribonian's claim to be one of the most influential figures in the history of Western legal thought. Also in 532, Justinian decided to employ another genius, the architect Anthemius of Tralles, to oversee the construction of a new Hagia Sophia to replace the church destroyed in the revolt. His achievement, likewise, stands to this day as one of the great triumphs of the human imagination.

It is plain that, despite January's disaster, Justinian remained ambitious, but while the reemployment of Tribonian and the decision to allow Anthemius to design the new church were predictable, given Justinian's devotion to major construction projects and to the reformation of the legal system, there was nothing in the previous years that made the decision to invade Africa or the choice of Belisarius to command the operation foreseeable. Belisarius had a good reputation as an officer—for instance, he had kept his men from looting their own people while on campaign (a quality unusual enough to be worthy of note by one contemporary), but he had not shown himself an especially brilliant tactician. He had been outmaneuvered by Azarethes, the Persian commander at the Battle of Callinicum in 531. All the same, along with Sittas, who, still in Armenia, had earned respect as a general, what Belisarius had that no other general could claim was a wife who had a close relationship with Theodora. And although that relationship would collapse a decade later, largely as a result of his own political ineptitude, at this stage, Belisarius was closely linked with the empress. Given that he was not the obvious choice to lead the expedition, Theodora's friendship may have been a decisive factor.[5]

Anyone interested in the chances of the expedition to North Africa succeeding would probably have turned, for a precedent, to the historical work of a man named Priscus. From Panium in Thrace, Priscus, whose career spanned the middle of the fifth century, and whose occasional service as a secretary to an imperial official puts him on a social par with Procopius, was a powerful witness to the fraught years when Attila and Geiseric threatened the empire. Throughout his history, Priscus' argument is that Roman failure was closely connected with bungling and incompetence rather than attributable to the superior skills of the enemy. This is a theme that comes through loud and clear in the summary history of the Vandal kingdom inspired by Priscus, with which Procopius introduces his account of the reconquest of North Africa. But then Procopius adds something of his own, something particular to his time and place. This Procopian addition is the sense that part of the empire had been lost and now must be recovered. Priscus, conversely, had seen the "Western Romans" as members of a separate state when he ran into some representatives of the Western court in the camp of Attila the Hun. Even now, the Senate in Rome worked with the Gothic king Theoderic in Ravenna, looking to traditions that went back to a period before there was an emperor. Malchus, the Greek historian of Zeno's time who reported that the latter agreed, in 476, that an emperor was no longer needed in the West, had apparently not thought the moment significant. The two halves of the empire had already gone their different ways.

This view of things would be shared by Jordanes, a younger contemporary of Theodora, whose short book on the history of the Goths was finished, in Latin, around 551. He reports that Zeno had charged Theoderic with the safety of the Roman Senate and that he had been advised to rule as king in Italy. The Roman Senate saw itself as a corporate body that had begun life with Romulus, the legendary founder of Rome, in the seventh century BC. There could have been no "fall of Rome," went the argument, because the most important institution, as its members saw it, was still functioning and exercising influence.

But in Constantinople, views were beginning to change. Even though a contemporary of Justinian's would refer to the Western empire as "the empire of Honorius"—implying that it was not part of *his* world—the official line was increasingly that the West was in need of liberation, and thus that the empire could be restored. Justinian had written that it had not been given to his predecessors to "liberate" Africa, and that the imperial insignia taken by the Vandals had been "restored" to *him*. Procopius' contemporary, Count Marcellinus, linked the fall of the western Roman Empire with the forced abdication of the young Emperor Romulus and the establishment of Odovacer as king of Italy in AD 476. Marcellinus had been Justinian's *cancellarius*, or secretary, before 527, and this view, adumbrated in his *Chronicle* (whose second edition was completed in 534), represented what was now the official line—just as it also made clear that the Nika Revolt was actually an attempted usurpation and that it was Justinian who ordered the executions of Hypatius and Pompeius.[6]

The new theory concerning the end of the Roman Empire, though not all that obviously correct or consistent when it surfaced in Justinian's time, would ultimately shape centuries of thinking about the history of Europe. Also in the air was a theory about how time itself should be measured, emerging in Rome, but heavily influenced by speculation at Constantinople. And this theory, too, influential as it has proved to be, was no more coherent or obvious at the time it was conceived than was Marcellinus' notion about the end of the western Roman Empire. The new theory emerged from questions about when to celebrate Easter, and ended by restating the relationship between time as measured by the Church and time as measured by the state.

For nearly a century before Justinian became emperor, the celebration of Easter had been set according to a table developed by the same Cyril of Alexandria who had played a significant role in the condemnation of Nestorius at the First Council of Ephesus in 431 (we met him in Chapter 5). Cyril's table correlated the beginning of the cycle to the beginning of the reign of Diocletian and the initiation of the fifteen-year tax, or indiction, cycles, that were used for official purposes. Working in Rome, where there had been some unhappiness with the Eastern system of computing dates for Easter, Dionysius Exiguus (the name celebrates his intellectual modesty) produced a new table for the Easter Cycle, beginning in AD 532, which combined existing systems of time-measurement with a new date for the birth of Christ. Given that many people still believed that the world would end after six thousand years, and that Jesus' birth was the year 5,500 from Creation, the fact that Dionysius could show that more than 500 years had passed since the Nativity meant that speculation about the year 6,000 could be deposited in the rubbish bin of theological speculation. The new dating system also served to separate the measurement of time from the memory of Diocletian, known as a vigorous persecutor of the Church. Before Dionysius proposed his changes, it was standard practice to date events by year within the empire's fifteen year tax assessment cycle, which Diocletian had set up. By breaking this connection, the chronology of Church history would no longer be dependent upon imperial history.

In the view of some of Dionysius' contemporaries, the new and improved Christian empire of Justinian should be able to do better with the measurement of time; so it was that Dionysius made a slight adjustment to received wisdom in setting the date of Christ's birth, *Anno Domini* 1, in the 754th year after the foundation of the city of Rome. The fact that both this date, and the date he was correcting, contradicted the evidence—irreconcilable—provided by the Gospel accounts of the birth of Christ does not seem to have bothered him. For the record, Jesus of Nazareth could not have been born both when Herod the Great was alive and when Quirinius—the Cyrenius of standard English Bibles—was governor of Syria, since the former died in 4 BC and the latter was governing in AD 6, by our reckoning.[7]

If the North African expedition was launched in an atmosphere of intellectual ferment, it also set off under a cloud of controversy. Even as resources were being gathered for the campaign, there was a great deal of concern amongst members of the Senate that the new expedition would fail as badly as the earlier one had. The situation was so dire, Procopius says, that no general wanted the job of leading the invasion, and John the Cappadocian even talked Justinian out of it, briefly, by stressing the high risk. It was now that a monk approached Justinian describing a dream in which God told him to speak with the emperor about the need to protect Christians from tyrants and promising His help against the Vandals. At this, Justinian's hesitation evaporated and he ordered the expedition to depart.[8]

The scene that Procopius creates here has deep roots in classical historiography, and there is no reason to believe that it represents what actually happened. On the other hand, the choice of this *topos* may well reflect concerns that were raised at the time, and the choice of the hated John to deliver bad advice was no doubt a measure of Procopius' own dislike of the man. As with Theodora's speech during the Nika Revolt, we need not believe in the literal truth of what was said in order to accept that it represents real concerns. The risk, however, may have been less than it seemed, and a careful observer would have been aware that Gelimir's seizure of the throne from his cousin Ilderich in 530 had not been greeted with joy on all sides. There was a rebellion against Gelimir in Sardinia in the summer of 533, which tied down a significant portion of the Vandal army as Belisarius was setting sail. It was also helpful that the government in Ravenna did not harbor positive feelings towards the Vandals, and would allow Belisarius to launch his invasion from its territory in Sicily.[9]

With the expedition under way, it is unlikely that Theodora had much to do with what ensued, though it is likely that she remained in touch with Antonina, who had accompanied her husband, Belisarius, on campaign. Theodora may also have been aware of the quarrels between Belisarius and his senior staff, of accusations that he was plotting against the emperor, and quite possibly of the decision, at the end of hostilities, to offer a public show of support via a triumph.[10]

Even as Belisarius was presenting his captives, a new and far more dangerous expedition was under discussion: the invasion of Italy, with a view to recovering the territory from the Goths. Ostensibly, this looked rather like a possible repeat of the Vandal invasion. The Gothic regime was in chaos after Theodahad—whose claim to the throne was based upon the co-regency with his cousin, Queen Amalasuintha, established after the death of her young son—split with the queen. She thought of fleeing to the east, but reconciled with Theodahad instead. Fleeing might well have been the wisest course, for the reconciliation was brief.

Theodahad imprisoned Amalasuintha on an island on Lake Balzano and then, as we know, had her murdered. Meanwhile, negotiations, probably concerned with guaranteeing the safety of the queen, were going on with Constantinople through the agency of Peter the Patrician, a favorite of Theodora's and himself a historian of some note.[11]

Amalasuintha had provided important assistance for the invasion of Africa in 533–534, and her murder would become the official cause of war between Constantinople and the Goths in 535. Even before that, discontented members of the governing classes had been coming east, bringing with them claims that the Gothic regime was tottering. Refugees from Vandal Africa had offered similar intelligence about the state of Gelimir's regime, and since the information they gave about Africa seemed to have been confirmed by events, Justinian was probably more disposed to listen to what the Italians had to say now. One of these was Dominicus—described by an anti-Chalcedonian historian who had debated with him as a "leader of the region"—who had fled Italy after a dispute with Theodahad. If people generally thought the way Dominicus did, surely they would welcome the invaders with open arms.[12]

Individuals like Dominicus who, sadly for Justinian, were almost by definition out of touch or out of sympathy with majority opinion in Italy, made very bad informants. Insofar as they sought to convince members of the Eastern court that the situation in Italy was like that in North Africa, they were not just bad informants, they were positively dangerous. In fact, members of the senatorial class appear to have gotten on reasonably well with the Gothic regime. The massive surviving correspondence of Cassiodorus, a member of one of the era's great families, suggests that the aristocracy had adjusted more easily than might have been anticipated to the regime in Ravenna. This regime was, truth be told, considerably more effective in guaranteeing the Italian peninsula's security and keeping the Vandals under control than had been the case when, from about 456 till 472, Ricimir ran the Western empire via a series of puppet emperors, several of them appointed from Constantinople.

Although self-identifying as "Arians," followers of the fourth-century heresy that had stressed Christ's human aspect, the Goths had not tampered with the strongly Chalcedonian line promoted by the bishops of Rome. Gothic tolerance constitutes one very big difference between the Gothic and the Vandal regimes, and the success of the interaction can be seen today in their capital of Ravenna, where the churches used by Arian congregations such as Sant' Apollinare Nuovo coexisted with churches for Catholics. Nor, it seems, do the Gothic kings appear to have infringed upon the prerogatives of the Roman aristocracy. Control of the Games in Rome, for instance, was left to the Senate, and it was either in the early 490s or shortly after 500 that the prefect of Rome, Basilius, carried out the last major repairs on the Colosseum, damaged by an earthquake. And it was to Rome that Theoderic came for chariot racing, respecting the authority of the Senate even though he had his own circus and chariot races in Ravenna. For leaders of the Roman aristocracy, it was possible to preserve the institutions and traditions of Rome without being politically subject to an emperor in Constantinople. Even Theoderic's brutal murder of two senior senators in 525 and 526 for treasonous communication with Constantinople had not permanently soiled the relationship.[13]

The chariot racing was significant not just for political reasons, but also because it represented the fact that, unlike Vandal North Africa, Italy had multiple capitals. To overthrow the Goths, a Roman army would have to take numerous major cities, and that would require, if people could not be counted on not to betray them, greater investments of time and money. Even if Constantinople was no longer so short of funds, it possessed a limited number of experienced troops, and Africa now required a garrison. Just as serious was the "grass is greener" phenomenon. Change always looks more inviting before it happens, and for Rome, there was already latent tension with Constantinople over religious affairs that had political implications, since the Ostrogothic court in Ravenna did not intervene in religious matters involving the Church at Rome. The Roman Senate had been placed in a supervisory position over the Church, whose leader, in turn, could act as a spokesman both for his institution, now one of the wealthiest in Italy, and for the Senate.[14] Furthermore, although generally supportive of the decisions of the Council of Chalcedon, which were based, after all, on doctrines promulgated by Pope Leo, popes were less than happy with the assertion that the patriarchs in Constantinople now stood second in primacy only to themselves. That was just too close, especially as some recent patriarchs had displayed doctrinal tendencies regarded in Rome as heretical.

So it was that, although members of the Ostrogothic governing élite were currently displaying spectacular incompetence and brutality towards each other, Italy's size prevented a rapid takeover of the kingdom, and Constantinople's failure to win a swift victory enabled the Goths to get their act together. It did not take long for them to rid themselves of the incompetent Theodahad and find efficient leadership in one Vitiges—and then, even more markedly, in a noble named Totila. The result was that the Gothic War would drag on for years.[15]

The Gothic War would not only hoover up men and money, it inevitably sharpened religious issues within the empire. If Justinian wanted to win support from the Pope, he would need to take a strong Chalcedonian line at home without alienating his anti-Chalcedonian subjects. It was in these negotiations that Theodora would play her most important role during the years to come—although, much as she might have influenced the choice of commanders for the Vandal expedition, her role was certainly not to manage a war. As the living embodiment of the Mother of God, her task was to deal with religion.

Religion had been playing a major role in relations between Rome and Constantinople even before the war was fully under way. Pope Hormisdas plainly regarded the imperial court as requiring instruction in the faith—hence his rejection of the "Suffering God" (Theopaschite) view that had interested Justinian in 519 (see Chapter 5) and would soon make a significant reappearance. His successor, Pope John, although more malleable, was likewise somewhat suspicious of what he regarded as potentially heretical proposals from the East. Even as the campaign was raging in North Africa, Justinian had summoned a three-day council at Constantinople at which he had attempted to persuade representatives of the Chalcedonian and anti-Chalcedonian factions to arrive at a compromise. Theodora, for her part, would turn over the Palace of Hormisdas, now embellished and in the process of being joined with the Great Palace itself, to act as a refuge for anti-Chalcedonian holy men (if she was not in fact already doing so). John of Ephesus, who stayed there for some time, says that at the height of the community's influence, it would provide quarters for some five hundred men, the space divided into cells as in a monastery. Theodora provided maintenance money for those living in the palace, whom she would visit, sometimes in the company of her husband—who, as John suggests, may have enjoyed discussing theological issues with the assembled company. The community appears to have been connected with the Church of Sergius and Bacchus; this may have caused additional irritation in Italy since the Latin Church of Peter and Paul, where Rome's emissaries worshiped, was adjacent.[16]

Justinian's occasional visits to the Palace of Hormisdas, and indeed his willingness to tolerate a large anti-Chalcedonian community on his own palace's doorstep, are emblematic of his desire to find a peaceful solution to the empire's religious divide. He had already allowed the restoration of monastic leaders to Amida and Edessa in the context of the Persian War—ordering Belisarius himself to make sure that it happened—presumably because he worried that the schism between hierarchy and laity occasioned by Justin's imposition of Chalcedonian bishops in the region had undermined security. Theodora, too, may have been mindful of this when she made a gift to a monastery near Callinicum on the Euphrates, which gave rise to one of several alternative versions of her earlier life that would circulate in later centuries, connecting her to this area. At the same time Justinian appears to have recognized the importance of the cross-border settlement established by the anti-Chalcedonians linking Christian communities within the Persian Empire with those in Roman territory. The Eastern monks responded by sending Justinian a declaration of faith and stating that they "beseech God, [who is] rich in gifts, that he bestow on your Tranquillity and the God-loving Empress good gifts from on high for our sake, making you deserving of peace and tranquillity, and [praying] that he place as a footstool every rebellious people." In the wake of the Nika Revolt, these were, no doubt, welcome sentiments.[17]

It was after the restoration of the monastic leaders and in the course of negotiating the treaty with Persia that Justinian summoned a meeting between Chalcedonian and anti-Chalcedonian leaders in 532, including John of Tella, of the anti-Chalcedonian community of Mesopotamia, who would be the central figure in constructing a virtual state within a state between the two empires. At this meeting, Justinian listened to statements from both sides and pressed his own Theopaschite formulations upon both groups, but without much success. The anti-Chalcedonian contingent replied that its members did not have the authority to give a definitive answer to the emperor's proposals. That said, the effort to get to grips with the issue was plainly appreciated. And even though he did not show up in person, Bishop Severus of Antioch, who had been invited, wrote a letter to the emperor assuring him of his loyalty. As he was the most prominent anti-Chalcedonian, Severus' sentiments carried some extra force, even though no agreement was forthcoming. Undeterred by his failure to win episcopal assent to his preferred formulation of the faith, Justinian still felt that he was right and continued to work to smooth over the differences, which he saw as minor. To the anti-Chalcedonian bishops, he had said: "I am not of the opinion . . . that you do not think in an orthodox fashion, but you do not wish to communicate [i.e., be in communion with Chalcedonians] out of excessive [scruples over] detail and because of [certain] names that have been put in the diptychs [recognized as legitimate bishops]."[18]

As Belisarius was sailing to Africa, it was evidently important for the emperor's understanding of the faith to be openly stated. On March 15, 533, Justinian issued an edict denouncing both extremes of the religious divide—Nestorianism (doctrines promulgated by the Bishop Nestorius we met in chapter 5 who believed that Mary was the Mother of Christ rather than of God) and Eutychianism (a doctrine promulgated by Eutyches of Constantinople so extreme in its assertion of the one nature of Christ that even the essentially Monophysite Second Council of Ephesus in 449 had condemned it). Justinian hereby declared that he did not innovate in the faith, but sought clarity by refuting error. Essentially quoting a letter he had sent to Hormisdas in 519, he proclaimed his belief in a consubstantial Trinity, and that:

> in the last days our Lord Jesus Christ, God's Only-Begotten
> Son, true God of true God, before the ages and without time,
> born from the Father, co-eternal with the Father, he from
> whom are all things and through whom are all things, having
> descended from the skies, became incarnate from the Holy
> Spirit and Mary, the Holy, Glorious Ever-Virgin and Mother
> of God, and assumed Man's nature and endured the cross for
> us in the time of Pontius Pilate.

Christ, he went on, had been consubstantial with God and with humans, and the Trinity had remained the Trinity. The language is here as it had been more than a decade earlier, very carefully chosen to appeal to those who could find a middle ground between the extremes of Nestorius and Eutyches. The problem was that, in a deeply polarized world, the middle ground tends to be a very slender patch, and that is what it continued to be in this case.[19]

The great victory in North Africa may have confirmed in Justinian the view that his path was the right one. A new sense of confidence appears in the handbook introducing the textbook of Roman law, the *Institutes*, produced on November 12, 533, stating that "now that Africa as well as innumerable other provinces have been restored to us after a long period of time through our victories granted by divine will," imperial majesty should be embellished by arms and fortified by laws. When a month later, on December 16, Tribonian's massive collection of the opinions of earlier jurists, the *Digest*, was given to the world, the emperor could say:

> God has given to us after the peace with the Persians, after the defeat of the Vandals and the entire acquisition of Libya and the recovery of most famous Carthage, to bring to conclusion the work of renewal of ancient laws—a thing which none of the emperors who had ruled before us even hoped to project for their minds and [which] even was considered wholly impossible for human nature.[20]

It is certainly the Justinian buoyed by victory that we see in John of Ephesus' account of the community assembled in the Palace of Hormisdas—both he and Theodora could set aside the usual formality of their positions in dealing with those they considered holy. Justinian did so because he enjoyed theological debate, appreciated the sacrifices of ascetics, and was hoping that officials of the Church would generally pursue an ascetic path. In 530, he issued a law laying down the directive that when religious foundations were looking for a new abbot or abbess, they should not simply elect the community's most senior member, but rather elect the person "whom good life, excellent character and the practice of asceticism" recommended to the community as a whole; he insisted on priestly celibacy as well. In 534, he discovered to his horror that there were priests dicing and gambling; blushing at the thought, he says, he ordered bishops to make sure no such thing happened on their watch. It was only if priests lived lives free from blame that they could set proper examples to others.[21]

Theodora's interest in the anti-Chalcedonian cause more probably stemmed from her appreciation of her and Justinian's life choices, though she was, by this point, scarcely a neophyte when it came to matters of the Trinity. We have a pamphlet by one Theodosius, a close friend of Severus, that is dedicated to her. At the time he wrote it, Theodosius held the important patriarchate of Alexandria. The work itself was a direct address to Theodora and was most likely intended to be read out to her at a public event. She will know, he says, "after such prophetic, evangelical, apostolic and patristic teachings," that Christ assumed human qualities in three ways. "But still," he continues, "we bring before you even the patristic testimonies of our God-bearing teachers so that on all sides those things that are said will cohere and be in concord. See now what Gregory, the Wonder Worker [a third-century bishop in northern Turkey] and most holy man, said in his work on the Incarnation. . . ."

Later she is invited to contemplate "the priestly and glorious trumpet of churches and lamp of true doctrines, our father Cyril [of Alexandria], the teacher of the shared mysteries of the Church who sublimely studied that mystery of the non-humanity of the Once Born as much as any man can do." As these passages suggest, the work is largely a compendium of quotations from earlier writers, showing that while Christ was subject to suffering and death in his human form, he could not suffer in his divine aspect, and at no point was his knowledge anything but fully divine—a crucial point for those who believe that the Gospels contain a fully accurate record of Jesus' statements. The implication of this was driven home in another work addressed to Theodora, this one by Constantine, Bishop of Laodicea: namely, that the Son's date for the end of the world is no different than the Father's.[22]

Procopius claims that Theodora and Justinian worked at cross-purposes so as to deceive their subjects.[23] That an empress and emperor should differ in matters of religion was not new—Ariadne had been as strong a supporter of the Chalcedonian cause in the era of her husbands Zeno and Anastasius as Theodora would prove to be of the anti-Chalcedonians. What Procopius is actually complaining about is that the empress and her husband were *faking* disagreements to fool their subjects (never mind that our dear friend documents in some detail an actual disagreement of considerable importance). It would have been more interesting if he had said that they had different work practices. If he had, he would for once have offered a helpful clue to their relationship, enabling us to see more clearly what it was that drew Justinian and Theodora together. They were very different people who reacted very differently to the same stimuli—for instance, Justinian thought of fleeing when Hypatius was attempting to take the throne; Theodora, of fighting.

In matters of religion, Justinian was drawn to theological speculation, whereas Theodora was much less keen on talk than on action. She was interested in helping those who had helped her, and those who made sacrifices for their faith, as may be best appreciated through a remarkable story John of Ephesus tells.

Sometime after 536, he records, she met with a deeply subsocial individual named Mare "the Solitary," who hailed from the Amida region. Mare made his own clothes from wool rags. (John says that he could not leave any written record of the things the man said to the imperial couple because no one would believe that anyone would speak the way he did to these two world rulers.) After listening to Mare's opening tirade, Theodora offered him a place in the Hormisdas palace community and had her treasurer offer him a very large sum of money to divide between his own needs and those of the poor. Mare took the bag from the treasurer, threw it across the room telling Theodora to go to hell (or so John says), and stormed out of the palace. She let him go, and when he had settled at Sycae (the modern area of Galata on the north side of the Golden Horn) she routinely sent her people there to try to win his friendship.

Mare appears to have become something of a celebrity, as all manner of important people would regularly visit him, which one night led to a band of brigands' attacking him because they thought he must be rich. Mare subdued them, but when men arrived the next day to arrest them, he insisted they be allowed to leave. By this time, as we shall see, staunch anti-Chalcedonians had reason to be irritated with Theodora, who had not been able to deliver as promised in a showdown with the Pope and her husband. By tolerating and assisting Mare, she was pointing out that her patronage was still important.[24]

Another figure with whom Theodora had close contact was the monk Zoora, mentioned earlier. Zoora, a small man (his name means "small" in Syriac), had begun his career as a holy man towards the end of Anastasius' reign by ascending a pillar in his neighborhood, and staying there. Indeed, he appears to have remained in place throughout Justin's reign, not climbing down and departing for Constantinople until Justinian was on the throne. Evidently already a celebrity—he came with his own entourage—he was greeted by Justinian before a large assemblage of senior officials and bishops. Zoora's arrival caused consternation in the ranks of the establishment—those awaiting him feared that they would be smitten with his clever words, not realizing that simple men come armed only with the hidden power of grace. The charge of his enemies that he was totally ignorant of Scripture may not be far from the truth.

Zoora greeted Justinian with a torrent of abuse for, he alleged, Justinian's persecution of the faithful—at which point the emperor, visibly angry, accused him of being an apostate and heretic, reminding him that he, Justinian, had decreed death to anyone who cursed the Synod. Zoora responded in no uncertain terms, saying that yes indeed, he joined with the angels in heaven in cursing the Synod. The meeting adjourned. The power of God then saved Zoora, for when Justinian's body swelled up, he was cured only after Theodora asked the monk to pray for him. Once Justinian was cured, she installed Zoora at Sycae, where people came from all around to see him, allowing him to hold the assemblies of his fellow anti-Chalcedonians, which had only recently been banned.[25]

Putting aside the issue of divine intervention, the key elements of Zoora's story, like Mare's, are his ascetic lifestyle and his fearlessness in speaking his mind (*parrhesia*)—which today we would see as practicing freedom of speech—thought to have been given him by God. Like Mare, Zoora was a man of limited educational attainment, whose asceticism bestowed on him enormous authority. Unlike with Mare, however, we have independent evidence for Zoora's importance at the Council of Constantinople in 536, where he is identified as a leader of the anti-Chalcedonian community, on a par with Bishop Severus, and endowed with priestly authority (on the evidence that he was conducting baptisms). In both cases, the agent assuring the security and influence of these people was Theodora.[26]

Given her attitude towards Mare and Zoora, what she probably admired most about Severus was that he lived in poverty as befitted a man of faith. Severus did not use his position to feather his own nest; he lived according to the values he preached. But the truth is that she found theology a bore; in the letter to the eunuch Misael revealing details of Theodora's reading habits, Severus is outraged that she made disparaging comments in public about an earlier theologian, whose work he is sure she did not understand. He is also worried that she will not appreciate the tract he has just sent her. Behind the exasperation is evidence of a long association, and some notion that in certain circumstances she would bend the rules in his favor—the work he sent her had been formally banned by her husband—something that he does not seem to think would matter all that much to her. Severus was, at the time of writing, on his way back from Constantinople to Egypt under her protection. One hostile contemporary would refer to members of the anti-Chalcedonian movement as "the Severans," while another referred to "Theodora's faction" as thwarting the interests of strict Chalcedonians.[27]

The difference between Theodora's approach and that of her husband became clearest in 535, even as tensions were brewing between Constantinople and Ravenna. The circumstances of this year and the next drew Mare to Constantinople in all his fury, though all would seem to have started very well, from the anti-Chalcedonian viewpoint, when the patriarchates of both Alexandria and Constantinople fell vacant within months of each other. When in 532 Justinian had asked the anti-Chalcedonian bishops how a union could be achieved, they had told him that, because they held only small sees, they could not speak for their movement as a whole. The solution that had not yet been tried was to put moderate anti-Chalcedonian bishops in charge of Alexandria and Constantinople.[28]

For Constantinople, Theodora's candidate was Anthimus, then Bishop of Trebizond and a participant on the Chalcedonian side at the consultation of 532. In the years since then, he had had a change of heart, and it was in the knowledge of this that Theodora was able to bring about his election as Patriarch. For Alexandria, she chose the Theodosius, whose theological writings we have already encountered. Both men looked to Severus for theological guidance, and it is two North Africans who provide the most important (if not unbiased) contemporary witnesses to what happened. These men are Liberatus, author of *A Short History of the Affair of the Nestorians and Eutychians*, and Victor from Tunnuna, who composed a chronicle covering the history of the world from Creation to AD 566, of which only the section from 444 to 566 survives.

Both assert that Anthimus and Theodosius were put in place through the influence of "Theodora's faction," which is no doubt to some degree true, although their statements conceal the crucial fact that it was Justinian who actually made the appointments. As John of Cappadocia's career abundantly testifies, Justinian was perfectly capable of making appointments his wife did not like, but in this case, there can be no doubt that he was doing what Theodora wanted him to do. Strict Chalcedonians had rejected his preferred theological stance anyway, so perhaps a different one would be more effective. Justinian's argument had been that his favored doctrine was compatible with both Chalcedonian and anti-Chalcedonian communities. What he needed now were a few bishops who agreed with him. The decision to move from an approach reflecting the church councils to the appointment of non-Chalcedonian bishops was a rather more radical step than the emperor was wont to take, and, as we shall see, he was willing to back down—not something he would usually do when it was a question of candidates he had a strong belief in (John of Cappadocia all over again). Victor's statement about the power of Theodora's "faction" may be based on no more than contemporary gossip, but in this case the gossip reflected reality. The episcopal nominations of 535 were Theodora's solution to the quest for a unified Church.[29]

The situation in both Alexandria and Constantinople was tense as the new bishops took up their sees. Theodosius may have had a friend in Severus, but he also had powerful opponents within the anti-Chalcedonian community at Alexandria. These individuals drove him out of the city until, on Theodora's orders, the *cubicularius* Narses descended from Constantinople with sufficient forces to put him back in charge. Reaction to Anthimus was less immediately violent, but there were technical reasons as well as doctrinal ones for people to object to his selection. Chief among these was that he was already Bishop of Trebizond, and there was a long tradition forbidding bishops to move from one city to another. Severus himself now arrived in Constantinople, taking up residence in the Palace of Hormisdas, and entered into communion with Anthimus.[30]

The large community of Chalcedonian monks in the city, especially the so-called sleepless monks, were unwilling to oppose him directly—this was possibly a legacy of the Nika Revolt, which might well have made anyone leery of threatening urban violence. What they could do was rally support from elsewhere, and they appealed to their colleagues in Palestine; these clerics promptly wrote to Pope Agapetus in Rome, who was on the verge of undertaking his own delicate mission in Constantinople.

In the extensive record of the council that would be held in May of 536 survives the letter that Marianus, Archimandrite of Dalmatios,

Constantinople's most successful monastery (and "administrator" of the others in the city), sent to Agapetus laying out their complaints: namely, that Anthimus was a heretic; that his election was illegal; and that something must be done about the other heretics in the city, especially Severus, Peter of Apamea, and Zoora. There may actually be a reference to this letter in John of Ephesus' account of Zoora's life, where he says that Agapetus came to Constantinople because he had heard of Zoora's importance. Could the fact that men like Zoora, and later Mare, were competitors for imperial support and offered an alternative path of communication between the palace and the city's population to the established Church hierarchy also have played a part? It is quite clear that Marianus found Zoora intolerable.[31]

According to Liberatus, Agapetus' mission was the consequence of a letter Theodahad had sent to the Senate in 535, threatening to murder its members en masse if the threatened invasion of Italy were not averted. There is some truth to this story, and the choice of Agapetus as the representative of the Roman aristocracy is emblematic of the Church's role as a conduit for diplomacy between East and West. In this case, Theodahad's public bellicosity concealed a very different agenda. Agapetus was actually carrying to Constantinople a proposal for a settlement in which Theodahad was offering to cede Sicily, amongst other concessions, if Justinian would halt the invasion. Under the circumstances, Justinian could not ignore the Pope, while it was in the Pope's interest to stress to the man who might well be his new ruler that he was a force to be reckoned with. Encouraged by signs of support from Eastern monasteries as well as Chalcedonian establishments in the capital, Agapetus arrived in February and wasted no time in causing a ruckus. He refused communion with Anthimus and, Liberatus thinks, excommunicated Theodora. Justinian, who may have decided that his wife's plan was unlikely to work—he had already sent troops to Alexandria to secure Theodosius' position—now acquiesced in Anthimus' removal from office on the grounds that he had been illegally consecrated. He then agreed to a council being held at the beginning of May—a date that suggests that the whole thing had been set up in advance, given that Justinian could not seriously have thought he was going to get a large number of Palestinian monks to show up at a mere two months' notice. (In fact, they did show up, and were no doubt already on the move by the time Agapetus arrived in town.)[32]

Anthimus plainly understood what his course of action must now be, as did Theodora. He surrendered his position and went into hiding (in the Palace of Hormisdas—which nicely underscores the political theatricality of the proceedings), where he remained during the conference. The conference was presided over by the new Patriarch, Menas, whom Agapetus consecrated on March 13. Having accomplished all of this, and agreed with Justinian that his confession of the faith was thoroughly orthodox, Agapetus died on April 22. John of Ephesus maintains that the cause of his death was a curse that Zoora laid on him.[33]

The conference, held at a convenient distance from the palace at the Church of St. Mary Chalkoprateia (St. Mary of the Copper Market), consisted of six sessions at which the assembled Chalcedonians assailed Severus, Anthimus, and Zoora. Repeated efforts were made to summon Anthimus, who stayed the whole time in the Palace of Hormisdas, along with Severus—the assembled bishops were well aware of his whereabouts, but there was nothing they could do to make him show up. The outcome of the council was to restore Chalcedonian dominance at Constantinople. On August 13, Justinian issued a rescript to Menas declaring Severus, Anthimus, Zoora, and Peter of Apamea heretics and banning them from the capital. Severus returned to Egypt, but Anthimus stayed put in the palace, presumably with Justinian's acquiescence. Zoora, too, seems to have remained in town for a while, before being moved to the city of Dercus in Thrace; we do not know where Peter ended up. The remaining significant anti-Chalcedonian bishop, Theodosius, was summoned to Constantinople at the end of 536 and deposed the next year; he was sent to join Zoora at Dercus until Theodora had the two of them moved to the Palace of Hormisdas.[34]

By the middle of May of 536, Theodora's approach to doctrinal issues was becoming shambolic, and the events of the next few months—especially Justinian's ban on the men condemned by the Council—raise questions about just how seriously claims about the personal piety of the imperial couple should be taken. Furthermore, it is impossible to imagine that Theodora and Justinian were unaware of the several elements of farce attaching to the recent proceedings.

The one thing that is incontrovertible is that Theodora chose the wrong people to act as her agents. She believed in her friends, in Severus above all, and in her choice of Theodosius as Patriarch of Alexandria—which was a huge mistake, as it set one group of anti-Chalcedonians against another when unity was of the essence; and she believed in Zoora, whose prominence at the Council of 536 is most readily explicable if he was indeed a respected figure in the area at the time. When her efforts failed, she made sure that her friends were safe, and was willing to take a certain amount of criticism as a consequence. She was able to admit a mistake, contrary to the image that emerges from Procopius' writings—that of a woman implacable in her hatred and single-minded in her pursuit of power. Indeed, the Theodora of 536 appears to be a person capable of compromise, who put the safety of her friends above the image of her own influence, which took something of a public beating in the course of the year. She does not appear to have pursued a vendetta against Menas, who remained Patriarch of Constantinople during the rest of her life.

Perhaps as significant as anything is that, as far as we can tell, her relationship with Justinian remained intact, despite their being seen quite obviously to have backed opposing sides. Their devotion to each other will also have helped Theodora protect Severus (who died in Egypt on February 8, 538), as well as Anthimus, Theodosius, and Zoora.

In John of Ephesus' picture of their relations with the holy men in the Palace of Hormisdas, we catch a glimpse of Justinian and Theodora's more private lives. She is now in her mid-forties, he in his fifties—and we find them in the company of ascetics. Justinian had always been extremely abstemious when it came to his choice of food, for instance, and perhaps his public views on the importance of clerical chastity and asceticism reflect his views of the proper lifestyle for the leader of the Christian empire. But if they do, Theodora must have shared them—even Procopius does not suggest that she had lovers on the side—and this may contribute to John's picture of her as the righteous queen true to her faith, and comfortable in the company of holy men. By this point, there is reason to think that their relationship, while marked by obvious personal affection, was minimally physical.

10

Plots and Plague

While the events attending the depositions of Theodosius and Anthimus were unfolding, one of the lasting memorials to Theodora's age was taking shape. Even as people were seeking Anthimus in the Palace of Hormisdas, a new monument to the centrality of religion in shaping the later Roman Empire was nearing completion in the heart of the city. The great basilica of Hagia Sophia dominates Istanbul's skyline to this day, and it remains one of the world's architectural marvels. It was dedicated on December 27, 537.

In his account of the new church, just north of the revamped square in front of the palace, Procopius describes the advice Justinian gave the architects when it seemed that the building might be unstable. The historian's implication is that the structure could not have been completed without the emperor's perceptive advice, and that he must have been channeling divine inspiration. For, Procopius says, the emperor knew nothing about architecture.[1]

Paul Silentiarius, who wrote a poem to commemorate the restoration of the church in 562–563 after its dome collapsed in the earthquake that struck Constantinople in 557, gives us an ampler vision of what the building represented. For Paul, it demonstrated the superiority of the Eastern capital, the "new Rome," over the old; and still, fourteen years after Theodora's death, it is presented as the imperial couple's joint work. It was Christ himself who guided the emperor, and the spirit of Rome arose to celebrate his triumphs around the world, urging him to restore this church, the most glorious symbol of his reign. As he praises the church, Paul shows how illusory are people's fears of the end of the world, triggered most recently by the earthquake and an outbreak of the

FIGURE 10.1. The church Hagia Sophia, which still dominates Istanbul's skyline, replaced the church of the same name that was destroyed in the Nika Revolt of 532. Dedicated in 537, the massive dome is an architectural wonder.

© JM Travel Photography

plague. Just as Justinian has survived a recent conspiracy, so, too, will the world survive. Hagia Sophia is the place where imperial and divine powers unite; and a place where one cannot forget the empress, whose monograms appear with those of her husband and who is depicted on altar cloths, joining hands with Mary and Jesus:

> This [connection with God] Mighty Master, makes the soul of the empress, she who is blessed, all excellent, lovely and all wise, to intercede with God on your behalf, she who was your pious collaborator when she was alive. But when she died, she provided for your subjects a supportive oath, an unbreakable oath, which you have not disregarded and would not willingly neglect.[2]

As the new church was going up, Theodora was at work on a project of her own, one that may be connected with other legislation enacted during these years. A law issued in 534 stated that if a woman did not want to appear on stage, no one could force her to do so, and if a provincial governor tried to compel her to do so, the local bishop should

FIGURE 10.2. View of the interior of Hagia Sophia from the loge of the empress, where the location of her throne is marked by a green stone. This is the view Theodora would have had of proceedings in the Church.

© Album / Art Resource, NY

stop him. Justinian, in restating a section of the law that had allowed his marriage, declared that actresses' daughters should have the same right. (Theodora's daughter had just married Probus' son or grandson, which makes this statement look quite timely.) In 537, the emperor issued an order that no one could force a woman to make an agreement to go on stage, and said that any such agreement had no legal force. A woman should be free to "live in chastity without danger." In regulations issued the next year on admissions to monastic life, Justinian went as far as to state that, in the worship of God, there was no distinction of gender or status, for all "are justly considered the same" in Christ. Procopius' rantings about the way Theodora corrupted the marriage laws, allowing women far more freedom than they had had in the past, tally with some of the provisions of a major law issued at the end of 542 outlining marriage practices—which prompts the thought, probably with good reason, that Theodora had a hand in drafting this piece of legislation, as well as that of earlier years on related issues. On another matter of great importance, the edict ending the purchasing of senior offices, Justinian announced that he had consulted with the empress.[3]

The thrust of the legislation Procopius complains about points to both greater equality between men and women and, despite what Procopius has to say, a notion that legislation could impose a higher moral standard on society. The law of 542 broke with earlier traditions of Roman marriage law in banning divorce based simply on incompatibility (Justinian would later reverse this). But in listing grounds for divorce, it gives a rather more plentiful list of male misdemeanors than female. In addition to adultery, for instance, it states that if a man lives with another woman in the same house as his wife, or keeps mistresses around town, his wife, after a family member has given notice that the behavior is unacceptable, shall be able to divorce him.[4] Such a provision addresses behaviors Theodora would have been intimately familiar with in her earlier life, and may not be unconnected with a significant initiative, undoubtedly associated with her, dealing with prostitution.

Theodora's personal initiative, alluded to above, was her establishment of a hostel for women who wished to escape their lives as prostitutes. In his book *On Buildings* (*De Aedificiis* in Latin), Procopius provides us with some interesting details. The hostel, called *Metanoia* ("Repentance"), was a former imperial palace located a few miles north of the city, he says, and had space for five hundred people (that the Palace of Hormisdas was redesigned at this same period is perhaps no coincidence). The women for whom Metanoia was intended were not high-class concubines, but rather, victims, by and large, of the ancient equivalent of sex trafficking: women from poor families who were brought to Constantinople and exploited by brothel owners. In what reads very much like a quotation from a law on the subject, Procopius explains that the emperor and Theodora, who "shared a common piety" in all they did, expelled the brothel keepers from the city. Recognizing that, in eliminating the brothels, they had deprived the prostitutes of the wherewithal to earn a living, Justinian and Theodora created Metanoia, a place where the women could go to recover from their trauma—or, as Procopius would see it, to repent of their past lives and turn to the worship of God as a way of cleansing their sins—and receive money to cover their basic needs.

In the *Secret History*, Procopius would say that the women did not want to be saved, and at night would throw themselves off the walls of the hostel (which is perhaps what we might expect him to say). In fact, such a measure combined practicality with the ideology of repentance, a notion that figures prominently in the laws concerning actresses. It also recognizes the differing circumstances of the two groups, pimps and prostitutes. Pimps are simply villains to be disposed of. As far as the women are concerned, there is no record of the creation of anything resembling the Metanoia at any other point in Roman history, and it reflects Theodora's deep concern for women who she felt were victims of the social order. As with her earlier efforts to protect child prostitutes, she treats prostitution, not as a moral issue, but as a social one, the result of economic deprivation, which she attempts to solve partly by giving pensions to Metanoia's residents.[5]

The legislation of the mid-530s, like the effort to install Anthimus and Theodosius as patriarchs in two of the empire's major cities, may well reflect Theodora's enormous influence within the palace, but that influence did not go unchallenged, for other interests could and did trump hers, as when Pope Agapetus intervened against Anthimus. The disagreements of 536 played out against a background of imperial stress, as the war in Italy dragged on and on, and tensions grew. John of Cappadocia had done a great deal to reform the empire's revenue stream, but this was not sufficient to fund a big enough army to overwhelm Gothic resistance and, more seriously, to guarantee the security of other frontiers.

The problem came to a head in 540, when Belisarius finally occupied the Gothic capital, Ravenna, and arranged a peace treaty whose crux was his salutation as Emperor by the Gothic nobility. He denied that this meant any challenge to Justinian; nonetheless, he was immediately recalled to Constantinople, accompanied by Gothic treasure and members of the Gothic royal family. There would be no triumph this time, and Belisarius was temporarily retired. The significance of these events, for public consumption, was depicted in a mosaic above the palace's Bronze Gate, facing the refurbished forum, which now displayed a gigantic mounted statue of Justinian in bronze. The mosaic showed the imperial couple gladly receiving the surrender of Africa and Italy, and Belisarius leading the army safely home. This, of course, he had not achieved, nor would it be achieved within Theodora's lifetime. War would soon break out once again in Italy, an event not unconnected with action taking place on the eastern frontier.[6]

The Gothic surrender had taken place in May of that year, and in June, the Persian king, Khusro, advanced up the Euphrates rather than taking the more normal invasion route across northern Mesopotamia. There were simply not enough men in the eastern army to offer him effective resistance. He therefore sacked Antioch, whose defenses had not been fully restored in the wake of the earthquake of 528, and carried off thousands of its citizens as captives to populate a new city, which he called "better Antioch," near the Persian capital, Ctesiphon. He went on to sack Seleucia, the ancient port city on the coast, taking time off to bathe in the Mediterranean, and at Apamea (modern Aleppo) he held chariot races, insisting that the Greens win. Thrusting ever onwards, Khusro collected two hundred pounds of gold from Edessa in return for not laying siege to the place, as well as large sums from other cities in compensation for not sacking them; not having to halt to lay waste enabled Khusro to move faster, to threaten more places en route, and to get some idea of what he might grab on a later expedition.[7]

The invasion was not a complete surprise, as relations between the two courts had been strained during the previous year when the king of the Jafnids, the Arab tribes aligned with Roman interests in the border region between the Roman and Persian empires, had attacked Khusro's Nasrid clients. With the bulk of the army still in Italy, it was a serious miscalculation to offer the Persian king an excuse to break the peace. In 541, Khusro launched an invasion through the Caucasus mountains towards the Black Sea, while Belisarius—in the emergency, forgiven his indiscretions—was placed in command of the garrison protecting Syria. Being rather more proactive than Bouzes, the nephew of Vitalian who had been in command the previous year and remained in post, Belisarius made cannier use of his troops by raiding Persian territory while the main army was away, and appears to have developed a decent relationship with his fellow commander.[8]

The failure on the eastern frontier encouraged the Goths—who may have felt cheated when it became clear that Belisarius was not going to be their ruler—to renew their war with Rome. It may also have given Theodora the opportunity to do something she had been itching to do for quite some time: namely, get rid of John the Cappadocian. Procopius' account, tinged as it is with his familiar antipathy towards both parties, suggests, as does John Lydus, that their rivalry was of long standing. This is not impossible, but it is perhaps significant that, in the law ending payment for offices, after having consulted his "most pious spouse," Justinian says, he has also spoken with John, which, as the law is addressed to John, might be taken as a signal to the collective official-dom that there was complete unanimity at the top and that they should abandon any notion of setting the two against each other on this issue.[9]

Although we are largely dependent on Procopius for understand-ing what exactly happened to John, we do get some helpful informa-tion from other sources. John Lydus' manuscripts *Concerning the Magistracies* contain, just before an entry plainly having to do with events in 542, a list of contents for the third and final book, which includes the tantalizing entry "concerning the pious Empress Theodora and how she assisted the state." It is probable that for John Lydus the "benefit" conferred at this point was John the Cappadocian's elimina-tion, while the chronicle tradition based on John Malalas reports that he was removed from office in August of 541 for participating in a plot with the patrician Antonina against the emperor.

The chronicle goes on to say that, once removed from office, he was sent to Cyzicus in Anatolia, where he was ordained as a deacon. While there, he joined in a plot with certain landholders to kill the local bishop, one Eusebius. Justinian was furious when he heard about this, and promptly sent a commission of inquiry consisting of four senior officials. When they found John guilty, Justinian exiled him to Antinoopolis in Egypt, where he remained until after Theodora's death. This account, which seems to be only moderately inaccurate, put-ting his exile in 540 rather than 541 and misreporting the month—he was removed from office between May and June of 541—is important because it confirms that essential elements of the story told at greater length by Procopius are not cut from whole cloth, but rather represent the official story circulating at the time. Procopius adds further details in his *Secret History*, some inverting elements of the official version, others suggesting that Theodora was preternaturally vindictive and that the bishop was killed in some sort of factional riot for which John was shown to be not entirely responsible.[10]

Before proceeding to the events surrounding John's fall from grace, it is worth noting the composition of the commission of inquiry, for these people were, more than likely, individuals with whom, to some degree, Theodora could work. One was Florus, a former palace official and the grandfather of Paul the Silentiarius; another was Phocas, who had replaced John as praetorian prefect in 532 after having been inves-tigated for his pagan beliefs a couple of years before; and the other two,

Paul and Thomas, are known only from this inquiry but are both said to have been members of the Senate, and Paul held an honorary consulship. The involvement of such senior officials might suggest that John's fall cannot be seen simply as a spat between two powerful people who hated each other, but as a major political issue. When Antonina is added to the mix, thereby bringing in Belisarius as well, the episode implicates even more deeply the whole governing élite.[11]

The story, as first reported by Procopius, is as follows. Theodora hated John of Cappadocia, who showed her no respect and slandered her to Justinian, but she could not persuade her husband to get rid of him. This much we have already observed. John, well aware of Theodora's loathing, feared she would send a barbarian to assassinate him in his sleep, which he now had trouble getting, even though he surrounded himself with many guards. Often when he woke, he made himself feel better by consulting with sorcerers, who assured him that he would become emperor. Furthermore, whenever he went to pray, John would dress in rough clothing like a pagan priest and mutter spells intended to control the emperor's mind. This last, which may have been publicly observable, is especially interesting because it suggests, paganism aside, that he dressed as an ascetic when he was not working, something that may well have endeared him to his ascetically inclined master.[12]

When Belisarius returned from Italy, Procopius continues, John, who drew hatred to himself with the force of an electromagnet, began to work actively against the general—though this may not be true, as John appears to have been out of Constantinople in the winter of 540–541. Antonina, perceiving that John was conspiring against her husband even as he was being sent to deal with the eastern front, and wishing to do the empress a favor, hit upon the following plan. John had a daughter named Euphemia, his only child, whom he loved deeply. One day, ostensibly bringing Euphemia into her confidence, Antonina complained to her that Justinian was ungrateful for her husband's success. Euphemia, who hated Theodora, was delighted to hear this, and asked if Belisarius might be interested in a regime change. This was not something Belisarius could do on his own, Antonina replied, but would need an insider's help. And, Procopius would later add, she swore the most powerful oaths a Christian could swear to win Euphemia's trust. Putting a less dramatic slant on events, it is possible that Antonina simply took advantage of the fact that John was out of town to strike up a relationship with his daughter.[13]

When Euphemia told John what was on Antonina's mind, he was delighted, immediately thinking that the prophecies about his taking the throne must be true. He asked his daughter to set up a meeting with Antonina as soon as possible. They could meet, not in the city, Antonina pointed out, but rather in the suburb of Rufinianae (which Belisarius happened to own). She then told Theodora what was going on. Theodora was delighted to have been informed, and urged her to spring the trap.

When the meeting at Rufinianae had been scheduled, Theodora went to Justinian and told him what was happening. She then dispatched troops, on her own authority, along with Narses the *cubicularius* and Marcellus commander of the palace guard, to arrest John when they caught him plotting with Antonina. Justinian, sensing that John was being entrapped, tried to get word to him that he should on no account meet with Antonina. But meet her John did, despite the emperor's warning, and when they overheard him plotting to seize the throne, the two imperial officials sprang their trap. They had not, however, counted on John's being able to escape with the protection of his bodyguards. He took refuge in a church—a big mistake, says Procopius, who thought that he might have gotten off scot free if he had just gone straight to Justinian. As it was, he gave Theodora an ideal opportunity to plot against him.[14]

Although John, his property confiscated, was dismissed and sent off to become a priest in Cyzicus, Justinian remained well disposed towards him and returned the bulk of what he had forfeited. It was then, however, that the Cappadocian was implicated in the murder of the Cyzicene bishop, investigated by the commission, stripped naked, flogged, and sent into exile; and, with but a single cloak to his name, he was ordered to beg in every town where the ship transporting him to exile in Egypt stopped along its way. He was ultimately relegated to Antinoopolis in southern Egypt, and not until after Theodora's death did he return to Constantinople.[15]

The portraits of both empress and emperor in this affair, penned after Theodora's death, are scarcely attractive. She comes across as conspiratorial and vindictive, while Justinian seems rather dim, unwilling to admit that his favorite—or indeed, both his favorites—might have some undesirable qualities. But what does this really tell us about Theodora?

The first thing, obviously, has to do with how people who disliked her interpreted her actions—what Procopius condemns is behavior that John Lydus would have praised as a sign of her devotion to the public good. Procopius will expand on the themes he introduces in his first account of John when he writes the *Secret History*, and there he also takes the opportunity to spice up the story. One of the main themes in the *Secret History*'s opening section is Antonina's domination of Belisarius, whose toleration of her well-advertised adulteries made him look foolish before any of this happened.

Initially, Antonina's unfaithfulness to Belisarius had angered Theodora. But Antonina was able to "make her manageable" by serving her in important matters: the first concerning Pope Silverius; the next, the affair of John of Cappadocia just recounted.

Regarding Silverius, and according to the writer Liberatus, Theodora had suborned Vigilius—then serving as the papal representative in Constantinople, a post he had held since 535—so that he would reinstate Anthimus, Severus, and Peter in their sees if she made him Pope. She then sent orders to Belisarius telling him what to do. On her instructions, Belisarius duly charged Pope Silverius with having plotted to let the Goths into Rome in 537, the year they had besieged Belisarius in the city. Silverius fled to a church for refuge, from which he was lured by Photius, Belisarius' son. He was exiled to Patara in Lycia. When he threatened to return to Italy, he was imprisoned on the island of Palmaria, where he died of starvation. Vigilius was duly enthroned as Pope in March of 537 and remained in office until his death in 555, steadfastly opposing Anthimus' restoration and the softening of the Chalcedonian position (which would suggest that rumors of deals struck with Theodora are no more than that).

It is an unpleasant tale, painting a picture of Theodora that Procopius could relish; it is also a tale marred by gross errors of fact, above and beyond those suggested by the facts of Vigilius' own career. Liberatus says Theodora's orders were sent to Belisarius when he was at Ravenna, which is interesting because it dates the story to 540. The siege of Rome had taken place in 537, as just noted, which is when, in his narrative of that event in his *History of the Gothic War*, Procopius tells us Belisarius deposed Silverius for plotting to betray the city to the Goths. Liberatus' story must date from the 540s, and its circulation needed no explanation when Procopius wrote the *Secret History*. It has nothing to do with what actually happened in Rome in 537 or the actual relationship between Antonina and Theodora. What is just as interesting is that Procopius writes that Theodora was offended by Antonina's personal life. Is this another hint that by 540 she and Justinian were leading lives of ascetic abstinence?[16]

In the *Secret History*, Procopius appears to be responding directly to comments such as those of John Lydus in his summary of Theodora's role in the praetorian prefect's downfall. Her actions, Procopius says, were motivated, not by her desire to further the interests of the state—the proof being that she did nothing about people who later behaved even more atrociously—but simply by the Cappadocian's slander of her. So vindictive was she, he goes on, that even four years later, she ordered the torture of two men accused of playing a role in the riot that saw Eusebius killed, in the hope that they would admit to John's direct complicity in the murder. They did not, so she had their hands cut off. This incident is also reported by John Malalas, who says that two brothers, Andreas and John, had their hands cut off for their participation in the riot. That the two should be named suggests that they were people of relatively high status within the faction, and that the case was somewhat more of a *cause célèbre* than Procopius allows. In fact, John Malalas' story presumably depended on public records. One being the trial of the brothers, the other being the trial of John himself; his statement also suggests that the earlier investigation of John's role had not yielded a definitive answer as to the nature of his role in the riot. That only came about as a result of the new trial in which the penalty for Andreas and John was devised, not by Theodora, but by the presiding judge. Theodora may have been the driving force behind John's fall, but she did not act alone.[17]

The main difference between Procopius' view and what we can glean of John the Lydian's—and, indeed, of Malalas' "official story"—is that, for Procopius, Theodora did the right thing for the wrong reason, and for John, she did the right thing for the right reason. For the general public, the Cappadocian's fall from power was more of a spectacle, a theatrical event playing out over the months between his initial denunciation and eventual exile. And it involved, not just the empress and her friend, but significant elements within the imperial hierarchy.

What is concealed behind all of this is the extent to which John's exit was linked to changes in fiscal policy. It may well be significant that his immediate replacement, Theodotus, made no significant changes in this department, and neither did Theodotus' successor, Peter Barsymes, noted as a particular favorite of Theodora's. Both Theodotus and Peter were experienced officials at the time they took office, so that John's fall from power possibly resulted from the fact that significant elements of the bureaucracy, following the catastrophic opening of the Persian war, thought he had too much influence with the emperor and that it was time for him to go, even though they had no actual alternatives to the policies he had devised. That Theodora was closely involved is confirmed more by John Lydus' praise than by Procopius' rant, which probably represents quite fairly what John the Cappadocian's supporters had to say.[18]

The choice of location for John's exile—Antinoopolis—is a further and final pointer to Theodora's involvement. At about the same time as she was hastening the end of John's career, an embassy arrived from a Sudanese tribe, the Nobadae, asking for a priest to provide them with spiritual leadership. According to John of Ephesus, Theodora, who had Theodosius with her in Constantinople, selected a priest named Julianus. Justinian wanted to send someone else, but Theodora wrote to the commander of the region, telling him that she would have his head if he allowed Justinian's priest to arrive ahead of hers. The commander in question made quite sure that Julianus arrived well ahead of Justinian's candidate—a smart move on his part, given that the emperor tended to think in terms of policy, whereas Theodora thought in terms of people. Also, in 547, the inhabitants of the city of Aphrodito, not far from Antinoopolis, who were at this point under Theodora's personal patronage, sent the empress an embassy asking that a local magnate named Julian not be allowed to add them to the areas under his control. Aphrodito was also home to a noted poet and anti-Chalcedonian thinker named Dioscorus. John was thus to be imprisoned in an area where Theodora's influence was especially strong.[19]

Even as John was heading south, something far deadlier than anyone had encountered in the recorded history of the Mediterranean was headed north. The great plague that entered the region in the summer of 542 shattered Justinian's ambitions, for the time being, anyway, and brought Theodora face to face with challenges greater even than the Nika Revolt.

The first instance of bubonic plague in Mediterranean history appears to have originated in central Africa. It spread steadily northwards, and first reports of deaths from the new and terrible disease appeared in Ethiopia and southern Egypt in 541. The next year the pestilence arrived in Constantinople, then raged throughout the eastern provinces for three long years.

Contemporary descriptions are explicit on the symptoms, and this has allowed modern researchers to identify the illness as stemming from the bacterium *Yersinia pestis*. The bacterium is ordinarily transmitted to humans via bites from the fleas of infected small rodents. Symptoms include the sudden onset of fever, weakness, chills, and one or more swollen and tender lymph nodes (these are the buboes that give this form of the plague its name). Whereas in modern populations it is treated with antibiotics, in the sixth century, the afflicted had recourse only to bathing, bed rest, and prayer. The widespread interest and belief in miraculous cures are to some degree a reflection of the fact that, for the average person who lacked access to the sort of physician who might treat a member of the imperial household, survival from a serious illness was something of a miracle. Indeed, in a society such as that of the Roman Empire of the time, which regarded illness as a punishment for sin, doctors and ascetic holy men were seen equally as potential agents of cure, and may have regarded each other as useful sources of information. The danger of the plague was that it struck too fast and spread too rapidly. One feature of medicine recognized during Theodora's time as well as in the modern world was that quarantine was the only way to prevent the spread of this disease, and of many others, too. One person we find trying to institute quarantine in southern Turkey in the 540s was a local holy man, Nicholas of Sion, the figure known more commonly today as Santa Claus.[20]

The effect of the plague on Alexandria in 541 was catastrophic, and ships from that city in the spring of 542 carried the infected rodents to Syria, Asia Minor, and Constantinople. Tribonian writes in March that, although "we hope that no [such] evil will ever befall the state," either divine will or the instability of human affairs brings evils that provide opportunities for imperial beneficence to be displayed. "Mortal danger," he continues, was spreading in every direction. In Constantinople, it took four months for the first outbreak to run its course. Tribonian himself would not live to the end of the year, and according to Procopius, he died of disease. Procopius and John of Ephesus, who were in the capital when the sickness came, saw it as both the vengeance of God and a play date for demons. Procopius writes that many people saw apparitions in human form that struck them down; John, that some demons appeared in the form of monks. Doctors knew not what to do about a disease they had never before met with; those who recovered did so for no obvious reason.

The death toll was horrendous. Between five thousand and ten thousand people perished in a single day on Constantinople alone; the full toll in the capital may have reached into the hundreds of thousands, possibly around half the city's population, while in one town on the Egyptian border, all but eight inhabitants were found dead. The pestilence recognized no difference in class or status; common people and nobles were smitten as one, citizens were seen to totter and fall in the streets, merchants or customers might be suddenly overcome in mid-transaction. In Constantinople, the story went around of a house filled with nothing but the dead, twenty bodies in all; of infants wailing as their mothers died. Theodore the *referendarius*, Justinian's personal messenger, was charged with burying the dead, using troops for the task or paying civilians to take out the bodies, filling the tombs around the city, digging up any corner where they could lay the dead, and as a last resort filling the towers in the defensive walls around Sycae. A victim of the plague would later recall how, when he was young during the first outbreak, he was afflicted with the swellings, and how later it took his wife, many of his children, relatives, servants, and tenants. For some, he said, the first symptoms were in the head, making the eyes bloodshot and the face swollen, then descending to the throat; others were suddenly smitten with a violent stomach disorder; while in those on whom the buboes swelled up, there was a raging fever, then death, if it came, by the third day.[21]

The plague's long-term impact is still to be fully measured. For now, it is clear that the economic expansion that had been taking place in the Syrian countryside came to an end in the mid–sixth century. There are also signs of major financial problems, as the basic source of revenue—the taxes on produce and persons—declined suddenly and rapidly, while transportation networks were interrupted and the state began to adjust its coinage to stretch its resources—sometimes without great success, as when Peter Barsymes tried to reduce the weight of the gold coinage in 542–543. Armies went unpaid, and it became next to impossible to fill their ranks; the campaign in Italy ground to a virtual halt.[22]

In Constantinople, there was a more immediate problem. Sometime after the plague took hold, buboes appeared on Justinian's groin. Doctors said that some of the victims would not regain full use of their faculties. What would happen if the emperor did not fully recover? People might get the idea that he was dysfunctional—and palace security was scarcely ironclad. He would survive, however, albeit incapacitated for a while.

In fact, nearly twenty years later—just months before Hagia Sophia's rededication—there was an attempt on Justinian's life. Paul the Silentiarius alludes to it in a poem, and Procopius gives details that may have emerged from the interrogation of those implicated in the plot. Justinian would be easy to kill because he stayed up late every night in a meeting room discussing Christian doctrine with some elderly priests. His nocturnal habits are attested to in a somewhat different way in the *Secret History*, and in the law eliminating payment for offices, Justinian himself refers to his "sleepless nights."

The point to all these accounts, for one who might want to kill him, is that Justinian seems not to have been surrounded by bodyguards, and that Theodora and he were not to be found in the same place at most hours of the night (if at all). But she was a good deal stricter about whom she would meet and when she would meet them.[23]

In the plague years, the generals on the Mesopotamian front, freed from the threat of immediate war as Khusro had cancelled a planned invasion when he got wind of the plague—which had penetrated his realm, too—met to decide what to do. Chief amongst them were Bouzes and Belisarius, who agreed that they would accept no new emperor from Constantinople. This, presumably, meant that Belisarius intended to declare himself emperor in the event of Justinian's death. Two other generals, Peter and John "the Glutton," reported back to Theodora the substance of these discussions, which could easily have evoked memories of untoward behavior on Belisarius' part; and not even Procopius would deny that the exchanges had taken place. As Justinian slowly recovered, Theodora insisted that Bouzes and Belisarius be recalled to the capital. They were both dismissed from their posts. Bouzes disappeared from public life for the next several years (though he probably did *not* spend two of them in a dark dungeon beneath Theodora's wing of the palace, as Procopius claims), and Belisarius was sent home, his now-vast estates confiscated.[24]

Procopius again portrays Theodora as vicious and vindictive. Unsurprisingly, she took the proposal that a new emperor from Constantinople not be accepted, in the now-unlikely event that the emperor should die, as an attack upon herself. Furthermore, says the historian, she persecuted Belisarius simply to please Antonina, who was estranged from her husband as a result of the lengthy and ill-concealed affair she was having with a younger man, which was nothing new—and indeed, Theodora had herself facilitated this particular fling. But this is to oversimplify the matter, and we must add, first of all, that Theodora would have every reason to regard the conversation reported to her as an attack upon herself, and, given that John the Glutton had risen through the ranks in Belisarius' service, to believe what she had been told.

Second, the fact that she was informed at all is a sign of the respect in which she was held. If people did not think her capable of ruling, they would not have kept her informed. As with the Cappadocian case, she was acting, not so much on her own, but rather with a group within the imperial government. As we have seen, during her years on the throne, Theodora had built up a powerful network of supporters of all sorts: Peter the Patrician, who acted in her interests in Italy was one; Peter Barsymes was another; as, quite likely, was Theodore the *referendarius*, who presumably would have been sending her bulletins during her husband's illness; as well, certainly as Narses and Marcellus, who had helped bring down John. Then, of course, there were large numbers throughout the eastern provinces who looked to her as a protector of their religious beliefs. Theodora had succeeded in bridging gaps of class, education, and experience to build a cohesive governing party based on loyalty to herself and to the emperor.

Whatever Procopius may assert, the person who stood at the center of this diverse group of officials, soldiers, and priests was unlikely to have been someone who owed her power and influence to sheer terror. People were well aware that she did not always get her way with her husband—the events of the Council of Constantinople of 536 made this clear, as did John the Cappadocian's long career, for instance. Absent absolute power, the qualities that would have drawn people to her were the same that attracted Justinian: she was smart, she was tough and vigorous, she was quite likely a very engaging person to be around. She was loyal to her friends. She had come from the provinces and made herself empress. In the crisis of 542, she once again did what was necessary to make sure both that she remained empress and that Justinian remained emperor. And it was through her ability alone that she would hold this title for the rest of her life.

11

Last Years

The years after the first outbreak of the bubonic plague were not easy. The pestilence recurred and spread. The supply system of the capital itself was threatened. Campaigns against the resurgent Goths were slowed; there were no significant reinforcements that could be sent with Belisarius, whom Justinian forgave and recalled, returning to him the bulk of his vast wealth. Campaigns against the Persians likewise ground slowly on, with neither side disposed to decisive action, and most of the fighting concentrated along the east coast of the Black Sea. In what became an important symbol of change, there would be no more consuls—a move made first, perhaps, because with the plague raging no one was eager to lend his name to the consular year; and with resources tight, the office was a luxury not readily affordable. As time passed, however, the failure to appoint a consul took on a different meaning. Justinian now looked less to Rome's history: the plague was foiling his ambitions to restore the empire, and with his regime weakened, he may well not have wanted to promote someone who would look like an obvious rival. Tribonian, the great spokesman of tradition and restoration, was now dead, and there was no one else to take up the cause. Justinian himself turned ever more to religion, so that a new, more priestly image of the imperial office began to take shape.[1]

For Theodora, traditional concerns would mingle with more forward-looking preoccupations as her family grew up. Her oldest grandson was approaching an age at which he might marry, and so was her niece, Comito's daughter Sophia by her now-deceased husband Sittas, who had perished in an Armenian ambush during 537 or 538. Indeed, Sophia was perhaps already showing signs of the strength and wit that would make her the most powerful woman of the next half-century. Theodora might also have been taking some pleasure in the success of her own daughter's marriage. In 542, she used the palace of her brother-in-law Probus to house John of Ephesus and at least one other anti-Chalcedonian clergyman, which suggests that everyone was getting along.[2]

Theodora continued to take a determined interest in the anti-Chalcedonian movement, which was now entering an important new phase. In 544, she was responsible for John of Ephesus' appointment to the bishopric of that name (he was originally from the Amida area of eastern Turkey). John's appointment signals two things: one, the continuing effort to find a middle ground between the Chalcedonians and the anti-Chalcedonians; the other, the coming of age of a new generation of leaders in the anti-Chalcedonian movement, which by 542 had already been experiencing a serious shortage of clergy, and without new clergy, the movement would fail. Theodora's most important contribution to the movement would be through enabling the creation of a new generation of leaders.

Some years before John's appointment, another John, John of Hephaestopolis, an Egyptian bishop and partisan of Theodosius, had departed Constantinople in secret and performed a number of ordinations, which, it appears, residents of the Palace of Hormisdas had agreed not to do. Claiming illness, he had asked if he could move out of the palace, and Theodora had set him up in another, the Palace of Anthemius, with an allowance. In his new home, he received groups from various places and performed ordinations, with the full knowledge of Theodosius and, it appears, of Theodora herself. John then asked to move outside the capital to continue his work, and again Theodora gave her permission.

At this point, rivals (unnamed) informed him that the empress had agreed with Justinian that he, John, was to be executed, presumably hoping that he would give up what he was doing and go into hiding. John did the opposite of what they might have expected and went straight to Theodora to demand an explanation. She was taken aback, and when she found out what had happened, she threatened those responsible for the trick with punishment. However, John prevailed on her not to kill them, to which she agreed. Having then asked him not to perform any more ordinations in the capital, she gave him permission to travel outside the city on the grounds of illness. He got as far as the borders of Syria before returning to Constantinople, where Theodora quashed accusations by Ephrem of Antioch that he had been carrying out illicit ordinations—which, of course, he had. Several years later, John set out on another, similar journey, in the course of which he met and ordained John of Ephesus, who arrived in Constantinople at about the same moment as the plague.[3]

The Theodora we see in this story is not too dissimilar from the Theodora we saw in the last chapter: as when she brought down John the Cappadocian and Belisarius, she was plainly willing to do things that Justinian would have preferred that she not do. At the same time, we get a taste of her sense of humor as she turns a blind eye to what John is doing—she seems rather like the police chief played by Claude Rains in the film *Casablanca*, who suddenly "discovers" gambling at Rick's. This is not the woman we know from Procopius, but more the woman we have perceived via the wide range of her friendships.

It was not long after John of Ephesus arrived in Constantinople that Theodora received an emissary from the Jafnid king—with the Persian war raging, it was important to keep him happy. This time there was no suggestion of pressing for a Chalcedonian alternative to an "orthodox" (in this case, anti-Chalcedonian) bishop. Theodosius duly consecrated two—Jacob Bar'adai as bishop of Edessa and Theodore as bishop of Bostra—with evidently no complaint from Justinian, who would not have been ignorant of what was going on in another part of his own palace. Bishop Jacob proved to be immensely influential: his achievement, essentially, was to create an alternative hierarchy for anti-Chalcedonian communities throughout Syria—which was not what Justinian had wished, for he still hoped it would be possible to unify the Church and later tried to have Jacob arrested. The result, instead, was the creation of institutions to support the community that is today the Syrian Orthodox Church. Similarly, efforts to maintain a single administrative structure in Alexandria led to the split that produced the Coptic Orthodox Church of that city.[4]

Clearly, Justinian was allowing Theodora to deal in her own way with the split in the Church, even before the elimination of her most serious political rival. This, too, is a measure of the institutional power that had accrued to her over the years and that enabled her to handle deftly both John of Cappadocia and the crisis of 542; it must also have helped that Justinian, as far as we can tell, got on quite well with Theodosius. But Chalcedon was not the only religious issue confronting the empire: for the plague was probably the catalyst for the return to an earlier policy of religious intolerance—plainly, God was very angry with the empire, and something needed to be done to put matters right.

On March 22, 544, Justinian announced publicly that God's chastisement had come to an end. One result of the plague had been the disruption of transportation networks and increasing prices for everyday items. In asserting that the plague had passed, Justinian was trying to restore order to the empire and, in this case, ordered people to stop inflating the prices they were charging for their goods. In that same year, he also embarked on what was essentially an antipagan witch-hunt. This was part of his motivation in appointing John as Bishop of Ephesus, for in that post, John would later claim to have converted above eighty thousand pagans from the countryside of western Turkey—most likely a considerable exaggeration—and to have dealt harshly with Montanist heretics, followers of a tradition of "new prophecy" that had inspired some Christians in the area since the second century. According to Procopius, the latter burned themselves alive in their churches. If John's campaign *was* responsible for the tragedy, he knew not to boast of it later, but persecution in the cause of religious "purity" was in the air. In Constantinople, a number of senior officials were arrested and tortured, while the elderly Phocas, who had proven himself a most loyal supporter of the regime both in the matter of John and in the Nika Revolt, committed suicide.[5]

In the post-plague years, Theodora herself may have been spending less and less time in Justinian's company. Procopius says that she was frequently residing in a palace at Herion on the far side of the Bosphorus. We do not know exactly when the palace, built by Justinian, was finished or when it became a favored residence, but the way Procopius describes it, "in the wake of the evils that beset all mankind," suggests that it was only after 542 that she began to make it her regular domicile. In fact, when the plague had finally abated and the capital was now faced with uncertainties of supply, it made sense for her to remove her large staff to another location. Procopius claims that this was hard on the latter because winter storms and the rampages of Porphyrius the whale made it hard to ship sufficient food to the place. Porphyrius was a wayward sperm whale that had moved in and out of the Bosporus from time to time in the course of the last few decades, "playing" with local fishing boats and generally terrorizing the nautical community. He was active again in the 540s until he beached himself and was killed by local peasants at the mouth of the Sangarius River around 550.[6]

Theodora's primary concern is unlikely to have been whale watching. Justinian would prove to be something of a demographic miracle for his day, living into his early eighties, but most people did not survive into their sixties, and by the mid-540s, Theodora would have been aware that she was unlikely to have a great deal of time remaining to her. She wanted the best for her family, and that involved the politics of marriage—a politics that would hopefully favor her relatives and disadvantage those of potential rivals.

She evidently made life something of a nightmare for Justinian's ablest cousin, Germanus, whom she disliked intensely. Knowledge of the empress's antipathy towards him evidently prevented people of high station from seeking alliances with Germanus, with the result, Procopius tells us, that his daughter was still unmarried at eighteen—a woman of her rank would ordinarily have been married by fifteen. In 545, Germanus finally persuaded John, a nephew of Vitalian, to arrange a marriage with his son—a scandal in Procopius' view, because John was of insufficiently high rank, and it was clear to all that Germanus was desperate. The issue in fact ran somewhat deeper, in that both men were on very poor terms with Belisarius; and John bore an undisguised animosity towards Theodora that was probably connected with the dismissal of his brother (or cousin) Bouzes in 542. What Procopius does not admit is that the proposed wedding was a statement of unity by Theodora's enemies that she could not prevent. This, too, should raise questions of how much people might actually have dreaded displeasing the empress—smart people do not make powerful people angry if they can avoid it, but both Germanus and John plainly felt they were never going to get along with Theodora, so they might as well do as they saw fit.[7]

On a more positive note, Theodora's niece Sophia married Justin, Justinian's nephew and the man emerging as the preferred heir apparent. Although rarely mentioned by Procopius—he was the only person to mention her by name—Comito must have remained a profoundly important friend to her sister all her life. Theodora also arranged a marriage between Ioanna, daughter of Antonina and Belisarius, and her grandson Anastasius; the wedding would take place shortly before her death. The marriage later collapsed (Procopius blamed Antonina), and we hear nothing more, for certain, of Anastasius. Theodora's two other grandsons went on to live longer and more prosperous lives. One of them, John, would rise to high administrative rank, while the other, Athanasius, would become a bishop. These were scarcely positions Theodora could have imagined for her grandchildren when her daughter was born, but now, thanks in part to the link with Emperor Athanasius' family, Theodora's descendants would occupy the highest level in Constantinopolitan society.

Theodora would not live to see her grandchildren grow up. She fell ill towards the end of 547 or in early 548. It may have been cancer. She died on June 28 that year, at the age of fifty-three (or thereabouts).[8]

Theodora may not have been the most powerful woman of her age—that title might attach more readily to her niece Sophia, or to Ariadne, wife of the emperors Zeno and Anastasius—but she was the most extraordinary. She had to make her own way in the world from a young age. She made her first career for herself, a career that gave her lifelong friends whom she did not forget when the palace became her home. One of the most important relationships in her life was with her older sister, whose talent as actress and dancer had eclipsed her own in her younger years. Comito may well have given her the support that appears to have been sadly lacking in her parents. Throughout her life, Theodora would be deeply loyal to those who helped her in her youth. Once she met Justinian, she built a wide-ranging network both inside the palace and as far as the frontiers of the empire. It is the extent of that network, ranging from semiliterate priests to soldiers, courtiers, and the aristocracy, that gave her so much clout. She understood that, in the world that she had made hers, it was not birth or education that guaranteed power, but access to office, and that the most important quality of one upon whom office was bestowed was loyalty.

Distinguishing the real Theodora from the one to be found in the pages of Procopius' *Secret History*, and seeing her as others saw her, we sense her brilliance—she moved in what was very much a man's world, a world where her own background was never forgotten, but this was a strength, not a weakness. She knew how to talk to people; her broad experience of the world had taught her that listening was as important as the ability to command, and it is precisely this quality that shines through so many of John of Ephesus' stories about her. Her linguistic facility—we know that she was trilingual, at least—together with her natural empathy meant she could speak the language of Zoora,

Mare and other have-nots and eccentrics, as well as that of bigwigs like Tribonian, Probus, and Narses. She was tough. Her enemies were right to fear her; she saved her throne and that of her husband at least once, during the Nika Revolt, and quite probably in the wake of the great plague. Her relationship with Justinian was plainly based, not just on passion (in fact, there seems to have been remarkably little of that, once it was clear by the early 530s that there would be no children), but even more on mutual respect. They disagreed profoundly on certain issues, and there were always other voices to whom Justinian would listen. But neither doubted that each one's first loyalty was to the other. Both understood that that was the way they must work.

Justinian's moment of prayer at her tomb in 559 was a public proclamation of his undying love. Theodora had changed his life and had helped shape their empire. As she had transformed herself, so she had transformed her world.

12

Legacy

No empress left so profound a mark on the imagination of her people as did Theodora. In the West, she was remembered more as a villain, the persecutor of popes; and her rumored role in the demise of Silverius was asserted in the medieval collection of papal lives known as the *Liber Pontificalis* (*Book of the Popes*) by means of a forged letter to Belisarius, ostensibly from Theodora, ordering him to eliminate the Holy Father.

Aimoin, a monk at Fleury who lived between the later years of the tenth and first years of the eleventh centuries, preserves an alternative and rather fractured version of Theodora's story in his history of the Franks. He tells us that Justinian and Belisarius walked into a brothel where they saw two young sisters, Antonia and Antonina, Amazons by birth who were being sold there as prostitutes. Justinian took up with Antonia, who subsequently interpreted an omen offered by an eagle as showing that Justinian would become emperor. She made him promise that when he took the throne he would not abandon her. When Justin died, the army proclaimed Justinian emperor, and he repaid the faith of his subjects by defeating the Persian king before returning in triumph to Constantinople. Once he returned, Antonia reminded him of his promise when she bribed her way into the palace after he had become emperor. Mindful of their love, Justinian took her to be his wife in the face of outrage from members of the Senate and the population at large. Once Justinian had killed a number of protestors, things calmed down, and here Aimoin's story ends.

Perhaps the most interesting thing about this story, which continues with an account of Belisarius' marriage to Antonina and the conquest of Africa, is that it has no obvious connection to any other written account of Theodora's life. Most likely it reflects oral traditions that survived even when her actual name was forgotten—she was the prostitute who became empress, and her memory was linked, too, with that of the Nika revolt, though not in any way that a reader of Procopius would recognize it.[1]

In areas where the anti-Chalcedonian cause flourished, things were different. In Egypt, people claimed her as their own; in later tradition she was regarded as Egyptian, and Patriarch Timothy of Alexandria was seen as her "spiritual father." Later, in Constantinople, visitors would be shown the Church of St. Panteleemon, which, it was said, was built on the site of a house where she had been employed as a weaver when she first arrived from Paphlagonia, a region bordering on the Black Sea. Others, contemplating an image of her at the Chalke Gate in Constantinople, might recall her as the once shameless hussy who mended her ways. There was also a story of a patrician named Bassus who committed suicide when he found out that she was angry with him. People visiting the Church of the Holy Apostles would be told that this was Theodora's church, upon which she had expended great effort; they would be told how she was inspired by a vision of the Apostles, and how she tricked Justinian so that she could dedicate it before he finished Hagia Sophia (the church was actually dedicated two years after her death).[2]

In Syria, some believed she was the daughter of a priest of Hieropolis whom Justinian had met by chance during Justin's time. Struck by her beauty, he had asked for her hand in marriage, but her father would agree to the match only if he allowed her to keep her anti-Chalcedonian faith. The story was later localized to the town of Daman near Callinicum and linked with her patronage of the monastery of Qadir, where she is said to have dedicated a pillar. A slightly different version of this tale appears in another Syriac source, the *Chronicle of 1234*, which again stresses her beauty and the comfort she brought to the Orthodox Christians when she became empress. Indeed, by the time Michael the Syrian was writing in the twelfth century, she appears as the faithful child of a faithful priest who had never strayed from the path of righteousness—a virtual embodiment of the Syrian Orthodox Church, in fact. Nicephorus Callistus, patriarch of Constantinople in the ninth century, added that her father was from Cyprus, in the belief that Justinian had made it an independent archbishopric—in this he was wrong, having confused Theodora's husband with Justinian II, who ruled from 669 to 711.[3] It was particularly for her piety that she was remembered for centuries after her death; and she was celebrated most strikingly, of course, in the mosaic at San Vitale, for in that image we perceive her beauty, brilliance, and power.

The memory of Theodora these traditions recall was revived on February 12, 2000, by Zakka I, Patriarch of the Syrian Orthodox Church in Damascus. In his encyclical letter of that day, he celebrated the fifteen-hundredth birthdays of Jacob Bar'adai, bishop of Edessa from 543 to 578, and of Theodora, announcing her beatification. She had long since been honored, along with Justinian, as a saint, and the two are celebrated on November 14 in the Eastern Orthodox Church. It is fair to say that Theodora's reputation has been somewhat tweaked over the centuries to play down her religious stance, as the Eastern Orthodox Church has remained firmly Chalcedonian. On the other hand, her actual stance is regarded, and quite reasonably so, as front and center in the Syrian Orthodox tradition; in announcing her beatification, Patriarch Zakka wrote:

> Contemporary, reliable, and honest historians who have full knowledge of her life have provided credible accounts on her origin, early life, pure conduct and her immaculate inner self and thoughts. At the forefront of those was the Syrian Chronicler St. John of Ephesus who had a close relationship with her family and knew her quite well. He wrote about her childhood and her marriage to Justinian the Caesar. The latter had promised her father that he would not force her to change her faith which rejects the Council of Chalcedon and its resolutions. He delivered his promise, indeed. Her staunch enemy, who was also an enemy of truth, the Chronicler Procopius, failed to deny her the glory that she earned with her wisdom and her courage in helping her husband Caesar Justinian. The dishonest and unjust Chronicler Procopius tried to smear her virtuous conduct. But the saying "the sieve cannot conceal the sunlight in the middle of the day" remains true.[4]

In Western Europe, where the Eastern tradition was long unknown, Procopius' vision predominated, even though the *Secret History* remained just that—secret, largely—until 1623, when Nicolò

Alemanni discovered the surviving manuscript in the Vatican Library. When he published the book, Alemanni omitted the racier sections of Chapter 9, which is where Procopius allowed his imagination to run wild on the subject of Theodora's youthful sex life. In publishing the work, Alemanni pointed out that it undermined the positive impression of Justinian's reign from contemporary sources and drew attention to the traditions about his ill treatment of Silverius, and "if anyone doubts what it contains about the infamous upbringing, life and habits of Theodora, (which we cannot translate without embarrassment or anger, which I suspect other readers will feel) there exists today the constitution of Justin which allows the marriage of fallen women to leading men."[5]

The missing bits of Chapter 9 were made available before long, in the *Menagiana*, a collection compiled to illustrate the wit of Gilles Ménage, a late–sixteenth-century French clergyman and intellectual. The impact of the *Secret History* on Justinian's reputation (and that of Theodora) was much as Alemanni suggested. Most significantly, for the future, in his *Considerations on the Causes of the Greatness and the Decadence of the Romans*, published in 1734, Montesquieu states that he prefers the evidence of the *Secret History* to that of Procopius' *Wars*, for two reasons (he lists three, actually): one, the weakness of the empire after Justinian's reign; two, he perceives in the *Codex Justinianus* so many legal changes of a sort he regards as petty that it can only mean that Justinian had put government up for sale. Finally, and most damningly, "that which did the most damage to the state was the project he conceived to reduce all men to the same opinion in matters of religion," which Montesquieu sees as in conflict with the general religious tolerance of the empire at its height. One of Justinian's greatest failings, Montesquieu continues, was that he "put on the stage a woman who had been a long-time prostitute, and she governed with a power that has no parallel in history, introducing into public affairs the passions and fantasies of her gender, she corrupted victories and fortunate successes."[6]

Edward Gibbon, whose *Decline and Fall of the Roman Empire* remains the most widely read book about the later years of the Roman Empire, was influenced in his thinking about Justinian and Byzantine history in general by Montesquieu. Despite his protestations to the contrary, Gibbon seems to have found the tale of Theodora's adventures amusing as well as significant. On one hand, he claims to find the *Secret*

History distasteful, noting that "such base inconsistency must doubtless sully the reputation, and detract from the credit of Procopius." But he also considers that "after the venom of his malignity has been suffered to exhale, the residue of the anecdotes, even the most disgraceful facts, some of which had been tenderly hinted in his public history, are established by their internal evidence, or the authentic monuments of the times." He footnotes at this point the passage from Montesquieu just quoted. Also, attracted by an inaccurate comment of Nicephorus Callistus' Gibbon has obvious fun describing the youthful adventures of the "fair Cyprian, whose merit appeared to justify her descent from the peculiar island of Venus." He points out, in another footnote, that a "learned prelate" he knows likes quoting Procopius on Theodora's routine with the geese. The pages he devotes to Theodora's early life set the tone for his very negative presentation of the Byzantine Empire as a whole, reducing the Byzantine period to a pale reflection of Rome's imperial past.[7]

The Theodora of Montesquieu and Gibbon became the Theodora of the ensuing century. Thus, for instance, the *Secret History* subsequently attracted favorable attention for Ernest Renan, the immensely influential nineteenth-century French orientalist and political theorist. It was Renan who, on one hand, had argued that the life of Jesus should be written (as he himself wrote it) as if he were a man, and on the other hand had argued that Jesus cast off the "taint" of Judaism to become an Aryan; who theorized that the essential element of a nation was that its people shared a common narrative, and, at the same time, argued that Jews constituted a religious group rather than an ethnic group. When he came across the *Secret History*, he found the work to be of the greatest interest. For Renan, Procopius undid the myth of Justinian as the great reformer at the end of antiquity. Instead, Procopius revealed Justinian as a disaster, a ruler who substituted his will for institutions, centralizing all institutions and removing all intermediaries between himself and his subjects. He humiliated men nurtured on the ancient understanding of personal dignity before his domestic servants and deprived them of their self-esteem. The *Secret History* is thus a punishment for those who made suspicion and evil credible.[8] Renan's views on the *Secret History* made him a natural to be invited to one of Paris's big events in 1884, the opening night of Victorien Sardou's *Théodora*.

Sardou's *Théodora*, with Sarah Bernhardt in the title role and music by Jean Massenet, attracted a great deal of attention, to which perhaps the most eloquent testimony is offered by two paintings by Benjamin Constant of Sarah Bernhardt in the role. The first, of 1887, *The Empress Theodora*, showing her slight, bejeweled figure on a throne that appears too big for her. Constant's *The Empress Theodora at the Colosseum* (*L'Impératrice Théodora au Colisée*) of about 1889 shows the red-headed(!) empress as she rests languidly on a couch in a building she never entered in a city she never visited, viewing the carnage of a beast hunt through a partially drawn curtain.[9]

Sardou's play, notable for its massive set pieces if not for the quality of its script, tells the story of Theodora's doomed affair with a nobleman named Andreas, who has fallen in love with her, not knowing who she is as she is wandering the streets in disguise. Andreas, it turns out, is deeply hostile to Justinian and is plotting his assassination, along with that of Theodora, whom he has evidently never seen in the flesh. After a series of increasingly improbable adventures and a massive riot in the Hippodrome, Theodora goes to an old friend who can provide her with

FIGURE 12.1. Benjamin Constant—Theodora on her throne.

© Jean Joseph Benjamin Constant. La Emperatirz Theodora. 1887. Museo Nacional de Bellas Artes.

a love potion with which she can control the men in her life (Andreas being at this point lodged in the palace dungeon). In the last scene, she gives the potion to Andreas, in an attempt to win him back, but the potion is in fact a poison concocted by a woman who has lost her son in the recent fighting and hopes that Theodora will murder Justinian with it. Andreas dies instead, just as the executioners approach Theodora herself, Justinian having in the meantime concluded that she has betrayed him. The executioners strangle her as the curtain comes down.[10]

Sardou's play not only inspired Constant, but created a new popular image for the empress. According to one contemporary, "for a whole week it was the most fashionable tea-table chatter in Paris to debate Theodora's chastity."[11] The play did very well, and there were two hundred performances in Paris, despite complaints in some quarters, as the *New York Times* reported on December 27, 1884:

> Sardou's "Theodora" was produced here this evening with splendid scenery. The dresses of the various characters were chiefly copies from the mosaics in the Church of San Vitale, at Ravenna. Sarah Bernhardt wore a reproduction of Theodora's mantle decked with heraldic peacocks and priceless gems. The music was by Massenet. The first act was received coolly, while the succeeding ones were vociferously applauded. M. [Ernest] Renan and other savants were present. The house was crowded to the ceiling. The critics express various opinions of the production, some accusing Sardou of mutilating history. The majority, however, are loud in their praises of the superb acting of Sarah Bernhardt and the intense dramatic nature of the various situations.[12]

The play was translated into English, opening in London in 1885, then in New York a year later. The French version played in New York in 1887 and 1891, again with Sarah Bernhardt in the leading role, then once more in 1902. We may well imagine that Theodora might not have minded seeing herself portrayed by the most famous actress of the time.

Subsequent Theodoras have been less successful. Xavier Leroux composed an opera, with a libretto by Sardou, that premiered to little acclaim at the Monte Carlo opera house in 1907. There was an epic silent film in 1921, making some use of Sardou's play, it also contains material about Theodora's youth (borrowed from Amoin). Starring

FIGURE 12.2. Sarah Bernhardt in her role as Theodora in Sardou's play.

© Culver Pictures / The Art Archives at Art Resource, NY

Rita Jolivet in the title role, the movie's theme is that Theodora could not move beyond her youth—she remains beautiful and passionate, and it is passion that finally leads to her ruin. Ten reels long, it is said to have cost the staggering sum of three million dollars and to have employed thousands to build its enormous sets; one contemporary reviewer, who thought the sheer spectacle "seldom if ever surpassed," found the story somewhat lacking in body and coherence, others were more positive and the movie played to large crowds.[13] On the stage and in film Theodora remained what she had been since Montesquieu—an idea based upon Procopius' account rather than on the actual person. Her image was not improved in the 1954 *Théodora, impératrice de Byzance*, released in English as *Theodora—Slave Empress*, in which the belly-dancing Theodora captivates Justinian, beats him in a chariot race, and then becomes enmeshed in the world of revolutionary politics. It is only in more recent years, in novels such as Gillian Bradshaw's *The Bearkeeper's Daughter* (told from the perspective of her fictitious son, John) and Stella Duffy's *Theodora: Actress, Empress, Whore* and *The Purple Shroud*, that a character has taken shape that responds to, rather than echoes, Procopius.

A curious side effect of Sardou's play was to inspire the French Byzantinist Charles Diehl, at the beginning of the twentieth century, to produce the first truly original portrait of Theodora. Diehl was the first scholar—and in a work written without footnotes—to successfully make use of non-Greco-Roman traditions to offer a far more nuanced vision of the empress, and to reveal the possibilities available in texts such as John of Ephesus' *Lives of the Eastern Saints*, even though the latter also remains to a degree under the spell of the *Secret History*. Indeed, not much has changed in this respect: as another Byzantinist, Hans-Georg Beck, nicely put it in 1986, we sense that she has remained the victim of Procopius, and, to some extent, Procopius of her.[14]

Diehl's approach was the right one in theory, if not entirely successful in execution. To find the real Theodora, we have to move beyond the framework imposed by Procopius and look at the world in which she lived, as well as at the wealth of material that survives outside the pages of the *Secret History*. The issue confronting any study of her is fundamental to the historiography of any era or any figure from the past: namely, how to deal with a persona that defies convention and stereotype. We cannot doubt that Theodora, an outsider to the establishment that she came to dominate, was a charismatic and politically influential woman in an age when what was mainly expected of an empress was public piety: pious Theodora was, but much else besides. The image of self-possessed power and dignity that radiates from the masterpiece on the walls of San Vitale recalls both the woman herself and the image she intended to bequeath.

Dramatis Personae

Agapetus Pope, May 13, 535, to April 22, 536; responsible for the deposition of Anthimus and summoning the Council of Constantinople.

Amalasuintha Queen of the Ostrogothic kingdom of Italy. Daughter of Theoderic, upon whose death in 526 she became regent for her son, Athalaric. When Athalaric died in 534, she appointed her cousin, Theodahad, her co-ruler. He murdered her, probably in April 535.

Anastasius Eastern Roman emperor, 491–518, born in Dyrrachium; information about his career before 491 is lacking; he was a *silentiarius* in 491, though not a senator. Ariadne chose him to succeed Zeno.

Anicia Juliana Daughter of the emperor Olybrius, she lived from 461 to 527–528. Staunch Chalcedonian, her good works include rebuilding the Church of St. Polydeuktos and improving the Church of St. Euphemia.

Anthemius of Tralles Distinguished mathematician and architect; he was charged with building the new Hagia Sophia after the destruction of the original church in 532.

Anthimus Anti-Chalcedonian Patriarch of Constantinople, 535–536; previously Bishop of Trebizond, in which role he appeared in the Chalcedonian delegation to the meeting concerning doctrine at Constantinople in 532; he was deposed before the second Council of Constantinople in 536, by which he was condemned.

Antonina Wife of Belisarius, friend of Theodora; former actress.

Apion Appointed by Anastasius to organize the military commissariat for the war with Persia, 503–504; correspondent of Bishop Severus of Antioch between 508 and 510; exiled in 510; recalled in 518 and appointed praetorian prefect by Justin, at which time he expressed allegiance to Chalcedonian theology.

Ariadne, Aelia Empress, 474–515. Daughter of Leo I, born before he became emperor in 457; she married Zeno in 466–467; their son Leo II became emperor in 474 with

Zeno as co-emperor; she supported Zeno during the revolt of Basiliscus in 475–476. Upon Zeno's death in 491, she married Anastasius, who succeeded Zeno.

Basiliscus, Flavius Usurper, brother of Verina; *magister utriusque militiae per Thracias* 464–467/8; consul 465; *magister utriusque militiae praesentalis* 468–472(?); botched the invasion of North Africa in 468; led revolt against Zeno in 475–476; although promised his life upon surrendering to Zeno, he was imprisoned under harsh conditions and allegedly starved to death.

Belisarius Justinian's leading general. Native of Germania, modern Sapareva Banya in Bulgaria; *bucellarius* of Justinian; *dux Mesopotamiae* 527–529; *magister utriusque militiae per orientem* 529–531; *magister utriusque militiae per orientem* (?) 532–542; reconquered North Africa (533–534); consul 535; defeated Goths in Italy 540; *comes sacri stabuli* 544–549, campaigning in Italy; *magister utriusque militiae per orientem et comes protectorum* 549–551; 559 commanded operation against the Huns; 562 convicted of participation in a plot against Justinian, exonerated in July 563; died March of 565.

Celer *Magister officiorum,* 503–518. A native of Illyricum, from 503–506, he was one of two commanders of the army in the war with Persia, and played a major role in the negotiations that ended the war. He was an associate of Severus of Antioch and, in 511, played a role in the plot against Macedonius.

Chrysomallo Friend of Theodora.

Comito Theodora's elder sister.

Fredegund Queen of the Franks, wife (probably before 568) of the Frankish king Chilperic; allegedly of very humble origins. She died in 597.

Gelimir King of the Vandals, 530–534, surrendered in March 534; was presented to Justinian in the triumph of 534; pensioned off on estates in central Turkey, where he died.

Germanus Nephew of Justin I, cousin of Justinian, *magister utriusque militiae per Thracias,* 518–527; *magister utriusque militiae praesentalis* and consul 536; commander in Africa 536–539(?); sent to Antioch to defend the city in 540; died in 550.

Hecebolus Theodora's lover; Governor of Cyrenaica under Anastasius; probable father of Theodora's daughter.

Hormisdas Pope, 514–523; many of his letters to senior officials at the court of Constantinople, defending Chalcedonian dogma, have been preserved. He was descended from a wealthy family in Campania.

Hypatius Nephew of Anastasius, consul in 500; *magister utriusque militiae praesentalis* in 503; as *magister utriusque militiae per Thracias* in 513, he was charged with suppressing Vitalian's first revolt, captured by Vitalian and imprisoned in a cage; he was later ransomed. *Magister utriusque militiae per orientem* 516(?)–518, and again in 527–529; executed in 532 for attempted usurpation during the Nika Revolt.

John of Cappadocia Praetorian prefect, 532–541; largely responsible for major fiscal reforms; exiled in 541 through the machinations of Theodora; returned to Constantinople after the death of Theodora in 548.

John of Ephesus Author and bishop, staunch anti-Chalcedonian, his principal works are *The Lives of the Eastern Saints* and the *Ecclesiastical History*. Born near Amida in 507; ordained by John of Tella in 529; in 542 appointed bishop in Asia to convert pagans; consecrated titular Bishop of Ephesus in 558. He was imprisoned, then exiled under Justin II from 571–574; the last datable events in his *Ecclesiastical History* occur in 588. It is likely that he died soon after the last events he records.

John the Lydian Author of three surviving works (composed during his retirement): *On the Months*, *Concerning Signs*, and *Concerning the Magistracies of the Roman State*; a native of Philadelphia in Lydia, he came to Constantinople in 511, entering the office of the praetorian prefect; praised by Justinian for his literary achievement, he was appointed to a professorial chair in Constantinople in 543; he retired in 551–552.

John of Tella Anti-Chalcedonian theologian, lived from 483 to 538 and played a major role in creating an anti-Chalcedonian hierarchy in the 530s.

Justin I Emperor, 518–527; uncle and adoptive father of Justinian, *comes rei militaris* 503–504; *comes excubitorum* 515–518.

Macedonius Patriarch of Constantinople, 495–511, deposed by emperor Anastasius. He died in 517.

Malalas, John Author of an important chronicle; probably a rhetorician, as "Malalas" is derived from the Syriac word for "rhetor" (*malal*). He may have moved from Antioch to Constantinople in the 530s.

Marinus Praetorian prefect 508(?)–512, and commander of Anastasius' fleet in the battle against Vitalian in 515. He was an associate of Severus of Antioch as well as a significant early supporter of Justin, who dismissed him in 518–519.

Marcellinus *Vir clarissimus comes*, author of an important Latin chronicle continuing that of Jerome, from the reign of the Eastern emperor Theodosius I to 534; *cancellarius* of Justinian in Justin's reign.

Narses Eunuch, *cubicularius*, 530–531/2; *spatharius* 532–535/6(?); *praepositus sacri cubiculi* 537/8–554 (or 558/9); commanded in Italy with Belisarius in 538/9; sent to arrest John of Cappadocia in 541; commander in chief in Italy 551–568; won decisive victories over the Goths at Busta Gallorum in 552 and over the Franks at Casilinum in

554; recalled to Constantinople in 568, he returned to Italy, where he died in 574 at the age of ninety-five. He was a staunch ally to Theodora.

Probus, Flavius, nephew of Anastasius, consul, 502; correspondent of Severus of Antioch; avoided being proclaimed emperor by the mob during the Nika Revolt in 532; in 533, his son married Theodora's daughter.

Procopius Writer, his surviving works are *The History of the Wars* (composed between 543 (probably) and 553, *Concerning Buildings* (c. 553), and the *Secret History* (c. 550). Born in Caesarea in Palestine, probably c. 500; served under Belisarius, possibly as *assessor* 527–531; and again with Belisarius during the invasion of Africa; returned to Constantinople in 534; probably also served with Belisarius in Sicily in 535; served briefly in Africa in 536; otherwise, participated in the Italian campaign until Belisarius' recall in 540.

Severus of Antioch Bishop and theologian; major leader of the anti-Chalcedonian movement. Born at Sozopolis in Pisidia, studied at Alexandria and Beirut; converted to Christianity and became leader of an ascetic community; arriving at Constantinople in 508, he played a role in the removal of Patriarch Macedonius; appointed Bishop of Antioch in 512, then removed in 518; exiled, and resided primarily in Egypt until his death in 538.

Silverius Pope, June 8, 536, to March 537; he was deposed for treasonable correspondence with Vitigis during the Gothic siege of Rome. He was the son of Pope Hormisdas.

Sittas Husband of Comito, Theodora's sister; *magister utriusque per Armeniam* 528; *magister utriusque militiae praesentalis* 530–538/9.

Theodahad King of the Ostrogoths, 534–536; deposed for incompetence in the face of Belisarius' invasion, he was assassinated in December 536.

Theoderic, Flavius King of the Ostrogoths, 471–526; ruler of Italy, 493–526; had been *magister utriusque militiae praesentalis* in 476/7–478; he rebelled against Emperor Zeno in 479 and 482; again appointed *magister utriusque militiae praesentalis* in 483–487; in 488 invaded Italy at Zeno's suggestion, murdering King Odovacer in 493 and claiming the kingship of Italy for himself.

Tribonian *Quaestor sacri palatii*, 529–532 and 535–541 (died 541/2); principal author of Justinian's legal reforms.

Verina, Aelia Empress, 457–484; arrested after the failure of the usurpation of her brother Basiliscus in 475–476; wife of Leo I, mother of Ariadne.

Vigilius Pope, 537–555, the son of John, a praetorian prefect under Theoderic. He was defeated in the papal election of 530, after which it was agreed that he would succeed Pope Boniface. Boniface later renounced the agreement, and Vigilius became papal representative in Constantinople. He returned to Rome in 536 and was elected pope after the deposition of Silverius.

Vitalian, Flavius Commander in Thrace where he led a rebellion against Emperor Anastasius, beginning in 513 when he briefly besieged Constantinople; he attacked Constantinople in 514, then withdrew, having received assurances of support for Chalcedonian clergy from Anastasius; *magister militum per Thracias* 514–515; exiled after defeat at Constantinople, then recalled; *comes et magister militum praesentalis* 518–520; consul 520; assassinated on Justin's orders in 520.

Zeno, Flavius Emperor, 474–491; in 466/7 he married Ariadne, by whom he had one son, Leo II, who succeeded Leo I; proclaimed emperor by Leo II on February 9, 474, becoming sole emperor after Leo II's death in November 474; recognized Odovacer as King of Italy in 476; November 474–August 476 exiled during the revolt of Basiliscus; in 488 he encouraged Theoderic to invade Italy.

Zoora Monk from the area of Amida, known for his years spent on top of a pillar; arrived at Constantinople in the early 530s; condemned for his staunch anti-Chalcedonian views at the Council of Constantinople in 536, he died several years later.

Timeline

517(?)	Theodora begins relationship with Hecebolus
518(?)	Birth of Theodora's daughter
518	Death of Emperor Anastasius; Justin I, Justinian's adoptive father, succeeds
520	Murder of Vitalian
521	Expulsion of anti-Chalcedonian community from Amida
522/23	Marriage of Justinian and Theodora
524	Massacre at Najran
525	Conference at Ramla
526	Ethiopian invasion of southern Arabia, defeat of Dhu Nuwas; massive earthquake destroys Antioch
527	Justinian becomes emperor; Theodora becomes empress; death of Justin
528	Establishment of commission to revise Roman laws, headed by Tribonian; earthquake destroys Antioch again; earthquake destroys Soloi Pompeiopolis
529	First edition of the *Codex Justinianus*; Samaritan revolt; persecution of "pagans" at Constantinople; closure of the philosophical school at Athens; legislation against child prostitution; outbreak of war with Persia
530	Battle of Dara
531	Battle of Callinicum; John the Cappadocian becomes praetorian prefect for the first time
532	Nika Revolt; peace with Persia; Council at Constantinople concerning Theopaschitism; John of Cappadocia reappointed as praetorian prefect
533	Invasion of Africa; defeat of the Vandals; completion of Justinian's *Digest* and the *Institutes*, textbook of Roman law; marriage of Theodora's daughter
534	Triumph of Belisarius; second edition of the *Codex Justinianus*
535	Invasion of Italy; appointment of Anthimus as anti-Chalcedonian Patriarch of Constantinople and of Theodosius as Patriarch of Alexandria; mission of Pope Agapetus to Constantinople
536	Death of Pope Agapetus; Council of Constantinople; deposition of patriarchs Anthimus of Constantinople and Theodosius of Alexandria
537	Siege of Rome; deposition of Pope Silverius; election of Pope Vigilius; dedication of Hagia Sophia
540	Belisarius captures Ravenna; Persians capture Antioch; Jacob Baradaeus appointed Bishop of Edessa
541	Bubonic plague in Alexandria; dismissal of John of Cappadocia
542	Bubonic plague in Constantinople
542/3	Dismissal of Belisarius at Theodora's behest
545	Treaty with Persia
548	Death of Theodora
557	Earthquake at Constantinople
562	Conspiracy against Justinian
563	Rededication of repaired Hagia Sophia
565	Death of Justinian

Abbreviations

ACO	*Acta Conciliarum Oecumenicorum*, ed. E. Schwartz and J. Straub (Berlin, 1914–1983)
AJA	*American Journal of Archaeology*
An. Tard.	*Antiquité Tardive*
AW	*Ancient World*
BASP	*Bulletin of the American Society of Papyrologists*
BÉ	*Bulletin Épigraphique*
BIFAO	*Bulletin de l'Institut Français d'Archéologie Orientale*
BMGS	*Bulletin of Modern Greek Studies*
BZ	*Byzantinische Zeitschrift*
CA	*Classical Antiquity*
CQ	*Classical Quarterly*
DOP	*Dumbarton Oaks Papers*
GRBS	*Greek Roman and Byzantine Studies*
HTR	*Harvard Theological Review*
JHS	*Journal of Hellenic Studies*
JLA	*Journal of Late Antiquity*
JNES	*Journal of Near Eastern Studies*
JÖB	*Jahrbuch der Österreichischen Byzantinistik*
JRA	*Journal of Roman Archaeology*
JRS	*Journal of Roman Studies*
JTS	*Journal of Theological Studies*
PBSR	*Papers of the British School in Rome*
PCBE Asie	S. Destephen, *Prosopographie chrétienne du Bas-Empire 2: Prosopographie du Diocèse d'Asie (325–641)*
PCBE Italie	C. Pietri, L. Pietri et al., *Prosopographie chrétienne du Bas-Empire 2: Prosopographie de l'Italie chrétienne (313–641)*
PIR²	*Prosopographia Imperii Romani* (2nd ed.)
PLRE 2	*Prosopography of the Later Roman Empire* vol. 2, ed. J. R. Martindale

PLRE 3	Prosopography of the Later Roman Empire, vol. 3, ed. J. R. Martindale
PO	Patrologia Orientalis
RhM	Rheinische Museum für Philologie
SEG	Supplementum Epigraphicum Graecum
T&MByz	Travaux et Mémoires
TAPA	Transactions of the American Philological Association
ZAC	Zeitschrift für Antikes Christentum
ZPE	Zeitschrift für Papyrologie und Epigraphik

Primary Sources[1]

Aet. Tetrab	Aetius of Amida, Tetrabiblos
Agath.	Agathias, Historiae
Anon. Peri pol.	Anonymous, Peri Politeias
Anon. Sev.	Anonymous, Vita Severi
Anth. Gr.	Anthologia Graeca; books 1–15 = Anthologia Palatina; Book 16 = Anthologia Paludea
AP	Anthologia Paludea
Apul. Met	Apuleius, Metamorphoses
Aug. de Trin.	Augustinus, de Trinitate
Candidus	Candidus (R. C. Blockley, The Fragmentary Classicizing Historians of Late Antiquity [Trowbridge, 1983])
Cass. Var.	Cassiodorus, Variae (ed. Mommsen)
Cedr.	Georgius Cedrenus, Compendium Historiarum
Chron. Pasch.	Chronicon Paschale
CJ	Codex Justinianus
Coripp. Iust	Corippus, In Laudem Iustini Augusti minoris Libri iv (ed. Averil Cameron)
CTh	Codex Theodosianus
Cyr. Scyth. V. Sabae	Cyril of Scythopolis, Vita Sabae (Life of St. Saba)
De Caer.	Liber de Caeremoniis
Evagr. HE	Evagrius, Ecclesiastical History
Greg. Tur. HF	Gregory of Tours, Historia Francorum
Joh. Ant, fr,	John of Antioch, Fragments (ed. Mariev)
Joh. Eph. Chron.	John of Ephesus, Chronicle, ed. W. J. Van Douwen and J. P. N. Land, Joannis Episcopi Ephesi Syri Monophysitae Commentarii de Beatis Orientalibus et Historiae Ecclesiasticae Fragmenta (Amsterdam, 1889)

1. Only the most frequently cited works are listed here, for other works please consult the list of abbreviations in the Oxford Classical Dictionary or in PLRE.

Joh. Eph. HE	John of Ephesus, *Ecclesiastical History*
Joh. Eph. V. SS. Or.	*Lives of the Eastern Saints (Vitae Sanctorum Orientalium)*, ed. E. W. Brooks (PO xvii, xviii, xix; 1923, 1924, 1926): page references are to the continuous numbering in Brooks' edition
Joh. Lyd. de mag.	John Lydus, *De Magistratibus Populi Romani*
Joh. Nik.	John of Nikiu, *The Chronicle of John of Nikiu,* tr. R. H. Charles
Just. *Nov.*	Justinian, *Novellae*
Lib. Pont.	*Liber Pontificalis*
Liberat. *Brev.*	Liberatus, *Breviarium causae Nestorianorum et Eutychianorum*
[Luc.] *As.*	[Lucian] *Asina*
Malal.	John Malalas, *Chronographia* (see J. Thurn, *Joannis Malalae Chronographis* [Berlin, 2000])
Malal. Fr.	John Malalas fragments, ed. Thurn, *Joannis Malalae Chronographis*
Malchus	Malchus of Philadelphia (R. C. Blockley, *The Fragmentary Classicizing Historians of Late Antiquity* [Trowbridge, 1983])
Marcell. com. s.a.	Marcellinus comes, *Chronicle* (ed. Mommsen, *Chronica Minora* II [Berlin, 1894]) (dates by year, *sub anno*)
Mart. Areth.	The Martyrdom of Arethas (ed. M. Detoraki, *Le martyre de Saint Aréthas et des compagnons* [Parin, 2007])
P. Perp. & Fel	*Passio Perpetuae et Felicitatis*
Par. Syn.	*Parastaseis Syntomoi Chronikai* (ed. Cameron and Herrin *Constantinople in the Early Eighth Century:* the Parastaseis Syntomoi Chronikai [Leiden, 1984])
P. Bingen	*Papyri in Honorem Johannis Bingen Octogenarii* (ed. H. Melaerts. Leuven, 2000)
P. Oxy.	*The Oxyrhynchus Papyri*
P. Harrauer.	*Wiener Papyri als Festgabe zum 60. Geburtstag von Hermann Harrauer* (ed. B. Palme. Vienna, 2001)
Procop. *Aed.*	Procopius, *Concerning Buildings*
Procop. *Anecd.*	Procopius, *The Secret History*
Procop. *Bell.*	Procopius, *Wars*
Ps.-Dion. *Chron.*	*Chronicon Pseudo-Dionysium vulgo dictum* (tr. W. Witakowski, Pseudo-Dionysius of Tel-Mahre, *Chronicle,* Part III)
Ps.-Zach. *Chron.*	*The Syriac Chronicle Known as That of Zachariah of Mitylene*
Sel.Pap.	*Select Papyri* (Loeb Classical Library 3 vols. Ed. A.S. Hunt, C.C. Edgar and D.L. Page, 1932–1941)
Sev. Ant. *Ep.*	Severus of Antioch, *Epistulae,* ed. and tr. E. W. Brooks (*PO* 12 [1915], 14 [1919])
Sev. Ant. *Ep. Sel.*	*The Sixth Book of the Select Letters of Severus, Patriarch of Antioch,* ed. and tr. E. W. Brooks (London, 1902–1914)
Sor. *Gyn*	Soranus, *Gynecology*

Tac. *Ann.*	Tacitus, *Annales*
Victor Tonn.	Victor Tonnensis, *Chronicle* (ed. Mommsen)
Theoph. *A.M.*	Theophanes *Chronographia* (dates by year of the world, *Anno Mundi*)
Zach. *V. Sev.*	Zacharias Rhetor, *Vita Severi*
Zon.	Ioannes Zonaras, *Epitome Historiarum*

Notes

Chapter 1

1. For the triumphal route and the purpose of the Capitolium, see C. Mango, "The Triumphal Way of Constantinople and the Golden Gate," *DOP* 54 (2000): 177; for a lucid study of the city based on the regionary catalogues (from which much that follows derives), see J. F. Matthews, "The *Notitia Urbis Constantinopolitanae*," in L. Grig and G. Kelly, eds., *Two Romes: Rome and Constantinople in Late Antiquity* (Oxford, 2012): 81–115; for Theodora's sarcophagus, see P. Grierson, C. Mango, and I. Sevcenko, "The Tombs and Obits of the Byzantine Emperors (337–1042); with an Additional Note," *DOP* 16 (1962): 30–32, 46.

2. G. Dagron, *L'hippodrome de Constantinople: jeux, peuple et politique* (Paris, 2011): 112.

3. There is no direct evidence for the date of her birth other than that she was still five in the reign of Anastasius. I think 495 more likely than 490, because she was still hoping to have a child in 530. C. Foss, "The Empress Theodora," *Byzantion* 72 (2002): 164–165, puts her birth around 490 or a little after, but Foss accepts the existence of her son John, which I do not: see p. 54–55. For her age in the reign of Anastasius, see Procop. *Anecd.* 9.2 and p. 14; for alternative birthplaces, see p. 206 with n. 2.

4. The basic study of the demography of the Roman world remains R. Bagnall and B. W. Frier, *The Demography of Roman Egypt* (Cambridge, 1994); see esp. pp. 84–90 for women; somewhat higher life expectancy emerges from data of the early Byzantine period, see E. Patlagean, *Pauvreté économique et pauvreté sociale à Byzance 4e-7e siècles* (Paris, 1977): 98–99; but those data come from funerary texts, which tend to yield higher figures for life expectancy, see B. W. Frier, "Roman Life Expectancy: The Pannonian Evidence," *Phoenix* 37 (1983): 335–344. For Theodora's grandsons, see p. 54; 201–202.

5. For Theodora's reading to herself, see p. 124, and p. 172 for her preparation of confidential reports before beginning her relationship with Justinian; for women's use of writing in general, see R. S. Bagnall and R. Cribiore, *Women's Letters from Ancient Egypt 300 BC-AD 800* (Ann Arbor, 2006): 5–24, noting that the women we meet in these letters are upper-middle class to upper class; for the relative social standing of Theodora's family, the lower end of the upper middle class would be appropriate; see p. 11 on her father's job, and M. Vesterinen, "Dancers and Professional Dancers

in Roman Egypt" (Ph.D. thesis, Helsinki, 2007): 102–107, showing that the average dancer made roughly 12 drachmas a day while the average worker made roughly one drachma 5 obols, which was basically the subsistence wage. I am extremely grateful to Dr. Vesterinen (now Satama) for allowing me to make use of her work. Dancers would have rated as "cheerleaders" on the distribution list discussed on p. 11, which indicates that at Theodora's family's social level, it might be expected that a girl would be educated. For Perpetua, see *P. Perp. & Fel., passim*; for Claudia Severa at Vindolanda, see http://vindolanda.csad.ox.ac.uk/TVII-291 (Tab. Vindol. II 291); see also R. J. Lane Fox, "Literacy and Power in Early Christianity," in A. Bowman and G. Woolf, eds., *Literacy and Power in the Ancient World* (Cambridge, 1994): 142–143; backwards extrapolation from the very low rates of female literacy in the later Middle Ages would not be appropriate: for these figures, see A. Laiou, "The Role of Women in Byzantine Society," *XVI. Internationaler Byzantinistenkongress* (Vienna 1981), *Akten* I/1= *JÖB* 31/1 (1981): 253–257.

6. Dagron, *L'hippodrome*, 108–115; C. Roueché, *Performers and Partisans at Aphrodisias in the Roman and Late Roman Periods. Journal of Roman Studies*, Monograph 6 (London, 1993): 44–47; for programs, see *P. Oxy.* 2707; *P. Harrauer* 56; *P. Bingen* 128; *P. Oxy.* 5215–18; the fact that Comito and Theodora had careers on the stage may be taken as virtual proof that their mother was an actress, given that the system of public entertainment was based on the hereditary attachment of families to the games, for which see E. Soler, "L'état romain face au baptême et aux pénuries d'acteurs et d'actrices, dans l'antiquité tardive," *An. Tard.* 15 (2007): 51.

7. Alan Cameron, *Circus Factions* (Oxford, 1976): 61–73.

8. Although the monetary amounts involved cannot be compared across time, the status these amounts represent can be, and although the occupations listed in the documents are older than the coinage—based on an eighth-century-AD currency system—we can be pretty certain that the specific cash payments were slotted into a preexisting list and attempted to represent an earlier system.

9. *De Caer.* 2.55 and discussion in Dagron, *L'hippodrome*, 111; M. Hendy, *Studies in the Byzantine Monetary Economy c. 300–1450* (Cambridge, 1985): 503–506.

10. For meat in general, see V. Grimm, "On Food and the Body," in D. S. Potter, ed., *A Companion to the Roman Empire* (Oxford, 2005): 361; on cereals, see P. Garnsey, *Famine and Food Supply in the Graeco-Roman World* (Cambridge, 1988): 43–53; for breads, see A. Dalby, *Flavours of Byzantium* (Totnes, 2003): 2, 25, 27–28, 163 (recipe for *konditon*); and, in general, Patlagean, *Pauvreté économique*, 36–44.

11. G. Dagron, "Poissons, pêcheurs et poissonniers de Constantinople," in C. Mango and G. Dagron, eds., *Constantinople and Its Hinterland: Papers from the Twenty-seventh Spring Symposium for Byzantine Studies*, Oxford, April 1993 (Aldershot, 1995): 57–73; G. C. Maniatis, "The Organizational Setup and Functioning of the Fish Market in Tenth-Century Constantinople," *DOP* 54 (2000): 29–30.

12. On the power of the dancing master, see R. Webb, *Demons and Dancers: Performance in Late Antiquity* (Cambridge, MA, 2008): 43; for the remarriage of widows, see *CJ* 3.8.1; 5.9.1 + 6.56.4 with A. Arjava, *Women and Law in Late Antiquity* (Oxford, 1996): 168–172; see also I. Mueller, "Single Women in the Roman Funerary Inscriptions," *ZPE* 175 (2010): 295–303.

13. Procop. *Anecd.* 9.2–7; for the population of Constantinople in this period, see D. Jacoby, "La population de Byzance à l'époque byzantine: un problème de démographie urbaine," *BZ* 41 (1961): 81–109; A. E. Müller, "Getreide für Konstantinopel.

Überlegungen zu Justinians Edikt XIII als Grundlage für Aussagen zu Einwohnerzahl des Konstantinopels im 6. Jh.," *JÖB* 43 (1993): 1–20, for a higher estimate.

14. D. S. Potter, *Constantine the Emperor* (Oxford, 2013): 259–268.

15. Grierson, Mango, and Sevcenko, "The Tombs and Obits of the Byzantine Emperors," *DOP* 16 (1962): 21–23.

16. See in general Averil Cameron and J. Herrin, *Constantinople in the Eighth Century: The* Parastaseis Syntomoi Chronikai (Leiden, 1984): 99, with note on pp. 212–213 (*Par. Syn.* 37); though for Leo, see K. R. Dark and L. R. Harris, "The Last Roman Forum: The Forum of Leo in Fifth-century Constantinople" *GRBS* 48 (2008): 57–69. Presumably, some memory of Septimius Severus, who had a major impact on the history of Byzantium, is hidden behind Severus, son of Carus.

17. J. H. G. W. Liebeschuetz, *Barbarians and Bishops: Army, Church and State in the Age of Arcadius and Chrysostom* (Oxford, 1990): 111–125; 273–278; see also Alan Cameron and J. Long with a contribution by L. Sherry, *Barbarians and Politics at the Court of Arcadius* (Berkeley, 1993). For Theodora's height, see Procop. *Anecd.* 10.11.

18. *De Caer.* 1.83 for the ceremony.

19. For Athanasius, see D. M. Gwynn, *The Eusebians: The Polemic of Athanasius of Alexandria and the Construction of the "Arian Controversy"* (Oxford, 2007); for the issue of the Gothic conversion, see P. Heather, "The Crossing of the Danube and the Gothic Conversion," *GRBS* 27 (1986): 289–319, although the "Arianism" of Valens is considerably overstated, see D. S. Potter, *The Roman Empire at Bay* AD *180–395*, 2nd ed. (London, 2014): 539–540.

20. For the councils at Ephesus, see esp. F. Millar, *A Greek Roman Empire: Power and Belief under Theodosius II 408–450* (Berkeley, 2006): 159–161, 189–190; M. Gaddis, *There Is No Crime for Those Who Have Christ: Religious Violence in the Christian Roman Empire* (Berkeley, 2005): 303–322; for the Council of Chalcedon, see R. Price and M. Gaddis, *The Acts of the Council of Chalcedon,* 3 vols. (Liverpool, 2005); and, for the events, R. Price, "The Council of Chalcedon (451): A Narrative," in R. Price and Mary Whitby, *Chalcedon in Context: Church Councils 400–700* (Liverpool, 2009): 70–91.

21. To hit on a general term to describe the theological opponents of Chalcedon is difficult, but to use the term "Monophysite" at this period is problematic as there was not a single coherent positive theology, hence my choice of the term "anti-Chalcedonian," which, while not ideal, comes closest to accuracy. On this, see N. Andrade, "The Syriac Life of John of Tella and the Frontier Politeia," *Hugoye: Journal of Syriac Studies* 12 (2009): 200 n. 3; for objections to the use of this term, see V. L. Menze, *Justinian and the Making of the Syrian Orthodox Church* (Oxford, 2008): 2–3; on the slow development of the Monophysite movement after Chalcedon, see Gaddis, *There Is No Crime,* 322–329; for the rationale, see A. Louth, "Why Did the Syrians Reject the Council of Chalcedon?" in Price and Whitby, *Chalcedon in Context,* 107–116.

22. K. G. Holum, *Theodosian Empresses: Women and Imperial Dominion in Late Antiquity* (Berkeley, 1989): 195–228.

23. The text quoted is from the opening of Zeno's *Henotikon,* for which see Evagr. *HE* 3.14, trans. Michael Whitby; for more on the *Henotikon,* see p. 6–67.

24. F. K. Haarer, *Anastasius I: Politics and Empire in the Late Roman World* (Cambridge, 2006): 164–179; M. Meier, *Anastasios I. Die Entstehung des Byzantinischen Reiches* (Stuttgart, 2009): 295–311 (noting on p. 296 that 514 might be a better date for the revolt's outbreak).

25. For the palace of Basiliscus, see *Patr.* 3.124; for the sources, see C. D. Gordon, *The Age of Attila* (with a new introduction and notes by D. S. Potter) (Ann Arbor, 2013): 120–121; Procop. *Bell.* 2.6; and p. 158.

26. For the statues, see *Par. Syn.* 29; 89 (Verina); 14 (Aspar); 67 (Leo); for literary sources see Gordon, *Age of Attila*, 131–146; and for a lucid narrative, A. D. Lee, *From Rome to Byzantium AD 363–565: The Transformation of Ancient Rome* (Edinburgh, 2013): 98–101.

27. *Par. Syn.* 89 (Verina the witch); for the circumstances of Illus' revolt, see H. Elton, "Illus and the Imperial Aristocracy under Zeno," *Byzantion* 70 (2000): 393–407.

28. For the succession of Anastasius, see Haarer, *Anastasius* 1–5; Meier, *Anastasios I*, 63–75.

Chapter 2

1. Malal. 18.43; Malal. Fr. 45, Theoph. A. M. 6026. Procop. *Anecd.* 16.7 with *PLRE* 3: 1051 (Priscus 1); Joh. Eph. *V. SS. Or.*, 189; *Parastaseis* 80 with n. ad loc. (Ariadne is named here, but Theodora is mentioned in the work's next section, making it more than plausible that the author simply confused the two women). It must be admitted that neither of these passages is without issue as evidence: in the case of the passage from John, despite Brooks's translation, widely followed, of *porneion* to mean "brothel," the meaning of the word in Classical Greek, I suspect John may simply be saying that she was an actress; for *pornê* as actress, see p. 39. For John of Ephesus' name, see *PCBE Asie*: 495. A central question in the study of this period is how to deal with the *Secret History* (*Anecdota*). The view of the work taken in the text derives from H. Börm, "Procopius, His Predecessors, and the Genesis of the *Anecdota*: Antimonarchic Discourse in Late Antique Historiography," in H. Börm (ed.), *Antimonarchic Discourse in Antiquity* (Stüttgart, 2015): 14–15, 22–25 (I am extremely grateful to Professor Börm for sharing this with me in advance of publication); and G. Greatrex, "Perceptions of Procopius in Recent Scholarship," *Histos* 8 (2014): 100–101. For other views, see esp. A. Kaldellis, *Procopius of Caesarea: Tyranny, History, and Philosophy at the End of Antiquity* (Philadelphia, 2004): 45–51; B. Rubin, *Die Zeitalter Justinians* (Berlin, 1960): 197–244; F. H. Tinnefeld, *Kategorien der Kaiserkritik in der byzantinischen Historiographie von Prokop bis Niketas Choniates* (Munich, 1971); see otherwise Averil Cameron, "Early Byzantine *Kaiserkritik*: Two Case Histories," *BMGS* 3 (1977): 1–17; for the basic themes of the *Anecdota*, see Averil Cameron, *Procopius and the Sixth Century* (London, 1985): 67–83. For the use of the *Anecdota* as a source, see S. A. Harvey, "Theodora the 'Believing' Queen: A Study in Syriac Historiographical Tradition," *Hugoye: Journal of Syriac Studies* 4 (2001) [2010]: 209–234; C. Foss, "The Empress Theodora," *Byzantion* 72 (2002): 141–176; E. A. Fisher, "Theodora and Antonina in the *Historia Arcana*: History and/or Fiction," *Arethusa* 11 (1978): 253–279; and L. James, *Empresses and Power in Early Byzantium* (Leicester, 2001). L. Brubacker, "Sex, Lies and Intertextuality: The Secret History of Prokopios and the Rhetoric of Gender in Sixth Century Byzantium," in L. Brubacker and J. M. H. Smith, *Gender in the Early Medieval World: East and West 300–900* (Cambridge, 2004): 83–101, argues that all the details of Theodora's early life are invented.

2. Procop. *Anecd.* 12.14–24 (demonic nature of husband and wife); Procop. *Bell.* 6.14.27 (mass rape of Vandal women); *Bell.* 7.1.12 (beauty of Vandal women and

Belisarius abstaining from raping them); *Bell.* 7.8.12 (rape punished by God); *Bell.* 8.10.5–6 (bad consequences for Persians who attempted to rape a Lazican woman); and Fisher, "Theodora and Antonina," 261–262. For sorcery, see Procop. *Anecd.* 27–28. For the pairing of Theodora with Antonina, see Cameron, *Procopius,* 72–74. For Procopius' religious views otherwise, see Procop. *Bell.* 2.12.22–23; *Bell.* 5.3.5–9; *Anecd.* 13.4; with J. A. S. Evans, "Christianity and Paganism in Procopius of Caesarea," *GRBS* 12 (1971): 91–100; G. Greatrex, "Recent Work on Procopius and the Composition of Wars VIII," *BMGS* 27 (2003): 62–67; G. Greatrex, "Perceptions of Procopius in Recent Scholarship," *Histos* 8 (2014): 76–121; see otherwise A. Kaldellis, "The Date and Structure of Procopius' *Secret History* and His Projected Work on Church History," *GRBS* 49 (2009): 607; Kaldellis, *Procopius of Caesarea,* 216–221. For the date of the *Anecdota,* see Börm, "Procopius," 17; Kaldellis, "The Date and Structure," 585–606; and Greatrex, "Recent Work," 60–61; for alternative views dating the work to 558–559, see J. A. S. Evans, "The Dates of Procopius' Works: A Recapitulation of the Evidence," *GRBS* 37 (1996): 309–313; B. Croke, "Procopius' *Secret History*: Rethinking the Date," *GRBS* 45 (2005): 405–431.

3. For Theodora and Comito, see Procop. *Anecd.* 9.9–10; for Theodora's acting career, see *Anecd.* 9.11–13; orifices, *Anecd.* 9.18; with A. Kaldellis, *Procopios: The Secret History with Related Texts* (Indianapolis, 2010): liv. For the son, see *Anecd.* 17. 16–23.

4. Procop. *Anecd.* 9.20–22.

5. Friends, see Procop. *Anecd.* 4.18–19 (Antonina); for Comito, see Malal. 429.16–430.11 (under "528"); Theoph. A. M. 6020; for Chrysomallo, see *Anecd.* 17.33; dungeons, Procop. *Anecd.* 4.4–11.

6. Procop. *Anecd.* 18.5–6, contrast Procop. *Aed.* 1.9.3; and Malal. 18.24 (Theodora and prostitutes); Procop. *Anecd.* 21.0–14 (corrupt practices of governors); Malal. 18.20 (law against corrupt practices); Malal. 18.19; 28; 40; 112 (aid to cities after earthquakes); Procop. *Anecd.* 18.36–45 (natural disasters); Procop. *Anecd.* 22.38, 25.11–12; Malal. 18.117 (coinage); with R. Scott, "Malalas, the *Secret History,* and Justinian's Propaganda," *DOP* 39 (1985): 101–102. Justinian as King of the Demons, see Procop. *Anecd.* 12.18–27.

7. Joh. Eph. *V. SS. Or.,* 24–25—the event is dated to some point before the arrival of Agapetus in February 536; see also p. 175.

8. For Ariadne and the death of Zeno, see Evagr. *HE* 3.29; Theoph. A. M. 5983 (epilepsy only); contrast Malal. 15.16 (death from dysentery); Zon. 14.2.31–35; Cedr. I. 622, 7–23 (entombment). For the development of the tradition, see L. I. Conrad, "Zeno the Epileptic Emperor: Historiography and Polemics as Sources of Realia," *BMGS* 24 (2000): 61–81; for the revolt of Illus, see Marcell. com. s.a. 484; Malal. 15.13; Theoph. A. M. 5972; for Ariadne and the false Leo, see Victor Tonn. s.a. 475; with B. Croke, "Basiliscus the Boy-Emperor," *GRBS* 24 (1983): 81–91; for the murder of Amalasuintha, see p. 139.

9. For Verina as a witch, see *Parastaseis Syntomoi Chronikai* 89; for her continued reach, see Malchus Fr. 20 (Blockley); for Verina's role in Basiliscus' revolt, see Candidus Fr. 1, 52–59 (Blockley).

10. For Geiseric and Eudoxia, see Joh. Ant. Fr. 224 (Mariev); for Honoria and Attila, see Joh. Ant. Fr. 223 (Mariev).

11. See, in general, James, *Empresses and Power,* 10–20, on expectations of empresses; for the death of Silverius, see p. 188.

12. Cass. *Var.* 10.32, 33 (Vitiges' letters about the wedding); L. Traube, *Cassiodori Orationum Reliquiae* in T. Mommsen *Cassiodori Senatoris Variae MGH* Auctorum Antiquissimorum 12 (Berlin, 1894): 465–482 (panegyric on the wedding, especially

interesting on the issue of usurpation); Procop. *Bell.* 3.11.27, 4.10.11–12 (interest in betraying Ravenna because of her abuse by Vitiges); 4.28.5–6 (burns grain supply in the city); see also *PLRE* 3: 851–852 (Matasuentha).

13. Greg. Tur. *HF* 4.28 (Galsuintha); 4.51 (murder of Sigibert); 6.46 (murder of Chilperic, whom Gregory calls the Herod and Nero of his time); *Liber Historiae Francorum* 35 (the story involving Landeric).

14. Greg. Tur. *HF* 5.39 (torture of Clovis's girlfriend and murder of Clovis); Leudast (5.49, 6.32); 6.35 (who tortures women and the prefect Mummolus); 8.31 (murder of bishop Praetextatus); 8.39 (widow of Badegisil); 4.25 (murder of Gutran's son); 4.25 (Charibert's marital career). See also Brubacker, "Sex, Lies and Intertextuality," 92–94; D. R. French, "Maintaining Boundaries: The Status of Actresses in Early Christian Society," *Vigiliae Christianae* 52 (1998): 316–317 and p. 39.

15. For Antonina's adulteries, see Procop. *Anecd.* 1.13, 16–17, 36; witchcraft, see *Anecd.* 1.26, 2.2, 3.2; Tower of Oblivion, see Procop. *Bell.* 1.5.7; with H. Börm, *Prokop und die Perser: Untersuchungen zu den römisch-sasanidischen Kontakten in der ausgehenden Spätantike* (Stuttgart, 2007): 216–217; for hatred of Priscus, see *Anecd.* 16.7; Agath. 2.29.1–30.3; with A. Cameron, *Agathias* (Oxford, 1970): 103–104; R. J. Lane Fox, "The Life of Daniel," in M. J. Edwards and S. Swain, eds., *Portraits: Biographical Representation in the Greek and Latin Literature of the Roman Empire* (Oxford, 1997): 206; J. T. Walker, "The Limits of Late Antiquity," *AW* 33 (2002): 65–67.

16. Agath. 2.29.1–30.3; with Averil Cameron, *Agathias* (Oxford, 1970): 103–104; Agath. 4. 21.5–227 (career of John); *PLRE* 3: 668 (Joannes 68); Evagr. *HE* 5.2 (Justin's head).

17. Joh. Lyd. *de mag.* 3.57–61; with Maas, *John Lydus and the Roman Past: Antiquarianism and Politics in the Age of Justinian* (London, 1992): 27, 81–82.

18. Joh. Lyd. *de mag.* 3.62; for Procopius' portrait, see p. 186.

19. Just. *Nov.* 8 praef. See also p. 184–185. For the circumstances, see E. Stein, *Histoire du bas-empire* 2 (Brussels, 1949): 464.

20. For the language of law, see Joh. Lyd. *de mag.* 3.42.1–3; *De mens frag. Incertae sedis* 7; with Maas, *John Lydus and the Roman Past*, 32 on Latin, and p. 13 on John's resultant insecurity; for John of Tella's literacy requirement, see Joh. Eph. *V. SS. Or.*, 316; for John of Ephesus' literary style, see S. A. Harvey, *Asceticism and Society in Crisis* (Berkeley, 1990): 40; for the importance of different career paths, see H. Börm, "Herrscher und Eliten in der Spätantike," in H. Börm and J. Wiesehöfer eds. *Commutatio und Contentio: Studies in the Late Roman, Sasanian and Early Islamic Near East in Memory of Zeev Rubin* (Düsseldorf, 2010): 179.

21. Procop. *Anecd.* 4.2–12; with p. 192–195.

Chapter 3

1. Just. *Nov.* 105.1 (28 December 537); with R. Webb, *Demons and Dancers: Performance in Late Antiquity* (Cambridge, MA, 2008): 8; *CJ* 5.4.33 (534); for return to the stage as *stuprum* (for the date and context, see T. A. J. McGinn, "The Legal Definition of Prostitute in Late Antiquity," *Memoirs of the American Academy in Rome* 42 [1997]: 103 n. 173); see also M. Vesterinen, *Dancing and Professional Dancers in Roman Egypt* (Ph.D. thesis, Helsinki 2007): 124–127; for *CJ* 5.4.23, the marriage law, see p. 91–93.

2. For Helena, see L. Brubaker, "Memories of Helena: Patterns in Imperial Female Matronage in the Fourth and Fifth Centuries," in L. James, ed., *Women, Men and*

Eunuchs: Gender in Byzantium (London, 1997): 52–75; for Thecla, see G. Dagron and M. D. La Tour, *Vie et miracles de sainte Thècle: texte grec, traduction et commentaire* Subsidia Hagiographica 62 (Brussels, 1978); for women in public life, see A. Laiou, "The Role of Women in Byzantine Society," *JÖB* 31 (1981): 233–260.

3. Vesterinen, *Dancing and Professional Dancers*, 107–110.

4. Choricius Gaz. *On Mimes* 19; see also Procop. *Anecd.* 9.14.

5. *P. Oxy.* 413; *Sel. Pap.* vol. 3 n. 76; H. Wiemken, *Der griechischer Mimus: Dokumente zur Geschichte des antiken Volkstheaters* (Bremen, 1972): 48–80; S. Tsitsiridis, "Greek Mime in the Roman Empire (*P. Oxy.* 413): *Charition* and *Moicheutria*," *Logeion* 1 (2011): 184–232.

6. Choricius Gaz. *On Mimes* 6; for the adulterous wife and Aesop, see *P. Oxy.* 413; *Sel. Pap.* vol. 3 n. 77; Wiemken, *Der griechischer Mimus*, 82–104; and, in general, R. W. Reynolds, "The Adultery Mime," *CQ* 40 (1946): 77–84; and, especially, P. H. Kehoe, "The Adultery Mime Reconsidered," in D. F. Bright and E. S. Ramage, eds., *Classical Texts and Their Traditions: Studies in Honor of C. R. Trahman* (Chico, 1984): 89–106.

7. *CTh* 15.7.12.1 (AD 394); for the new mime script, see *P. Oxy.* 5189.

8. See esp. *CTh* 15.7.13; see also Choricius Gaz. *On Mimes* 17.

9. Passages quoted here are Severus of Antioch, *Hymn* 269 (tr. Brooks) in E. W. Brooks, *James of Edessa: Hymns of Severus of Antioch and Others*; vol. 2, *Patrologia Orientalis* 7.5: 716–717 (adapted); see also, on the Antiochene Olympic games, Cathedral Homily 91 in M. Brière, *Les Homélies Cathédrales de Sévère d'Antioche: Patrologia Orientalis* 25.1: 25–26 (pp. 469–470 in the continuous series); Cathedral Homily 107 in M. Brière, *Les Homélies Cathédrales de Sévère d'Antioche: Patrologia Orientalis* 25.4: 191–192 (pp. 697–698 in the continuous series).

10. The words in quotation marks spoken by the defender of the pantomime are my paraphrase of Jacob's Homily 5: see C. Moss, "Jacob of Serugh's Homilies on the Spectacles of the Theater," *Le Muséon* 48 (1935): 108–109; for the quotations from Jacob, see Moss, "Jacob of Serugh's Homilies," 109; 105 (they appear in the text here in the order indicated). For Choricius, see esp. n. 6 above.

11. *CTh.* 15.7.11; Jacob the Deacon, *Life of St. Pelagia the Whore* 2; 7.

12. Procop. *Anecd.* 9.26; see also Wiemken, *Der griechischer Mimus*, 173–183, on the organization of a troupe; see also P. Cesaretti, *Theodora: Empress of Byzantium*, tr. R. M. Giammanco Frongia (New York, 2004): 76.

13. Procop. *Anecd.* 9.15–16; for the thoroughly literary background to this passage in particular, see B. Baldwin, "Sexual Rhetoric in Procopius," *Mnemosyne* 40 (1987): 150–152.

14. For Nero and Acte, see Tac. *Ann.* 13.12, 46; 14.2; Suet. *Nero* 50; *PIR²* C 1068. For a wide-ranging summary of views on prostitution in the modern world, see C. A. McKinnon, "Trafficking, Prostitution and Inequality," *Harvard Civil-Rights Civil-Liberties Law Review* 46 (2011): 271–309 (I am indebted to Suellyn Scarnecchia for bringing this to my attention); for a different approach, see R. Weitzer, *Legalizing Prostitution: From Illicit Vice to Lawful Business* (New York, 2011): 17–21; for an important comparative study of the economics of Roman prostitution, see T. A. J. McGinn, *The Economy of Prostitution in the Roman World: A Study of Social History and the Brothel* (Ann Arbor, 2004): 14–77.

15. For the legal status of actresses, see McGinn, "The Legal Definition of Prostitute in Late Antiquity," 73–116.

16. For Caenis, see *PIR²* A 888; for Marcia, see *PIR²* M 261. For a vivid evocation of the Roman *demimonde*, see J. Griffin, "Augustan Poetry and the Life of Luxury,"

JRS 66 (1976): 87–105, upon which the use of sixth-century poetry in what follows is modeled.

17. *Anth. Gr.* 5. 302; Joh. Lyd. *de mag.* 3.28; with M. Maas, *John Lydus and the Roman Past* (London, 1992): 31.

18. *Anth. Gr.* 5. 299 (Agathias); 300 (Paul); 272.

19. *Anth. Gr.* 5. 272 (Paul); 222 (Agathias); 217 (Paul); 240 (Macedonius); 255 (Paul sees the girl he wants in public with another man); 256 (Paul and Galatea); 250 (Lais).

20. *Anth. Gr.* 5. 247 (Macedonius); 218 (Agathias); 248 (Paul).

21. Sor. *Gyn.* 60–63; see also A. Roussel, *Porneia: On Desire and the Body in Antiquity*, tr. F. Pheasant (Oxford, 1988): 40–45, on the nature of Soranus' writing.

22. On Aëtius, see J. Scarborough, "Theodora, Aëtius of Amida and Procopius: Some Possible Connections," *GRBS* 53 (2013): 742–762 (I am very grateful to Professor Scarborough for sharing this splendid piece with me in advance of publication). On the treatment of uterine fibrosis, see Aet. *Tetrab.* 16.97; on uterine sores, see Aet. *Tetrab.* 16.92; menstrual cramps, Aet. *Tetrab.* 16.77. For abortion, see Aet. *Tetrab.* 16.18. For the chemical effects of these herbs, I have consulted botanica.com, http://botanical.com/botanical/mgmh/r/rue---20.html (rue); WebMD, http://www.webmd.com/vitamins-supplements/ingredientmono-729-WORMWOOD.aspx?activeIngredientId =729&activeIngredientName=WORMWOOD(wormwood);and WebMD,http://www.webmd.com/vitamins-supplements/ingredientmono-774-MARSHMALLOW.aspx?a ctiveIngredientId=774&activeIngredientName=MARSHMALLOW (marshmallow). For vaginal suppositories and contraceptive potions, see Aet. *Tetrab.* 16.17 (the first recipe quoted is the first in this section; for the medicinal uses of pine bark extract, see Memorial Sloan Kettering Cancer Center, http://www.mskcc.org/cancer-care/herb/pine-bark-extract). See also *Midrash Genesis Rabbah* 23.2, quoted in the next note, for awareness of the effectiveness of herbal contraception.

23. On clitoridectomy, see Aet. *Tetrab.* 16.103; with Scarborough, "Theodora," 755–756; for masturbation, see Aet. *Tetrab.* 16.82; for the rabbinic view, see *Midrash Genesis Rabbah* 23.2 (not very positive—the passage reads: "the men of the generation of the Flood used to act thus: each took two wives, one for procreation, the other for sexual gratification. The former would stay a widow throughout her life, while the latter was given a potion of roots, so that she should not bear, and then she sat before him like a harlot" [tr. H. Freedman and B. Simon, eds., *Midrash Rabbah* (London, 1939) 1: 194]).

24. [Luc.] *As.* 8–9; on which, see also *P. Oxy.* 5204, for issues of the vocabulary; Apul. *Met.* 3.20; Procop. *Anecd.* 9.14–15.

25. For the ages at which actresses might retire, see Vesterinen, *Dancers and Professional Dancing*, 112–113; for Hecebolus, see Procop. *Anecd.* 9.27, 12.30. The history of her daughter's progeny is crucial for determining the chronology of Theodora's early years. It is likely that Theodora's oldest grandson was around fifteen at the time of his wedding in 548 (see further, C. Foss, "The Empress Theodora," *Byzantion* 72 [2002]: 164). Theodora's two other grandsons, Athanasius and John, seem not to have been of marriageable age before her death. For Anastasius, see *PLRE* 3: 63 (p. 63); Athanasius, see *PLRE* 3: 147 (Athanasius 5); for John, see *PLRE* 3.676–677 (Joannes 90); see otherwise T. Pratsch, *Theodora von Byzanz: Kurtisane und Kaiserin* (Stuttgart, 2011): 44. For average ages at marriage, see S. Treggiari, *Roman Marriage: Iusti Coniuges from the Time of Cicero to the Time of Ulpian* (Oxford, 1991): 39–43; 399–400. For a later chronology, see Foss, "The Empress Theodora," 167.

26. For John, see Procop. *Anecd.* 17.16–23.

27. See p. 137–138; 182–183.

28. See, in general, A. Arjava, *Women and Law in Late Antiquity* (Oxford, 1996): 205–210; S. Treggiari, "*Concubinae,*" *PBSR* 49 (1981): 59–81; T. A. J. McGinn, "Concubinage and the Lex Julia," *TAPA* 121 (1991): 335–375. For the issues of children, see esp. Arjava, *Woman and Law*, 208–210.

29. J. G. Pedley, "The History of the City," in R. G. Goodchild, J. G. Pedley, and D. White, *Apollonia: The Port of Cyrene. Excavations by the University of Michigan 1965–1968, Supplements to Libya Antiqua* IV (1976): 11–15, on the site; for the silphium problem (Synesius claims to have been cultivating some in the fifth century despite Pliny's claim of its extinction during the first), see K. Parejko, "Pliny the Elder's Silphium: First Recorded Species Extinction," *Conservation Biology* 17 (2003): 925–927.

30. *SEG* 9.356; with further discussion in J. Reynolds, "The Inscriptions of Apollonia," in Goodchild et al., *Apollonia*: n. 37 (p. 309); and F. K. Haarer, *Anastasius I: Politics and Empire in the Late Roman World* (Cambridge, 2006): 215, and, more generally, 213–216.

31. R. G. Goodchild, "The 'Palace of the Dux'," in Goodchild et al., *Apollonia*: 245–265.

32. Pedley, "The History of the City," 21, pointing out that the city was represented at the Councils of Ephesus in 431 and 449. The province was not represented at Chalcedon.

Chapter 4

1. Procop. *Anecd.* 12.28–30; J. A. S. Evans, *The Empress Theodora: Partner of Justinian* (Austin, 2002): 17–18. A. Kaldellis, *Prokopios: The Secret History with Related Texts* (Indianapolis, 2010): 60 n. 108, notes the awkwardness with which Macedonia fits into the story; in fact, *Anecd.* 9.27, which states that she was destitute, is contradicted by the statement she lost money on the trip back from Pentapolis. P. Cesaretti, *Theodora: Empress of Byzantium,* tr. R. M. Giammanco Frongia (New York, 2004): 133, notes the story's literary aspect.

2. For Theodora's place in this network, see esp. S. A. Harvey, "Theodora the 'Believing' Queen: A Study in Syriac Historiographic Tradition," *Hyoge* 4.2 (2001) [2010]: 224–225; and idem, *Asceticism and Society in Crisis: John of Ephesus and the Lives of the Eastern Saints* (Berkeley, 1990): 78–81; see otherwise V. L. Menze, *Justinian and the Making of the Syrian Orthodox Church* (Oxford, 2008): 211–216.

3. For the pagan intellectual community, see esp. E. J. Watts, *City and School in Late Antique Athens and Alexandria* (Berkeley, 2006).

4. Severus, *Homily* 26 (M. Brière and F. Graffin, *Les Homélies Cathédrales de Sévère d' Antioche. Homilies XXVI-XXXI. PO* 36.4 [Turnhout, 1974]: 544–557); for Antioch in general, G. Downey, *A History of Antioch in Syria from Seleucus to the Arab Conquest* (Princeton, 1961): 496–526, remains a valuable introduction; but see more recently, C. Kondoleon, *Antioch: The Lost City* (Princeton, 2001); and G. W. Bowersock, *Mosaics as History: The Near East from Late Antiquity to Islam* (Cambridge, MA, 2006) is particularly important for the cultural context.

5. On the deposition of Macedonius, see F. K. Haarer, *Anastasius I: Politics and Empire in the Late Roman World* (Cambridge, 2006): 145–156; for the riots of 512, see M. Meier, "Σταυρωθεὶς δι' ἡμᾶς: Der Aufstand gegen Anastasios im Jahr 512," *Millennium* 4 (2008): 157–238, which is fundamental on historiographic questions; and Haarer, *Anastasius*, 156–157.

6. *Anth. Gr.* 15.50, 16.350; with Alan Cameron, *Porphyrius the Charioteer* (Oxford, 1973): 126–130; Haarer, *Anastasius*, 164–175; for the religious and economic dimensions of the revolt, see also D. Ruscu, "The Revolt of Vitalianus and the 'Scythian Controversy'," *BZ* 101 (2008): 773–779.

7. For Severus' childhood, see Zach. *V. Sev.* 11; for the charge that Severus was a pagan in his youth, see Zach. *V. Sev.* 8–10. Severus as much as says he was a pagan up until the point of his conversion, which he attributes to Leontius, see F. Alpi, *La route royale: Sévère d'Antioche et les églises d'orient (512–518)* (Beirut, 2009): 40–45; P. Allen and C. T. R. Hayward, *Severus of Antioch* (London, 2004): 5–11. For the pagans in Alexandria, see Zach. *V. Sev.* 1.7–47; with E. J. Watts, *Riot in Alexandria: Tradition and Group Dynamics in Late Antique Pagan and Christian Communities* (Berkeley, 2010): 2–22; for Beirut, see Zach. *V. Sev.* 58–63; for paganism in this period, see C. P. Jones, *Between Pagan and Christian* (Cambridge, 2014): 126–143.

8. Zach. *V. Sev.* 145–146; Haarer, *Anastasius 1*, 144–145; Allen and Hayward, *Severus of Antioch*, 5–8.

9. For monastic society in Constantinople at this point, see P. Hatlie, *The Monks and Monasteries of Constantinople ca. 350–850* (Cambridge, 2007): 90–132. For Daniel the Stylite, see esp. R. J. Lane Fox, "The Life of Daniel," in M. J. Edwards and S. Swain, eds., *Portraits: Biographical Representation in the Greek and Latin Literature of the Roman Empire* (Oxford, 1997): 201–206. For Clementinus and Eupraxius, see Zach. *V. Sev.* 146, with *PLRE* 2: 303 (Clementinus); and *PLRE* 2: 426 (Eupraxius), with E. W. Brooks, *A Collection of Letters of Severus of Antioch from Numerous Syriac Manuscripts Patrologia Orientalis* 14.1 (Paris, 1920) nn. 65 (very long), 67, 68 (both fragments 67 and 68 are addressed to Eupraxius and Phocas, the latter being *PLRE* 2: 881 [Phocas 4]). For Theodore *PLRE* 2: 1095 (Theodorus n. 54) and the torch, see Sev. Ant. *Ep. Sel.* 10.3; if he is the addressee of 10.5, then he was very well connected, since he is described as the brother-in-law of prefects. For the letter of Conon the *silentiarius*, see Sev. Ant. *Ep. Sel.* 10.4; *PLRE* 2: 307 (Conon 5).

10. For the text of the *Henotikon* quoted here, see Evagr. *HE* 3.14; tr. M. Whitby, *The Ecclesiastical History of Evagrius Scholasticus* (Liverpool, 2000): 147–149.

11. *V. Dan.* 73–83; Joh. Ant. Fr. 234, 3 (Mariev); Evagr. *HE* 3.26; Theoph. A. M. 5971–5972; Candidus Fr. 1, 89–103 (Blockley); *PLRE* 2: 717–718 (Fl. Marcianus 17).

12. For the history of the Trisagion, see S. Brock, "The Thrice Holy Hymn in the Liturgy," *Sobornost* 7.2 (1985): 24–34, esp. p. 29. For the rationale behind the anti-Chalcedonian addition, see Ps.-Zach. *Chron.* 9.49 (G. Greatrex, ed., *The Chronicle of Pseudo-Zachariah Rhetor: Church and War in Late Antiquity*, tr. R. R. Phenix and C. B. Horn, with contributions by S. P. Brock and W. Witakowski (Liverpool, 2011): 265–267; Ps.-Dion *Chron.* s.a. 506–7 9 (W. Witakowski, *Pseudo-Dionysius of Tel-Mahre, Chronicle Part III* [Liverpool, 1996]: 13–15); M. Meier, "Σταυρωθεὶς δι' ἡμας," 211–226, on *Henotikon* politics. The text quoted is from the "Tome of Leo" in the version read at the Council of Chalcedon (Session 2.22), tr. R. Price and M. Gaddis, *The Acts of the Council of Chalcedon: Volume 2* (Liverpool, 2005): 20–21. Note also the important discussion in P. Brown, *Poverty and Leadership in the Later Roman Empire* (Hanover, 2002): 109.

13. For Severus' account of the events of 511, the passage quoted is from the "Coptic First Letter of Severus to Soterichus," translated in J. Dijkstra and G. Greatrex, "Patriarchs and Politics in Constantinople in the Reign of Anastasius (with a Re-edition of *O. Mon. Epiph.* 59," *Millennium* 6 (2009): 241. For Severus' election and

his actions on being elected, see Ps.-Dion. *Chron.* s.a. 511–512; also on the election, Zach. *V. Sev.* 153–154; Anon. *Sev.* 56.

14. For the prospects of each, see the valuable discussion in Greatrex, "Hypatius," 126–135.

15. *De Caer.* 1.92. For the role of silentiaries, see A. H. M. Jones, *The Later Roman Empire 284–602: A Social, Economic and Administrative Survey* (Oxford, 1964): 571–572; for Ariadne's Chalcedonianism, see Cyr. Scyth. *V. Sabae* 145; tr. R. M. Price, *Lives of the Monks of Palestine by Cyril of Scythopolis* (Kalamazoo, 1991): 154; and Harrar, *Anastasius I*, 1–6 (accession), 152 (Ariadne).

16. See, in general, A. A. Vasiliev, *Justin the First: An Introduction to the Epoch of Justinian the Great* (Cambridge, MA, 1950): 68–82, esp. p. 75, on the crucial point that the senate and officials made the initial choice; for Patricius' general unpopularity, see Greatrex, "Hypatius," 126–127.

17. *De Caer.* 1.93.

18. For Amantius and Justin on the day of Justin's accession, see Ps.-Zach. *Chron.* 8.1; (G. Greatrex, ed., *The Chronicle of Pseudo-Zachariah Rhetor*: 281); Malal. 17.2; Theoph. A.M. 6011; Marcell. com. s.a. 518–519; Evagr. *HE* 4.2; for the "conspiracy of Amantius," in addition to the texts cited above, see Procop. *Anecd.* 6.26; for Justin and Amantius, see also G. Greatrex, "The Early Years of Justin I's Reign in the Sources," *Electrum* 12 (2007): 99–105. See also p. 150 on the view that Justin "pushed aside" Anastasius' relatives (Procop. *Bell.* 1.11.1).

19. Joh. Lyd. *de mag.* 3.49.

20. For the function of holy men and women, P. Brown, "The Rise and Function of the Holy Man in Late Antiquity," *JRS* 61 (1971): 80–101, remains foundational.

21. The structure of the sixth-century economy is a matter of considerable debate; the view adopted here tracks most closely that in J. G. Keenan, "Notes on Absentee Landlordism at Aphrodito," *BASP* 22 (1985): 137–169 (especially his concluding remarks on p. 169); see also R. Bagnall, *Egypt in Late Antiquity* (Princeton, 1993): 148–153, favoring a picture adumbrated in J. Gascou, "Les grands domaines, la cité et l'état en Égypte byzantine: recherches d'histoire agraire, fiscale et administrative," *T&MByz* 9 (1985): 1–90. For a different view, see J. Banaji, *Agrarian Change in Late Antiquity: Gold, Labour and Aristocratic Dominance* (Oxford, 2001); and P. Sarris, *Economy and Society in the Age of Justinian* (Cambridge, 2006). The view that the attractions of imperial office undermined traditional civic government is also the central tenet of J. H. G. W. Liebeschuetz, *The Decline and Fall of the Roman City* (Oxford, 2001) (with which I am also in substantial agreement). The problem with the view that Sarris and Banaji put forward is simply that the estates they are talking about are not so large and profitable as they assume; see T. Hickey, *Wine, Wealth and the State in Late Antique Egypt* (Ann Arbor, 2012). For the model of relations adopted here, see especially P. N. Bell, *Social Conflict in the Age of Justinian: Its Nature, Management and Mediation* (Oxford, 2013) esp. pp. 341–345; and E. Patlagean, *Pauvreté économique et pauvreté sociale à Byzance 4e–7e siècles* (Paris, 1977): 203–231.

22. See esp. P. Brown, *Power and Persuasion in Late Antiquity: Towards a Christian Empire* (Madison, 1992): 30–34 (admittedly drawing on earlier evidence) on the local connections of imperial administrators; for the transformation of the Roman aristocracy's economic position in the period after the Vandal conquest, see p. 164–165.

23. For Theodosius II on provisioning, see *CTh* 15.10.1–2; on the *Palmati*, see Cameron, *Circus Factions*, 8; for chariot horses, see *CTh* 15.7.5–6; for the accountant of the theater and the chariot horses, see *CTh* 8.7.21–2.

24. The crucial study of the implantation of circus factions in urban districts is J. Gascou, "Les institutions de l'hippodrome en Égypte byzantine," *BIFAO* 76 (1976): 185–212; see also the important discussion in C. Roueché, *Performers and Partisans at Aphrodisias in the Roman and Later Roman Periods, JRS* Monograph 6 (London, 1993): 147–151; for faction headquarters in provincial cities, see *SEG* 1987 n. 1548; *BE* 1989 n. 993 (Jerash); J. P. Rey-Coquais, *Inscriptions grecques et latines de Tyre* (Beirut, 2006) nn. 127–146; with C. Roueché, "Spectacles in Late Antiquity: Some Observations," *An. Tard.* 15 (2007): 62.

25. G. Greatrex, "The Nika Revolt—A Reappraisal," *JHS* 117 (1997): 64–65; Bell, *Social Conflicts*, 150–160.

26. Malal. 14.2, with Michael Whitby, "The Violence of the Circus Factions," in K. Hopwood, ed., *Organized Crime in Antiquity* (Swansea, 1998): 237.

27. Procop. *Anecd.* 9, with *AP* 16.355.3–6, and Alan Cameron, *Porphyrius the Charioteer* (Oxford, 1973): 163; on Porphyrius, see *AP* 16.338. 5–6; for the Antiochene situation, see Malal. 16.6; for the riot at Antioch, see esp. Cameron, *Circus Factions*, 151, with *PLRE* 2: 215 (Basilus 8) (p. 215); on the dancers, see Malal. 15.12.

28. For Zeno and the Greens, see Malal. 15.15, and *PLRE* 2: 1092 (Theodorus 33) with further references.

29. Malal. *n* 16.4; Mal., Fr. 37; *Chron. Pasch.* p. 608; with Mary Whitby and Michael Whitby, *The Chronicon Paschale AD 284–628* (Liverpool, 1989): 100 n. 316, on the problem of the date; I favor 507 because of Marcell. com. s.a. 507: *seditio popularis in circo facta miles ei armatus obstitit.*

30. Malal. 16.2: with *PLRE* 2: 251 (Calliopius 3); (p. 251); 313 (Constantius 13); 558 (Hierius 6).

31. Malal. Fr. 39; Joh. Ant. Fr. 214c; Marcell. com. s.a. 501; and *PLRE* 2: 313 (Constantinus 13).

32. Bell, *Social Conflict*, 343–344.

33. *PLRE* 2: 248 (Caesaria 2); with Joh. Ant. Fr. 214b, and *PLRE* 2: 2478 (Caesaria 1); *PLRE* 2: 248–249 (Caesaria 3); *PLRE* 2: 763–764 (Misael); for Eupraxius, Phocas, and Conon, see n. 66 n.9.

34. *PLRE* 2: 794 (Oecumenius); see esp. Brooks, *Letters* 1, 2; dealing with priests, see Sev. Ant. *Ep.* 23; for the Conon of Sev. Ant. *Ep. Sel.* 1.45, see *PLRE* 2: 307–308 (Conon 6), the Conon of *Sel. Ep.* 6.1, 10.4; Sev. Ant. *Ep.* n. 78, see *PLRE* 2, 307 (Conon 5) and n. 9 above; for the letter to Celer, see Sev. Ant. *Ep.* n. 21 with *PLRE* 2: 277 (Celer 2 on this letter); 954 (Rufinus 12); for letters to Timostratus, brother of Rufinus, the *magister militum per Thracias* in 515, see *PLRE* 2: 1119–1120 (Timostratus); *PLRE* 2: 954–957 (Rufinus 13); for their father, see *PLRE* 2: 1011 (Silvanus 7); see also Brooks, *Letters,* nn. 19–21; 62; 95 to Isidorus the *comes* (also theological), and *PLRE* 2: 631 (Isidorus 7).

35. Sev. Ant. *Ep.* n. 29 (monks of Isaac); Sev. Ant. *Ep. Sel.* 1.14 (to Antoninus of Beroia); Sev. Ant. *Ep. Sel.* 1.26 (to Solon on obnoxious priests); Sev. Ant. *Ep. Sel.* 1.33 (the situation at Pompeiopolis); Sev. Ant. *Ep. Sel.* 1.35 (to Eustacius on slaves as priests); Sev. Ant. *Ep. Sel.* 1.18; 1.30; 1.32; 1.46 (selecting bishops); Sev. Ant. *Ep. Sel.* 1.27 (ordering magistrates of Anazarbus not to ordain a priest); Sev. Ant. *Ep. Sel.* 1.30 (priests of Apamea quoting a pagan author).

36. For Severus' dealings with martyr shrines and journeys, see P. Allen and C. T. R. Hayward, *Severus of Antioch* (London, 2004): 22–23; for Sergius and Bacchus, see E. K. Fowden, *The Barbarian Plain: Saint Sergius between Rome and Iran* (Berkeley, 1999): 1–26; 106–112; 117–120; Haarer, *Anastasius*, 37–39; and p. 102–104.

37. Procop. *Anecd.* 12.28–30, with p. 86–87, for Theodora's initial meeting with Justinian. For alternative versions in the Syriac tradition, see p. 206. For her admiration of Severus, see Cyril Scyth. *V. Sab.* pp. 172–174; Ps.-Zach. *Chron.* 9.19; for a very different view of her interest in the anti-Chalcedonian community, see p. 94, n. 14. For Severus on the games, see p. 62.

38. For this version of Eve (in a letter written by Severus to a wealthy woman, Procla), see Brooks, *Letters*, n. 92. For the recognized connection with Severus, see previous note.

39. For Severus on social inequality, see Alpi, *La route royale*: 172–178; Brown, *Poverty and Leadership*, 109–110.

40. For the poet/priest, see Sev. Ant. *Ep. Sel.* 1.27.

Chapter 5

1. For the view that Justinian was responsible for Vitalian's murder, see Victor Tonn. s.a. 523; Procop. *Anecd.* 6.27–28. The official explanation for the assassination appears in Theoph. A.M. 519/20; Malal. 17.8; Malal. Fr. 43; Joh. Nik. 90.11–2. For the geography of this part of the palace, see R. Guilland, "Les quartiers militaires," *Byzantinoslavica* 17 (1956): 71–85, and idem, *Études de topographie de Constantinople byzantine* (Amsterdam, 1969): 14–24; J. Kostenec, *Walking through Byzantium: Great Palace Region*, 2nd ed. (Istanbul, 2008): 136. The view of Justin's reign in what follows is heavily influenced by B. Croke, "Justinian under Justin: Reconfiguring a Reign," *Byzantinische Zeitschrift*, 100 (2007): 13–55; see also n. 98–100 for more on the palace's structure.

2. See Stein, *Histoire du Bas-Empire* 2, 275–276.

3. For Justin's early career, see A. A. Vasiliev, *Justin the First*, 42–85; for the Isaurian campaigns, see Haarer, *Anastasius I*, 22–28; for the opening of the Persian war, see G. Greatrex, *Rome and Persia at War* (rev. ed.), *502–532* (Cambridge, 2006): 79–115.; for Diogenianus, see Malal. 16.2, Diogenianus as relative of Ariadne; for his recall, see Malal. 17.3; Theoph. A.M. 6011; see in general *PLRE* 2: 362 (Diogenianus 4).

4. For the battle in the harbor, see Malal. 16.16; for Proclus, see *PLRE* 2: 919 (Proclus 8); probably identical with *PLRE* 2: 919 (Proclus 9) as noted in Whitby and Whitby, *Chronicon Paschale*, 103 n. 324; Apion, see next n.

5. For Apion, see *PLRE* 2: 111–112, and works cited in ch. 4, n. 21 (his Oxyrhynchite estate is the centerpiece for studies of the contemporary economy; for his appointment as praetorian prefect, see Malal. 17.3; *Chron. Pasch.* s.a. 519; Theoph. A.M. 6011; *CJ* 7.63.3a for the date (he is in office by December 1); for Philoxenus, see Malal. 17.3; *Chron. Pasch.* s.a. 519 with *PLRE* 2: 879–880 (Philoxenus 8).

6. For the situation from a Western perspective, see J. Moorhead, *Theodoric in Italy* (Oxford, 1992): 194–120.

7. Procop. *Anecd.* 12.28–32. For the view that this was the way Theodora met Justinian, see also J. A. S. Evans, *The Empress Theodora: Partner of Justinian* (Austin, 2002): 17–18; and idem, *The Power Game in Byzantium: Antonina and the Empress Theodora* (London, 2011): 45–47; M. Angold, "Procopius' Portrait of Justinian," in *ΦΙΛΕΛΛΗΝ, Studies in Honor of Robert Browning* (Venice, 1996): 31–32.

8. For the text, see *ACO* 4.1: 199–200 (it is contained in the records of the seventh session of the Council of Constantinople, May 26, 553). For Theodoret and Nestorius,

see Millar, *A Greek Roman Empire*, 24–25, 183, 200, 222; T. Urbainczyk, *Theodoret of Cyrrhus: The Bishop and Holy Man* (Ann Arbor, 2002): 23–29; Gaddis, *There Is No Crime*, 289, 301–303; for a list of the bribes Cyril provided to the court, see Cyril, *Ep.* 96.

9. For the role of a *defensor*, see Haarer, *Anastasius I*: 209–211.

10. For the pregnancy, see *V. Theod. Syk.* 3.10 with S. Mitchell, *Anatolia: Lands, Men, And Gods in Asia Minor* (Oxford, 1993): 122.

11. For his sleeping and dietary habits, see Procop. *Anecd.* 13.28–29, 15.11; for Justinian and Theopaschitism, see *CA* n. 187 (hostile), 188 and 191 (accepting), 196.6 (quoting Aug. *de Trin.* 2.16); the Scythian monks who were promoting the doctrine in 519–520 were connected with Vitalian, see *CA* 216.5; J. Moorhead, *Theodoric in Italy* (Oxford, 1992): 204–211; Ruscu, "The Revolt of Vitalianus," 779–783.

12. T. Honoré, *Tribonian* (London, 1978): 13–14, on the characteristics of those closest to Justinian; ibid., 64–66, on the issue of Tribonian's possible paganism (see also p. 115–116).

13. *CJ* 5.4.23; on Demosthenes, see *PLRE* 2: 533–534 (Demosthenes 4); Joh. Lyd. *de mag.* 3.42; and C. Foss, "The Empress Theodora," *Byzantion* 72 (2002): 169. The basic analysis of this law remains D. Daube, "The Marriage of Justinian and Theodora: Legal and Theological Reflections," *Catholic University Law Review* 360 (1966–967): 380–399. There is no reason to follow Procopius (*Anecd.* 9.51) and date the law to after Euphemia's death: though, see G. Tate, *Justinien: l'épopée de l'Empire d'Orient* (Paris, 2004): 92–98, who does not believe they met until after 522.

14. On the person-specific nature of the third clause, see Daube, "The Marriage," 393; Alan Cameron, "The House of Anastasius," *GRBS* 19 (1978): 271.

15. Joh. Eph. *V. SS. Or.*, 192–195 (with p. 26, n. 1); see also S. A. Harvey, *Asceticism and Crisis in Society: John of Ephesus and the* Lives of the Eastern Saints (Berkeley, 1990): 78–79. On the date of the expulsions from Amida, see Greatrex, *Rome and Persia at War*, 131; for "palace watching," see Millar, *A Greek Roman Empire*, 192–196. For a different understanding of the expulsions, see V. L. Menze, *Justinian and the Making of the Syrian Orthodox Church* (Oxford, 2008): 213–214, whose views seem difficult to reconcile with Pseudo-Dionysius of Tel-Mahre, *Chronicle* pp. 29, 32; and B. Croke, "Justinian, Theodora and the Church of Saints Sergius and Bacchus," *DOP* 60 (2006): 32–36. For the context of these restorations, see p. 134; 167 with n. 17.

16. Michael the Syrian, *Chron.* 9.24 (V. Chabot, *Chronique de Michel le Syrien* 2 (Paris, 1901): 206–207; the significance of the passage is noted by Evans, *Empress Theodora*, 70.

17. The date of Euphemia's death is nowhere recorded: see *PLRE*, also Croke, "Justinian under Justin," 41–42, for conventional views of her death. For her burial, see P. Grierson, C. Mango, and I. Sevcenko, "The Tombs and Obits of the Byzantine Emperors (337–1042); with an Additional Note," *DOP* 16 (1962): 27, 45–46. The only reason to think that she died as early as 521–522 is the date of the marriage law.

18. *Anth. Gr.* 16.78 (Paul Silentiarius) on her hair color, with P. Cesaretti, *Theodora: Empress of Byzantium*, tr. R. M. Giammanco Frongia (New York, 2004): 296.

19. Malal. 17.12 for the first version (see also Theoph. A.M. 6012); Joh. Nik. 90.16–19 (version 2); Procop. *Anecd.* 9.33–43; on his non-readership in antiquity, see Averil Cameron, *Procopius and the Sixth Century* (Berkeley, 1985): 4; for a fourth version, this one from a palace insider, see Marcell.com. s.a. 523; for a somewhat different take on this material, see Croke, "Justinian under Justin," 39–40. For Theodotus, see *PLRE* 2: 1104–1105 (Theodotus 11).

20. For the title "patrician," see Jones, *Later Roman Empire*, 106; for the ceremony, my version is a simplified rendering of the version found in *De Caer.* 1.47-48, which is from a later period.

21. See J. Bardill, "The Great Palace of the Byzantine Emperors and the Walker Trust Excavations," *JRA* 12 (1999): 216-230.

22. J. Bardill, "Visualizing the Great Palace of the Byzantine Emperors at Constantinople: Archaeology, Text and Topography," in F. Bauer, ed., *Visualisierungen von Herrschaft-frühmittelalterliche Residenzen Gestalt und Zeremoniell* Byzas 5 (Istanbul, 2006): 5-23, on the upper palace; although Bardill corrects his topography in a number of significant ways, there is still great value in the discussion of literary texts in R. Guilland, *Études de topographie de Constantinople Byzantine* 1 Berliner byzantinische Arbeiten 37 (Amsterdam, 1969): 3-93.

23. For the palace as Olympus, see Coripp. *Iust* 3.178-190; for details of the *consistorium*, see Coripp. *Iust* 3.191-209; for the golden couches, see Coripp. *Iust* 3.216.

24. For the trade with India, see G. K. Young, *Rome's Eastern Trade: International Commerce and Imperial Policy 31* BC-AD *305* (London, 2001): 27-89 (trade with India and Africa through Egypt); H. Sidebotham, *Berenike and the Ancient Maritime Spice Route* (Berkeley, 2011); for Farasan, see *AE* 2004 n. 1643.

25. For the contact with Tiberias, see A. Moberg, *The Book of the Himyarites* (Lund, 1924): 7; Malal. 18.15; for the timing of the attack and for the chronology of events, see *Mart. Areth.* 3; for the possible connection with the Koran, see Moberg, *The Book of the Himyarites*: xlvi; for an overview of the sources connected with the massacre, see M. Detoraki, *Le martyre de saint Aréthas et de ses compagnons (BHG 166)* (Paris, 2007): 13-56; and for the events, see G. W. Bowersock, *The Throne of Adulis* (Oxford, 2013): 84-91; for Simon's role, see I. Shahîd, *The Martyrs of Najrân. Subsidia Hagiographica* 49 (Brussels, 1971): 113-178, esp. 159-167; see also Procop. *Bell.* 1.20.

26. For Abraham, see *PLRE* 2: 3 (Abramius); for father, an ambassador to Kinda in central Arabia, see *PLRE* 2: 425 (Euphrasius); for the career of Nonnosus, see Bowersock, *The Throne of Adulis*, 135-142; Croke, "Justinian under Justin," 38-39, suggests that the initiative was Justin's.

27. See, in general, I. Shahîd, "Byzantino-Arabica: The Conference of Ramla AD 524," *JNES* 23 (1964): 115-131.

28. See Greatrex, "Hypatius," 139-140, for a reasonable assessment of his retention in command (and the likelihood that Justin made no significant changes).

Chapter 6

1. Malal. 17.9; *Chron. Pasch.* 613.3-615.4; the events are misrepresented at Procop. *Bell.* 1.11.28-30; see further Vasiliev, *Justin the First*, 264-265; Greatrex, *Rome and Persia at War*, 133-134.

2. Proc. *Bell.* 1.11.23-30; Theoph. A.M. 6013 (displacing the event to 520/1); Greatrex, *Rome and Persia at War*, 135-136; Vasiliev, *Justin the First*, 266-268; Croke, "Justinian under Justin," 43-44 for 525; H. Börm, *Prokop und die Perser*, 312-313; for the earlier negotiation concerning Theodosius II, see Agath. 4.26.6-7; Procop. *Bell.* 1.2.1-10 with A. Cameron, "Agathias on the Sassanians," *DOP* 23/24 (1969/1970): 149; and Börm, *Prokop und die Perser*, 309-310 with whom I am in agreement; see otherwise G. Greatrex and J. Bardill, "Antiochus the 'Praepositus.' A Persian Eunuch at the Court of Theodosius

II," *DOP* 50 (1996): 171–180. For Kavadh and the Mazdakite heresy, see P. Pourshariati, *Decline and Fall of the Sasanian Empire: The Sasanian-Parthian Confederacy and the Arab Conquest of Iran* (London, 2008): 82–83.

3. These details are derived from *De Caer.* 1.43; for the relevance to Justinian, see Croke, "Justinian under Justin," 46–47.

4. For the legend, see Fowden, *The Barbarian Plain*, 7–26; for the walls, see Proc. *Aed.* 2.9.3–9; with Fowden, *The Barbarian Plain*, 93–94, on the date.

5. B. Croke, "Justinian, Theodora, and the Church of Sergius and Bacchus," *DOP* 60 (2006): 49–51, contra J. Bardill, "The Church of Sts. Sergius and Bacchus in Constantinople and the Monophysite Refugees," *DOP* 54 (2000): 1–11.

6. M. Harrison, *A Temple for Byzantium: The Discovery and Excavation of Anicia Juliana's Palace Church in Istanbul* (Austin, 1989): 33–35, 137–142; A. M. Yasin, *Saints and Church Spaces in the late antique Mediterranean: Architecture, Cult and Community* (Cambridge, 2009): 112–115; 138–140.

7. L. Brubaker, "The Age of Justinian: Gender and Society," in M. Maas, *The Cambridge Companion to the Age of Justinian* (Cambridge, 2005): 438–441.

8. L. James, *Empresses and Power in Early Byzantium* (Leicester, 2001): 149.

9. *Anth. Gr.* 1.10.1–13; see further Mary Whitby, "The St. Polyeuktos Epigram (AP 10): A Literary Perspective," in S. F. Fitzgerald, ed., *Greek Literature in Late Antiquity: Dynamism, Didacticism, Classicism* (Aldershot, 2006): 159–188.

10. L. Brubaker, "Memories of Helena," in L. James, ed., *Women, Men and Eunuchs: Gender in Byzantium* (London, 1997): 56.

11. For Anthemius, see *PLRE* Procopius, Anthemius 9 (p. 99); for Anicius Olybrius, see *PLRE* Olybius 3 (p. 795); for Areobindus, see *PLRE* Fl. Areobindus Dagalaiphus Areobindus 1 (p. 143–144).

12. For Daniel, see p. 66; for the monasteries of the period, see P. Hatlie, *The Monks and Monasteries of Constantinople ca. 350–850* (Cambridge, 2007): 133–171.

13. Anon. *Peri pol.* 5.68–76; for the dialogue as a whole, see P. N. Bell, *Three Political Voices from the Age of Justinian* (Liverpool, 2009): 49–79; for the "activation" of group identities, see the important discussion in P. N. Bell, *Social Conflict in the Age of Justinian: Its Nature, Management and Mediation* (Oxford, 2013): 150–160; P. Hatlie, "Monks and Circus Factions in Early Byzantine Political Life," in M. Kaplan, ed., *Monastères, images, pouvoirs et société à Byzance* (Paris, 2006): 21–23; on the role of ceremony, see Averil Cameron, "The Construction of Court Ritual: The Byzantine *Book of Ceremonies*," in D. Cannadine and S. Price, eds., *Rituals and Royalty: Power and Ceremonial in Traditional Societies* (Cambridge, 1987): 106–136.

14. Procop. *Anecd.* 9.31–32; *CJ* 7.37.3 (in 531 on her property rights, showing that, as empress, she had full title); see also Evans, *Theodora*, 29; Diehl, *Theodora*, 57.

15. The work drawn upon in the text is identified in the manuscripts as *How a Man Should Order His Life on a Monthly Basis, by Herophilus the Philosopher* Ἱεροφίλου φιλοσόφου πῶς ὀφείλει διαιτᾶσθαι ἄνθρωπος ἐφ'ἑκάστῳ μηνί; edited in A. Delatte, *Anecdota Atheniensa et alia* II *Textes grecs relatifs à l'histoire des sciences*, Bibliothèque de la Faculté de Philosophie et Lettres de l'Université de Liège 88 (Liège, 1939): 456–466. For a translation, see Dalby, *Flavours*, 161–169.

16. For glossaries, see *P. Oxy.* 5162 (thematic), 5161 (verbs).

17. See the excellent discussion in Maas, *John Lydus*, 67–82; esp. p. 73 on Tribonian; and C. P. Jones, *Between Pagan and Christian* (Cambridge, MA, 2014): 126–144, on differing encounters between pagan and Christian and *passim* for a sensitive discussion

of the often blurred lines between traditional belief and Christianity; for John the Cappadocian, see Procop. *Bell.* 1.24.10; for the *excubitores*, see Joh. Lyd. *de mag.* 3.12.

18. Joh. Lyd. *de mag.* 3.30; for suggestions, see Millar, *A Greek Roman Empire*, 207–214.

19. Joh. Lyd. *de mag.* 3.30. For venal office-holding, see Kelly, *Ruling the Later Roman Empire*, 60–113 and esp. 64–68; 79–81, 100–101 (discussing John); for the list of fees at Timgad, see A. Chastagnol, *L'Album municipal de Timgad* (Bonn, 1978): 75–88; and Kelly, *Ruling the Later Roman Empire*, 138–142.

20. *De Caer.* 1.94–95 for the ceremonies and the date.

21. *De Caer.* 1.43; the ceremony here, from which I have selected the most traditional elements, is of a later date. My inclusion of the True Cross may be incorrect—I include it because it is integral to the ceremony in the triclinium; but the True Cross appears to have been less significant at this period than it would be later. For the date, to April, see next n.

22. The tradition stemming from Malalas states that Theodora was crowned along with Justinian on April 4; see Malal. 17.18; *Chron. Pasch.* p. 616; but this date is most likely wrong; on the other hand, it is not impossible that Theodora's coronation occurred on April 4. At the time of her death on June 28, 548, she is said to have reigned for 28 years and three months. Other sources mention April 1 for the proclamation of Justinian only: see Marcell.com. s.a. 527; Cyril Scyth. *V. Sabae* 68. The crucial evidence, in my view, is provided by the presentation of the coronation in the *Liber de Caeremoniis*.

Chapter 7

1. Procop. *Aed.* 1.1.6–11.

2. For the significance of the new leadership, see G. Tate, *Justinien: l'épopée de l'Empire d'Orient* (Paris, 2004): 351–364, though the details stressed are different from those discussed in this text. For Tribonian, see T. Honoré, *Tribonian* (Ithaca, 1978), 12–13; for the creation of the first edition of the Justinianic Code, see S. Corcoran, "Anastasius, Justinian, and the Pagans: A Tale of Two Law Codes and a Papyrus," *JLA* 2 (2009): 184–185; for Constantine, see *PLRE* 3, 340 (Constantinus 1); for Germanus, see *PLRE* 2, 505–507; he made his reputation as a general while *magister militum per Thracias* from 519 to 527, and was out of office from 527 to 536; for Sittas, see *PLRE* 3, 1160–3; the praetorian prefects from 528 onwards are Atarbius (March–June 528); Menas (June 528–April 529); Demosthenes (September 529–March? 530); Julianus (March 530–February 531). For Menas and Theodora, see p. 139, and see *PLRE* 2, 755 (Menas 5); Demosthenes is the same man who received the law allowing Theodora's wedding: see *PLRE* 2, 353–355 (Fl. Theodorus Petrus Demosthenes); for Atarbius, see *PLRE* 3, 140 (Atarbius); for Julianus, see *PLRE* 3, 729–730 (Julianus 4); the praetorian prefecture attested for Basilides before 528 may have been honorary—he was an associate of Tribonian and a member of the commission to produce the code, see *PLRE* 3, 172–173 (Basilides). On the denigration of the traditional bureaucracy, see M. S. Bjornlie, *Politics and Tradition between Rome, Ravenna and Constantinople: A Study of Cassiodorus and the Variae, 527–554* (Cambridge, 2013): 75–77.

3. Meier, *Das andere Zeitalter Justinians*, 118–136.

4. J. Herrin, *Unrivaled Influence: Women and Empire in Byzantium* (Princeton, 2013): 221–222, on the size of the entourage. For the murder of Amalasuintha, see p. 30; 163–164.

5. Procop. *Anecd.* 15.6–9; Brooks, *Letters* n. 63; see also p. 78; 172.

6. For San Vitale, see D. Deliyannis, *Ravenna in Late Antiquity* (Cambridge, 2010): 240–242; and M. P. Canepa, *The Two Eyes of the World: Art and Ritual Kingship between Rome and Sassanian Iran* (Berkeley, 2009): 118, pointing out that the three Magi on Theodora's robe represent Sasanian client kings coming over to Rome; for the Diptych of Justin, see K. Weitzmann, ed., *Age of Spirituality: Late Antique and Early Christian Art, Third to Seventh Century*. Catalogue of exhibition at the Metropolitan Museum of Art November 11, 1977, through February 12, 1978 (New York, 1979), n. 51; for the San Clemente Theotokos, see J. L. Osborne, "Early Medieval Painting in San Clemente, Rome: The Madonna and Child in the Niche," *Gesta* 20 (1981): 299–310 (esp. pp. 300–304); for the public image of an empress, see L. James, *Empresses and Power in Early Byzantium* (Leicester, 2001): 26–45. For Theodora's hair, see *Anth. Gr.* 16.77 (Paul Silentiarius).

7. For fourth-century panegyrics on empresses, see H. Leppin, "Kaiserliche Kohabitation: Von der Normalität Theodoras," in C. Kunst and U. Riemer, eds., *Grenzen der Macht: zur Rolle des römischen Kaiserfrauen* (Stuttgart, 2000): 81–82; for the development of the position of empress, see H. Leppin, "Theodora und Iustinian," in H. Temporini and G. Vitzthum, *Die Kaiserinnen Roms von Livia bis Theodora* (Munich, 2002): 439–441; for the connection of the empress with Mary, see Averil Cameron, "The Theotokos in Sixth-Century Constantinople: A City Finds Its Symbol," *JTS* 29 (1978): 87–88, 97–98, 104; J. Herrin, *Women in Purple: Rulers of Medieval Byzantium* (Princeton, 2001): 21–22; Herrin, *Unrivaled Influence* (especially on both the connection with Mary and representations of female authority figures): 165, 170–173; C. Pazdernik, "'Our Most Pious Consort Given Us by God': Dissident Reactions to the Partnership of Justinian and Theodora, 525–548," *CA* 13 (1994): 267–268; see, in general, James, *Empresses and Power*, 90–95.

8. Procop. *Anecd.* 30.23 tr. Kaldellis; for a more positive image, see Corippus, *In Justinum* 3.155–169; see also Tate, *Justinien*, 340–343; and Canepa, *Two Eyes of the World*, 150–153, pointing out that Justinian was aligning his own court practice with the Sasanian court, which made it easier to demand prostration from Sasanian emissaries.

9. See Evans, *Theodora*, 22.

10. M. Maas, "History and Ideology in Justinianic Reform Legislation" *DOP* 40 (1986): 25; T. Honoré, *Tribonian* (Ithaca, 1978): 125–126. The text quoted above is *Summa praef.* The confirmation of the code is as printed in P. Krueger, *Codex Iustinianus*, 14th ed. (Zurich, 1967): 2–3.

11. *CJ* 1.5.12; Malal. 18.30, 42; with Stein, *Histoire du Bas-Empire* 2, 369, on the date. For the Samaritan revolt, see Malal. 18.35, 54; Theoph. A.M. 6021; Cyril. Scyth. *V. Sab.* pp. 163, 172–173; Procop. *Anecd.* 11.24–30, 27.8–9, with Stein, *Histoire du Bas-Empire* 2, 287–288; for the Manichaean situation, see also *CJ* 1.5.15; Malal. 18.30, which may suggest that the measure was sparked by a Persian pogrom against Manichaeans, though the formulaic nature of anti-Manichaean legislation may make this an unnecessary assumption; for Manichaean texts in the Roman Empire, see I. Gardner and S. N. C. Lieu, *Manichaean Texts from the Roman Empire* (Cambridge, 2004): 35–45.

12. K. L. Noethlichs, "*Quid possit antiquitatis nostris legibus abrogare*: Politische Propaganda und praktische Politik bei Justinian I im Lichte der kaiserlichen

Gesetzgebung und der antiken Historiographie," *ZAC* 4 (2000): 116–132 = M. Meier, ed., *Justinian: neue Wege der Forschung* (Darmstadt, 2011): 39–57.

13. For Simeon's request, see Joh. Eph. *V. SS. Or.*, 157; for Khusro, see *Anecd.* 2.32–36; for her dealings with the Ostrogothic court, see pp. 139 and 164; for the Nobadae in the Sudan, see Joh. Eph., *HE* 4.6 and p. 190.

14. For negotiations with the Huns, see Ps.-Zach. *Chron.* 9.2.5; Procop. *Bell.* 1.13.2–8; Malal. 18.14; *Chron. Pasch.* 618; Stein, *Histoire du Bas-Empire* 2, 283; for Palmyra, see Malal. 18.2; for al-Mundhir, see Stein, *Histoire du Bas-Empire* 2, 284; for the purpose, see Greatrex, *Rome and Persia at War*, 151 n. 6.

15. Procop. *Aed.* 3.2.10–13; Malal. 18.5 for Martyropolis; for the reorganization of the eastern frontier, see *CJ* 1.29.5; for Comito's marriage in this year, see Theoph. A.M. 6020.

16. For the Church of St. Michael, see Malal. 17.19, and possibly Procop. *Aed.* 2.10.25 (dubiously attributing it to Justinian); with W. Mayer and P. Allen, *The Churches of Syrian Antioch (AD 300–638)* (Leuven, 2012): 99, 109, 160; and G. Downey, *A History of Antioch in Syria from Seleucus to the Arab Conquest* (Princeton, 1974): 545 n. 21; for the Church of the Theotokos, see Malal. 17.19; Procop. *Aed.* 2.10.24; with Mayer and Allen, *The Churches*, 107–109. See L. James, *Empresses and Power*, 148–159 (esp. p. 157 on the "public culture of sovereignty").

17. Malal. 17.19.

18. Ps.-Dion. *Chron.* 29–32.

19. Malal. 18.19 (Soloi Pompeiopolis); Malal. 18.27; Theoph. A.M. 6021 (Antioch). For the ideological significance of natural disasters, see the important discussion in M. Meier, *Das andere Zeitalter Justinians: Kontingenzefahrung und Kontingenzbewältung im 6. Jahrhundert n. Chr.* (Göttingen, 2004): 345–356.

20. Malal. 18.18; see also *CTh* 9.7.6; Zon. 14.7; Procop. *Anecd.* 16.18–22 Theoph. A.M. 6021; Cedr., 645, 17–21; M. Meier *Das andere Zeitalter Justinians*, 201–202, 595; J. J. O'Donnell, *The Ruin of the Roman Empire* (New York, 2008): 211–212. For paganism in this context, see H. Leppin, *Justinian: das christliche Experiment* (Stuttgart, 2011): 105; for the nature of the penalties, see E. Watts, "Justinian, Malalas, and the End of Athenian Philosophical Teaching in AD 529," *JRS* 94 (2004): 174 n. 6. The law of 559 is in Just. *Nov.* 141; for a somewhat different view, see Honoré, *Tribonian*, 14–15.

21. *CJ* 1.11.10, with Corcoran, "Anastasius, Justinian and the Pagans," 198–203; Malal. 18.47, with Watts, "Justinian," 168–182; for the return, see Agath. 2.30.3–4, with Watts, "Justinian," 180; Jones, *Between Pagan and Christian*, 28–29; 30–31; 128–129; for dice oracles, see D. S. Potter, "Lot Oracles from Asia Minor," *JRA* 24 (2011): 764–772.

22. Malal. 18.23; for Theodora's capricious behavior, see Procop. *Anecd.* 17.7–14; for John Lydus, see Joh. Lyd. *de mag.* 3.68.

23. Malal. 18.24; *CJ* 7.15.3 (issued on November 1, 531).

24. Malal. 18.25; Theoph. A.M. 6025; for the discrepancy in the date, see Mango and Scott, *Theophanes*, 286 nn. 2 and 3; and Diehl, *Theodora*, 57, on the salubrious nature of the Pythian spring. For Menas, see *PLRE* 2, 755 (Menas 2); and on bureaucratic corruption, esp. *CJ* 1.53.1 (restricting the ability of officials to purchase properties or receive donations in places where they were serving); *CJ* 7.54.2, 10.8.3 (lowering to 1% a month the interest that debtors must pay after a payment order was issued, though the *fiscus* might charge up to 6%); *CJ* 9.4.6 (with *CJ* 1.3.43, 1.4.22–23, 9.5.2, 9.47.26) stating that only imperial officials could order imprisonment; *CJ* 12.33.6 (slaves should not be taken into the imperial service without their master's knowledge); *CJ* 12.34.1 (barring people doing business with the state from positions in the imperial service).

25. Procop. *Anecd.* 6.1 (Theodora's fears of competition); *Anecd.* 6.3–5 (murder); *Bell.* 5.4.25, stating that Amalasuintha was dead before Theodora's agent arrived; Cassiodorus *Var.*, 10.20, 21; the passage quoted is 10.20.4, tr. Barnish. See also p. 163–164.

26. For the career of John of Cappadocia, see *PLRE* 3 Joannes 11 (pp. 627–635); for John Lydus, see Joh. Lyd. *de mag.* 3.69; with Maas, *John Lydus*, 95.

27. *CJ* 6.40.2 on women's purpose; 5.27.11 on the legitimacy of children born before marriage, promulgated March 18, 531.

28. Cyril Scyth. *V. Sab.* pp. 172–174. For the Samaritan revolt, see n. 11 above.

Chapter 8

1. See M. Meier, "Zur Funktion der Theodora-Rede im Geschichtswerk Prokops (BP 1, 24, 33–37)," *RhM* 147 (2004): 91; A. Cameron, *Procopius and the History of the Sixth Century* (London, 1985): 69; J. A. Evans, *The Empress Theodora: Partner of Justinian* (Austin, 2002): 45.

2. Malal. 18.52 (for the text, reading *kometes* on the basis of Theoph. A.M. 6023, see J. Thurn, *Joannis Malalae Chronographis* [Berlin, 2000] ad loc.); John of Ephesus, *Chron.* s.a. 541.

3. Kavadh's demand needs to be seen in the context of the Persian king's shortage of cash; see esp. P. Pourshariati, *Decline and Fall of the Sasanian Empire: The Sasanian–Parthian Confederacy and the Arab Conquest of Iran* (London, 2008): 78–81; Z. Rubin, "The Reforms of Khusro Anushirwan," in A. Cameron, ed., *The Byzantine and Early Islamic Near East* 3: *States, Resources and Armies* (Princeton, 1995): 227–297.

4. For John, see esp. Joh. Lyd. *de mag.* 3.50 (dating the "demon-driven" troubles caused by him to the 540s); 3.62 (reflecting the charges Theodora manufactured in 541); 3.62; 3.64 on second-term gluttony; 3.65 referring to Just. *Nov.* 82 (August 8, 539); 3.69, Theodora warns Justinian that he must rein John in, failure to do so leading to the Nika Revolt (3.70); see further, Maas, *John Lydus*, 79–81, 87–88, 93–96; and G. Greatrex, "The Nika Revolt: A Reappraisal," *JHS* 117 (1997): 60 n. 5.

5. For Pseudo-Zachariah, see G. Greatrex, ed., with R. R. Phenix and C. B. Horn (tr.), *The Chronicles of Pseudo-Zachariah Rhetor: Church and War in Late Antiquity* (Liverpool, 2011): 343–344 (Ps.-Zach. *Chron.* 9.14).

6. For the legal records alluded to in the text, see for inheritance *CJ* 2.3.30, 2.40.5, 6.37.25, 5.27.12, 6.58.13, 7.15.3 (this might, however, have been part of another measure, if not free-standing, as it concerns the rights of slave concubines); for arbitration *CJ* 3.1.17, 3.1.18; for financial transactions *CJ* 4.18.3, 4.27.3, 4.31.14, 4.39.9, 3.37.27, 8.37.14; for rights of women in marriage *CJ* 6.40.3, 5.11.7, 5.14.11; for adoption 8.37.14, 8.48; for the end of Latin rights *CJ* 7.6.1.

7. Procop. *Bell.* 1.24.1–6; *Dial.* 5.103–107; Procop. *Aed.* 1.1.20; *Anecd.* 12.12.18.32; 9.12; the view of Justinian's essential culpability accords with Greatrex, "The Nika Revolt," 80; see also P. N. Bell, *Social Conflict in the Age of Justinian: Its Nature, Management and Mediation* (Oxford, 2013): 158; for a very different view, see M. Meier, "Die Inszenierung einer Katastrophe: Justinian und der Nika-Aufstand," *ZPE* 142 (2003): 273–300, arguing that Justinian allowed the revolt to develop in order to uncover resistance to his policies.

8. For the movement of people into the city, see Greatrex, "The Nika Revolt," 61, though it is possible that this is backdated from the later 530s, as is the other material

in John Lydus; the appointment of the *quaestor* is in 539, see *N*. 80. For the integrative function of factions, see Bell, *Social Conflict*, 156. For date of the *Akta dia Kalapodion*, see Meier, "Inszenierung," 286.

9. For the date, see Meier in the previous note; for the case that the incident took place on the 10th, see E. Stein, *Histoire du Bas-Empire* 2, 450 n. 1; correcting J. B. Bury, "The Nika Revolt," *JHS* 17 (1897): 106. G. Greatrex, "The Nika Revolt: A Reappraisal," *JHS* 117 (1997): 68 n. 41, offers a good survey of views on the *Akta dia Kalopodion*, which Bury argues is the incident that triggered the riot. For the textual tradition and problems therein, see Mango and Scott, *The Chronicle of Theophanes Confessor* (Oxford, 1997): 281–282 n. 8; I am inclined to agree with the reasoning in Mary Whitby and Michael Whitby, *Chronicon Paschale AD 284–628* (Liverpool, 1989): 113–114; and now the thorough analysis in Meier, "Inszenierung," 278–286; for an alternative view, see Alan Cameron, *Circus Factions* (Oxford, 1976): 322–329. For the inappropriate nature of Justinian's response, see Cameron, *Circus Factions*, 169.

10. The sections quoted are lines 1–5, 23–24, 51–52; for the factions as self-appointed representatives of orthodoxy, see D. S. Potter, "Anatomies of Violence: Entertainment and Violence in the Eastern Roman Empire from Theodosius I to Heraclius," *Studia Patristica* 60 (2011): 61–72.

11. Malal. 18.71; Theoph. A.M. 6024.

12. Malal. 18.71; Procop. *Bell*. 1.24.8–9; with Bury, "The Nika Revolt," 106, 116.

13. Malal. 18.71; Procop. *Bell*. 1.24.11–18.

14. See Procop. *Bell*. 1. 24.19–20; though, see also Meier, "Inszenierung," 295; *Bell*. 1.24.39–40, on the state of affairs with the guard; and *Chron. Pasch.* pp. 624–625, on the role of the *candidatus* Ephraem (for the position of *candidatus*, see A. H. M. Jones, *The Later Roman Empire*) and *Chron. Pasch.* p. 626.12–14 with Whitby and Whitby, *Chronicon Paschale*, 125 n. 363 on the *scholarii* and *excubitores*. For Justin's accession in this context, see Procop. *Bell*. 1.11.1; with H. Börm, "Procopius, His Predecessors and the Genesis of the *Anecdota*," 6–7.

15. *Chron. Pasch.* p. 623, tr. Whitby and Whitby.

16. Malal. 18.71; Theoph. A.M. 6024 on the language of the crowd; for the delivery of the insignia, see Procop. *Bell*. 1.24.22–31. For a different view, see Greatrex, "The Nika Revolt," 76; and Meier, "Inszenierung," 295–296. For the reasons given in the text, I think Hypatius was trying to take the throne.

17. Procop. *Bell*. 1.24.33–37.

18. For Belisarius as a basic source for Procopius, see Meier, "Zur Funktion der Theodora-Rede," 89, 97; for the echo of Dionysius I at Isocrates 6.45 and its possible resonance, see Meier's comments on pp. 99–101; and for the notion that Theodora's speech takes up that of Origen (otherwise unknown, see *PLRE* 3, 957 [Origenes]), see his comments on pp. 103–104. These good observations do not, I think, invalidate the basic point that the portrayal of Theodora's role reflects contemporary understanding of her personality; see also C. D. Pazdernik, "'Our Most Pious Consort Given Us by God': Dissident Reactions to the Partnership of Justinian and Theodora AD 525–548," *CA* 134 (1994): 271–272; for the essential accuracy of the narrative placing Theodora's intervention at this stage, see Greatrex, "The Nika Revolt," 78.

19. *Chron. Pasch.* pp. 624.19–625.8; this incident is central to Meier's view that Hypatius was acting as Justinian's agent and that it was only upon hearing the news that Justinian had fled that his enemies revealed themselves; see Meier, "Inszenierung," 296.

20. Death toll: Marcell.com. s.a. 532: *innumeris passim in circo populis trucidatis*; Malal. Fr. 46, 30,000; Procop. *Bell*. 1.24.54, more than 30,000; Malal. 18.71; *Chron*.

Pasch. p. 627; Theoph. A.M. 6024, 35,000; Joh. Lyd. *de mag.* 3.70, 50,000; and Ps.-Zach. *Chron.* 9.14.b, 80,000. The discrepancy between Malal. Fr. 46 and the epitome is likely to be the result of an error in transmission that influenced the author of the *Chronicon Paschale* and Theophanes. For Theodora's alleged role in the deaths of Hypatius and Pompeius, see Ps.-Zach. *Chron.* 9.14.b; for other punishments, see Theoph. A.M. 6024; Procop. *Bell.* 1.24.57–58.

Chapter 9

1. Procop. *Bell.* 4.9.1–14; Malal. 8.81; Ps.-Zach. *Chron.* 9.17 with M. McCormick, *Eternal Victory: Triumphal Rulership in Late Antiquity, Byzantium and the Early Medieval West* (Cambridge, 1986): 124–129; see also *CJ* 1.17.2 on divine agency; Joh. Lyd. *de mag.* 2.2 on Justinian's regalia, and H. Börm, "Justinians Triumph und Belisars Erniedrigung. Überlegungen zum Verhältnis zwischen Kaiser und Militär im späten Römischen Reich," *Chiron* 43 (2013): 66–75, on the politics of the procession; M. Meier, "Das Ende des Konsulats im Jahr 541/42 und seine Gründe: kritische Anmerkungen zur Vorstellung eines 'Zeitalters Justinians'," *ZPE* 138 (2002): 287–288, on the ideological aspects.

2. *CJ* 1.27.1 (Justinian's thanks); *CJ* 1.27. 6–7, imperial ornaments; Procop. *Bell.* 4.9.5–7, on the treasures from Jerusalem; for other treasures of Solomon said to be with the Visigoths after Alaric's sack, see Procop. *Bell.* 5.12.41–42.

3. For Basiliscus, see A. Merrills and R. Miles, *The Vandals* (Oxford, 2010): 468–469; and p. 22; for Belisarius' campaign, see Merrills and Miles, *The Vandals*, 228–233.

4. For the restorations of senators, see Alan Cameron, "The House of Anastasius," *GRBS* 19 (1978): 264 and p. 272 on the marriage; for the Persian peace, see Procop. *Bell.* 1.22.19; Malal. 459; 110 *centenaria* or 800,000 solidi was roughly 25% of the annual budget: see M. Hendy, *Studies in the Byzantine Monetary Economy c. 300–1450* (Cambridge, 1985): 170; for the strategic issues, see E. Luttwak, *The Grand Strategy of the Byzantine Empire* (Cambridge, 2009): 53–55, 81.

5. Procop. *Bell.* 3.9. 25–26 says that Belisarius was relieved of his command in the East without being told that he was being given the African command, but see Ps.-Zach. *Chron.* 9.17; with G. Greatrex, *Rome and Persia at War* (1998): 194–195; Procop. *Bell.* 3.10.21 says he was given the command just before the expedition departed. For the notion that the Nika Revolt (and financial issues) inspired the invasion, see also B. Rubin, *Das Zeitalter Iustinians* 1 (Berlin, 1960): 320; and idem *Das Zeitalter Iustinians* 2, ed. C. Capizzi (Berlin, 1995): 16; H. Leppin, *Justinian: das christliche Experiment* (Stuttgart, 2011): 152; P. N. Bell, *Social Conflict in the Age of Justinian: Its Nature, Management, and Mediation* (Oxford, 2013): 308.

6. For the liberation of Africa, see *CJ* 1.27.6–7; for Marcellinus, see Marcell.com. s.a. 476; and idem, s.a. 454 (on the death of Aëtius); for the historiographic creation of the year 476 as a pivotal moment in world history, see B. Croke, "A.D. 476: The Manufacture of a Turning Point," *Chiron* 13 (1983): 81–119 = B. Croke, *Christian Chronicles and Byzantine History, 5th–6th Centuries* (Aldershot, 1992) no. V; for Eustathius, see also Evagr. *EH* 2.16. For Marcellinus and Justinian, see J. J. O'Donnell, *The Ruin of Rome* (New York, 2008): 212–216; B. Croke, *Count Marcellinus and His Chronicle* (Oxford, 2001): 28–31, on the implications of Cassiodorus, *Institutiones* 1.17; M. S. Bjornlie, *Politics and Tradition between Rome, Ravenna and Constantinople: A Study of*

Cassiodorus and the Variae, 527–554 (Cambridge, 2013): 90–94. For Jordanes, see *Get.* 292, 295; K. L. Noethlichs, *"Quid possit antiquitatis nostris legibus abrogare*: politische Propaganda und praktische Politik bei Justinian I im Lichte der kaiserlichen Gesetzgebung und der antiken Historiographie," *ZAC* 4 (2000): 117–120 = M. Meier ed. *Justinian: neue Wege der Forschung* (Darmstadt, 2011): 40–43. See also A. Glotz, "Die 'Ende' des Weströmischen Reiches in der frühbyzantinischen syrischen Historiographie," in A. Glotz, H. Leppin, and H. Schlange-Schoningen, eds., *Jensits der Grenzen: Beiträge zur spätantiken und frühmittelalterlichen Geschichtsschreibung* (Berlin, 2009): 169–198.

7. R. Syme, "The *Titulus Tibertinus,"* *Akten des VI Internationalen Kongress für Griechische und Lateinische Epigraphik* (Munich, 1972): 585–601 (reprinted in R. Syme, *Roman Papers,* ed. A. Birley [Oxford, 1984]: 869–884) is masterful on the issues involved; for Dionysius, see also M. Meier *Das andere Zeitalter Justinians: Kontingenzefahrung und Kontingenzbewältung im 6. Jahrhundert n. Chr.* (Göttingen, 2004): 463–466; for the computational issues, see G. Declercq, "Dionysius Exiguus and the Introduction of the Christian Era," *Sacris Erudiri* 41 (2002): 165–246. Dionysius did not date the Incarnation to December 25, but rather to March 25.

8. Procop. *Bell.* 3.10.1–22.

9. For the circumstances, see Procop. *Bell.* 3.10.22–24; 11.22 (revolt against Gelimir in Tripolitania); 3.10.25–11.1.22–24; Ps.-Zach. *Chron.* 9.17 (revolt in Sardinia); Procop. *Bell.* 3.14.5, 5.3.22–24 (relations with the Goths); E. Stein, *Histoire du Bas-Empire* 2 (Brussels, 1949): 313–314; H. Leppin, *Justinian: das Christliche Experiment* (Stuttgart, 2011): 152. For the size of the expeditionary force, see M. Whitby, "Recruitment in Roman Armies from Justinian to Heraclius (ca. 565–615)" in Averil Cameron, ed., *The Byzantine and Early Islamic Near East* 3: *States, Resources, Armies* (Princeton, 1995): 101.

10. Procop. *Bell.* 4.8.1–8.

11. For Peter's embassy, see Procop. *Bell.* 3.3.30, 4.17–22; Cass. *Var.* 10.19–20, 22–24; Procop. *Anecd.* 16.2–4; with *PLRE* 3: 994–998 (Petrus 6); and p. 139 and next n.

12. For the anti-Vandal lobby, see Procop. *Bell.* 4.5.8; Ps.-Zach. *Chron.* 9.; with Stein, *Histoire du Bas-Empire,* 312; and B. Croke, "Justinian's Constantinople," in M. Maas, *The Cambridge Companion to the Age of Justinian* (Cambridge, 2005): 75; Merrills and Miles, *The Vandals,* 230. For the Vandal use of Arianism as a way of creating a unified governing group, see Y. Modéran, "Une guerre de religion: les deux églises d'Afrique à l'époque vandale," *An. Tard.* 11: 27; Y. Modéran, "L'établissement territorial des Vandales en Afrique," *An. Tard.* 10 (2002): 87–122; for the Gothic situation, see especially P. Brown, *Through the Eye of a Needle: Wealth, the Fall of Rome, and the Making of Christianity in the West, AD 350–550* (Princeton, 2012): 454–477; for Dominicus, see Ps.-Zach. *Chron.* 9.18a; with G. Greatrex et al., *The Chronicle of Pseudo-Zachariah Rhetor: Church and War in Late Antiquity* (Liverpool, 2011): 365 n. 278, on his identity; and J. Moorhead, *Theoderic in Italy* (Oxford, 1992): 171–172, on the context. For the political situation in Italy, see Cass. *Var.* 10.20–21 (Theodahad and Gudeliva to Theodora, usually taken as referring to her interest in Amalasuintha's demise, though it is highly unlikely that the Gothic royals would be discussing what was in fact an official *casus belli* in this way at this point, see Procop. *Bell.* 5.4.30 and Wolfram's observation of the context, *History of the Goths,* 339); Cass. *Var.* 10.22 (Theodahad most likely mentioning Pope Agapetus' forthcoming trip to Justinian). For the chronology of Peter's journey, see Stein, *Histoire du Bas-Empire* 2, 339 n. 1. He left Constantinople in December of 534, arriving in Italy in March 535. See, in general, Stein, *Histoire du Bas-Empire* 2: 338–339; Amalasuintha may have been murdered on April 30, 535;

the war broke out in June. See also J. A. S. Evans, *The Empress Theodora: Partner of Justinian* (Austin, 2002): 63–66.

13. The formulation at the end of the paragraph is borrowed from Stein, *Histoire du Bas-Empire* 2: 336; see also J. Moorhead, *Justinian* (New York, 1994): 72–74, for a succinct summary of the differences between the Vandal and Ostrogothic states. See also J. J. O'Donnell, *Cassiodorus* (Berkeley, 1979): 33–102; and idem, *The Ruin of the Roman Empire* (New York, 2008): 107–147; Bjornlie, *Politics and Tradition*, 7–33; and the important discussion of the *edictum Theoderici* in S. D. W. Lafferty, *Law and Society in the Age of Theoderic: A Study of the* Edictum Theoderici (Cambridge, 2013): 22–100. For persecution by the Vandals, see *CJ* 1.27.2–5; Procop. *Bell.* 3.8.3–4 (possibly influenced by the preceding); and Victor Vitensis, *Historia Persecutionis* (admittedly earlier); Merrills and Miles, *The Vandals*, 141–176, 204–227, correcting the overall picture somewhat; but Modéran, "Une guerre de religion," 37–42, shows that the Vandals took control of major religious centers. For the churches in Ravenna, see D. Deliyannis, *Ravenna in Late Antiquity* (Cambridge, 2010): 139–144; for circuses, see J. H. Humphrey, *Roman Circuses: Arenas for Chariot Racing* (Berkeley, 1986): 632–633.

14. Brown, *Through the Eye of A Needle*, 476.

15. For the Gothic War, see H. Wolfram, *History of the Goths*, tr. T. J. Dunlap (Berkeley, 1988): 339–362; for the impact of the war, see esp. C. Wickham, *Framing the Early Middle Ages: Europe and the Mediterranean 400–800* (Oxford, 2005): 644–656.

16. For the development of the Palace of Hormisdas, see Proc. *Aed.* 1.10.4, which requires modification in light of Harvard syr. 22.3 and the discussion in B. Croke, "Justinian, Theodora and the Church of Saints Sergius and Bacchus," *DOP* 60 (2006): 40–44; contra J. Bardill, "The Church of Saints Sergius and Bacchus in Constantinople and the Monophysite Refugees," *DOP* 54 (2000): 9–10; though I suspect as suggested in the text that Bardill is correct that the community began to take shape prior to 536 because Anthimus used it as a hideout in that year: see p. 176 n. 29; see also S. Brock, "The Conversations with the Syrian Orthodox under Justinian (532)," *Orientalia Christiana Periodica* 47 (1981): 92 n. 17 (reprinted in S. Brock, *Studies in Syriac Christianity: History, Literature and Theology* [Brookfield, VT, 1992]). For the community there, see Joh. Eph. *V. SS. Or.*, 475 (number of residents), 476 (arrangement of rooms), 479–480 (visits by Theodora and Justinian).

17. For the restorations and possible connection with the Persian war, see W. H. C. Frend, *The Rise of the Monophysite Movement* (Cambridge, 1972): 261–262, 264; Croke, "Justinian, Theodora and the Church of Saints Sergius and Bacchus," 34–35; for Theodora and the monastery of Qadir near Callinicum, see Michael Syrus, *Chron.* 18.5. The passage quoted is Ps.-Zach. *Chron.* 9.15b, the translation minimally adapted from Greatrex et al., *The Chronicle of Pseudo-Zachariah Rhetor*, 347.

18. The passage quoted is Harvard syr. 12.36, tr. Brock, "The Conversations," 108. For John of Tella and the cross-border community, see N. J. Andrade, "The Syriac Life of John of Tella and the Frontier Politeia," *Hugoye: Journal of Syriac Studies* 12 (2009): 199–234. Ps.-Zach. *Chron.* 9.16 preserves Severus' letter.

19. *CJ* 1.1.6, tr. Coleman-Norton, *Roman State and Christian Church*, n. 636.

20. *D. Tanta*, tr. Coleman-Norton; with F. Millar, "Rome, Constantinople and the Near Eastern Church under Justinian: Two Synods of C.E. 536," *JRS* 98 (2008): 66–67.

21. For the amiable Justinian, see Joh. Eph. *V. SS. Or.*, 478. For regulations on priestly conduct, see *CJ* 1.3.46 (530) (succession); 1.3.44 (530) (clerical celibacy); 1.3.41 (528), 1.3.47 (530) (episcopal celibacy); 1.4.34 (534) (on gambling). On the dichotomy in John of Ephesus between Justinian the persecutor and Justinian the discussant, see

C. Pazdernik, "'Our Most Pious Consort Given Us by God': Dissident Reactions to the Partnership of Justinian and Theodora," *CA* 13 (1994): 260–261; Harvey, *Asceticism and Society in Crisis*, 90.

22. A. van Roey and P. Allen, *Monophysite Texts of the Sixth Century: Orientalia Lovaniensia Analecta* 56 (Leuven, 1994): 16–20, on the theology; the sections quoted in this text are lines 96–97, 111–113, and 211–215. See also van Roey and Allen, *Monophysite Texts*, 66–71, on Constantine of Laodicea.

23. Proc. *Anecd.* 10.15.3; see also Evagr. *HE* 4.10; with Pazdernik, "'Our Most Pious Consort,'" 264–266, pointing out that Evagrius' comment, unlike Procopius', is limited to ecclesiastical affairs; see also P. Allen, *Evagrius Scholasticus the Church Historian* (Louvain, 1981): 182–183; H. Leppin, "Kaiserliche Kohabitation: Von der Normalität Theodoras," in C. Kunst and U. Riemer, eds., *Grenzen der Macht: zur Rolle des römischen Kaiserfrauen* (Stuttgart, 2000): 75–85; and p. 199.

24. Joh. Eph. *V. SS. Or.*, 428–439; with Pazdernik, "'Our Most Pious Consort Given Us by God'": 277–278; S. A. Harvey, *Asceticism and Crisis in Society: John of Ephesus and the* Lives of the Eastern Saints (Berkeley, 1990): 84–88; idem, "Theodora the 'Believing' Queen: A Study in Syriac Historiographical Tradition," *Hugoye: Journal of Syriac Studies* 4 (2001)[2010]: 228–229, especially on the point of the acceptability of Mare's rudeness to Theodora. See, in general, L. James, *Empresses and Power in Early Byzantium* (Leicester, 2001): 86–87, on the tendency of an empress to deal with individuals rather than systems.

25. Joh. Eph. *V. SS. Or.*, 19 (the beginning of his career before the Hun invasion of 515); he was the pupil of the holy man Habib (see pp. 17–18); for the meeting with Justinian, see pp. 21–24; for Theodora's intervention, see pp. 24–25; with Harvey, *Asceticism and Crisis*, 84–85, 88–89; for the connection between this story and one in Procopius, see p. 29. The date of Zoora's arrival in Constantinople cannot be determined with precision, but John (p. 26) says that he had been in the city for some time before Agapetus' arrival. For his ignorance of Scripture, see *ACO* 3, 148 *Collectio Sabbaitica* 5 n. 69 (*epistula episcoporum Orientalium et Palestinorum ad Agapetum*). For the scene envisaged when Zoora arrived at Constantinople, compare F. Nau, "Textes Monophysites 6: Le Colloque Monophysite de 531," *Patrologia Orientalis* 13 (1919): 193. See also Harvey, "Theodora the 'Believing' Queen: A Study in Syriac Historiographical Tradition," 227–228.

26. For Zoora's baptisms, see *ACO* 3, 131 *Collectio Sabbaitica* 5 n. 59 (*libellus monachorum ad Iustinianum*); *ACO* 3, 138 *Collectio Sabbaitica* 5 n. 68 (*libellus monachorum ad Agapetum*); with Menze, *Justinian and the Making of the Syrian Orthodox Church*, 189; for the reason this was an issue, see Nau, "Textes Monophysites," 193–194; Elias, *Life of John of Tella*, 59; 139 *Collectio Sabbaitica* 5, n. 68; for Zoora's equation with Severus, see *ACO* 3, 138.

27. The letter is in Brooks, *Letters* n. 63 (on which, see p. 124); for the circumstances under which it was written, see p. 176. For definitions of faction, see, for instance, *ACO* 4: 169 for "those who left the Church with Severus"; Victor Tonn. s.a. 529, 537, 543, on "the faction of Theodora."

28. Harvard syr. 12.40.

29. Anthimus was resident in the Palace of Hormisdas before his election, suggesting a prior connection with Theodora; see *ACO* 3, 175 *Collectio Sabbaitica* 5, n. 113 (*Gesta Synodi de Anthimo*). The view taken in this text tracks with that of Frend, *Rise*, 268–271; see also T. Pratsch, *Theodora von Byzanz: Kurtisane und Kaiserin* (Stuttgart, 2011): 68–69; Cameron, "The House of Anastasius," 272; see otherwise Menze, *Justinian*

and the Making of the Syrian Orthodox Church, 199–201. John of Ephesus' compressed account of the five patriarchs does not suggest that Theodora played a role in his selection, but he does have Theodora rescue him from Justinian's anger (Joh. Eph. *V. SS. Or.*, 385–386).

30. For the situation in Alexandria, see B. Evetts, *History of the Coptic Patriarchs of Alexandria: Patrologia Orientalis* 1 (1907): 195–196; Victor Tonn. s.a. 538, 539; Liberat. *Brev.* 20; but see Anon. *Sev.* 75, which has Severus convert Anthimus after his election.

31. *ACO* 3, 138 *Collectio Sabbaitica* 5 n. 68 (*libellus monachorum ad Agapetum*); Joh. Eph. *V. SS. Or.*, 26; see also *ACO* 3, 32–33 *Collectio Sabbaitica* 53 n. 12 (*libellus monachorum ad imperatorem*); *ACO* 3, 43 *Collectio Sabbaitica* 5 n. 14 (*libellus monachorum ad Menam*); *ACO* 3, 181 (*Gesta Synodi de Anthimo* 128). For the importance of Dalmatios, see Hatlie, *Monks and Monasteries*, 93.

32. Liberat, *Brev.* 21 (the threat), confirmed by Cass. *Var.* 11.13; see also Procop. *Bell.* 5.6; Stein, *Histoire du Bas-Empire* 2: 343, on the peace offer; and, in general, Leppin, *Justinian: das Christliche Experiment*, 163.

33. Joh. Eph. *V. SS. Or.*, 30–31; for the date, see *Lib. Pont.* 59.

34. For awareness of Anthimus' location, see *ACO* 3, 159–160, 175; *Collectio Sabbaitica* 5 n. 80, 82, 113 (*Gesta Synodi de Anthimo*); Just. *Nov.* 42 for the ban on Severus' writings; Joh. Eph. *V. SS. Or.*, 35 has Zoora join Theodosius at Dercus; he does not mention the Palace of Hormisdas as the site of relocation, but he says the two of them were moved together. For Theodosius, see Joh. Eph. *V. SS. Or.*, 326–327 (life of John of Hephaestopolis).

Chapter 10

1. For the date of the dedication, see Theoph. A.M. 6030; Procop. *Aed.* 1.1.71 on divine guidance; for Paul Silentiarius' *Descriptio Sanctae Sophias*, see Mary Whitby, "The Occasion of Paul the Silentiary's *Ekphrasis* of S. Sophia," *CQ* 35 (1985): 218–219; R. Macrides and P. Magdalino, "The Architecture of Ekphrasis: Construction and Context of Paul the Silentiary's Poem on Hagia Sophia," *BMGS* 12 (1988): 54–60, 68–69.

2. The translation of lines 58–65 in this text is from P. N. Bell, *Three Political Voices from the Age of Justinian* (Liverpool, 2009): 192; see also Macrides and Magdalino, "The Architecture," 71, on other reminders of Theodora in the church.

3. *CJ* 1.4.33; 5.4.29 (marriages of actresses); Just. *Nov.* 51 (forbidding people to take sureties) (September 1, 537); for consultation with Theodora, see Just. *Nov.* 8.1; see also Procop. *Anecd.* 17.24–26. See also J. A. S. Evans, *The Empress Theodora: Partner of Justinian* (Austin, 2002): 37–38; C. Diehl, *Theodora: Empress of Byzantium*, tr. S. R. Rosenbaum (New York, 1972): 139–142.

4. Just. *Nov.* 117.8 (ban on divorce without specific cause); Just. *Nov.* 117.9 (man living openly with other women). Note also Just. *Nov.* 117.6 validating marriages between women of low status and men of high status; the recipient of the Novel is Theodotus (see n. 18), who was also the recipient of Just. *Nov.* 115, which included a provision allowing parents to disinherit children who they discovered are non-Chalcedonian.

5. Procop. *Aed.* 1.9.1–10; *Anecd.* 17.5–6; B. Baldwin, "Three-Obol Girls in Procopius," *Hermes* 120 (1992): 255–257.

6. Procop. *Aed.* 1.10.5 (statue of Justinian); 16–19 (painting at the Chalke Gate); for the negotiation of terms with the Goths, see Procop. *Bell.* 6.29.19–20; with E. Stein, *Histoire*

du Bas-Empire (Paris, 1949) 2: 367; J. Moorhead *Justinian* (New York, 1994): 85 n. 20. For Belisarius' recall, see the contradictory stories at Procop. *Bell.* 2.19.49 and *Anecd.* 3.4. For the additional revenues from John's *aerikon*, which amounted to roughly 30 *kentenaria* or 216,000 solidi, see M. Hendy, *Studies in the Byzantine Monetary Economy c. 300–1450* (Cambridge, 1985): 237–238, which is out of a total budget of roughly 550 *kentenaria* or 4 million solidi: on which, see Hendy, *Studies*, 170–171. The bulk of the new revenue (increasing revenue from 440 *kentenaria* = 3,200,000 *solidi*) was the result of the acquisition of Africa; see further, E. Stein, *Histoire du Bas-Empire* 2 (Brussels, 1949): 463–480; see also Michael Whitby, "Recruitment in Roman Armies from Justinian to Heraclius (ca. 565–615)," in Averil Cameron, ed., *The Byzantine and Early Islamic Near East* 3: *States, Resources, Armies* (Princeton, 1995): 103.

7. In theory, the eastern army should have had a strength of 105,000 men (see Agath. 5.13); see otherwise, Whitby, "Recruitment in Roman Armies," 73–74, 101–103. For the defenses of Antioch and the sack of the city, see G. Downey, *A History of Antioch in Syria from Seleucus to the Arab Conquest* (Princeton, 1961): 533–546. For the strength of the army in the next year, see Procop. *Bell.* 2.16 (vague, but presumably fewer than the 30,000 men at Procop. *Bell.* 2.24.16, with Whitby, "Recruitment in Roman Armies," 74). For the sack of Antioch, see Procop. *Bell.* 2.8.1–13; Joh. Lyd. *de mag.* 3.54; *V. Sym. Styl. Iun.* 57 (in G. Greatrex and S. N. C. Lieu, *The Roman Eastern Frontiers and the Persian Wars* Part II: *363–630* [London, 2002]: 104–105). For Bouzes' conduct, see Procop. *Bell.* 2.6.1–8, esp. 3–4; it appears that the total strategic reserve was just 300 men; see Procop. *Bell.* 2.6.9. For the chariot races, Procop. *Bell.* 2.11.31–35; for Seleucia, see Procop. *Bell.* 2.11.1; for Edessa, see Procop. *Bell.* 2.12.31–34; for the new Antioch, see Procop. *Bell.* 2.14.1–4.

8. Procop. *Bell.* 2.16.1–19.49; Evag *HE* 4.25–26.

9. Just. *Nov.* 8.1.

10. Joh. Lyd. *de mag.* 3.76 (index only); Malal. Fr. 47 (an extended version preserved in *Excerpta de insidiis*, 172–173); Procop. *Bell.* 1.25; *Anecd.* 1.14, 2.15–16, 17.38–45; for the chronology, see Just. *Nov.* 109 (7 May 542) and Just. *Nov.* 111 (1 June 542 to Theodotus as praetorian prefect); Honoré, *Tribonian* (Ithaca, 1978), 61.

11. *PLRE* 3: 490 (Florus); *PLRE* 2: 881–882 (Phocas 5); *PLRE* 3: 977 (Paulus 11); *PLRE* 3: 1316 (Thomas 9).

12. Procop. *Bell.* 1.25. 4–10.

13. Procop. *Bell.* 1.25. 11–18; with *Anecd.* 2.15–16, on the oaths Antonina swore; see also J. A. S. Evans, *The Power Game in Byzantium: Antonina and the Empress Theodora* (London, 2011): 148; see also Stein, *Histoire du Bas-Empire* 2: 481.

14. Procop. *Bell.* 1.25.23–30.

15. Procop. *Bell.* 1.25.31–44.

16. For a view of the portrait of Theodora here, see Averil Cameron, *Procopius and the Sixth Century* (London, 1985): 70. For Silverius, see Procop. *Anecd.* 1.14; Liberatus, *Brev.* 21; *Lib. Pont.* 60, which leaves out the detail about Ravenna, but directly cites Liberatus, so it cannot be considered independent testimony. For Silverius' deposition in 537, see Procop. *Bell.* 5.25.13 and Prokop. *Anekdota: Geheimgeschichte des Kaiserhofs von Byzan*, tr. O. Veh with introduction and notes by M. Meier and H. Leppin (Düsseldorf/Zurich, 2005): 284. For a different approach to Liberatus' narrative, see B. Rubin, *Das Zeitalter Iustinians* 2, ed. C. Capizzi (Berlin, 1995): 109–110; J. Moorhead, *Justinian* (New York, 1994) 81–82.

17. Procop. *Anecd.* 17.38–45; Malal. Fr. 47 (*Excerpta de Insidiis*): 172–173 with A. Kaldellis, *Prokopios: The Secret History with Related Texts* (Indianapolis, 2010): 80 n. 169.

18. For Theodotus, see Procop. *Anecd.* 22.1–2, 6; with *PLRE* 3: 1301 (Theodotus 3); note also Just. *Nov.* 112 emending but not replacing the procedure implemented in Just. *Nov.* 96 (issued to John); for Peter Barsymes, see *Anecd.* 22.3–38, *PLRE* 3: 999–1002 (Petrus 9).

19. For the embassy to the Nobadae, see Joh. Eph. *HE* 4.6; with E. Stein, *Histoire du Bas-Empire* (Paris, 1949): 2; W. H. C. Frend, *The Rise of the Monophysite Movement* (Cambridge, 1972): 298–299; for Aphrodito, see *P. Cairo Maspero* I 67024; with *PLRE* 3: 734–735 (Julianus 13); and P. Sarris, *Economy and Society in the Age of Justinian* (Cambridge, 2006): 108.

20. For the plague, see "Centers for Disease Control and Prevention: Plague," http://www.cdc.gov/plague/symptoms/index.html; for significant contemporary descriptions, see esp. Procop. *Bell.* 2.22; Ps.-Dion. *Chron.* s.a. 543/4, esp. p. 95; with P. Horden, "Mediterranean Plague in the Age of Justinian," in M. Maas, ed., *The Cambridge Companion to the Age of Justinian* (Cambridge, 2005): 139–146; R. Sallares, "Ecology, Evolution, and the Epidemiology of Plague," in L. K. Little, ed., *Plague and the End of Antiquity: The Pandemic of 541–750* (Cambridge, 2007): 231–289. For the plague's chronology, see M. G. Morony, "'For Whom Does the Writer Write?': The First Bubonic Plague Pandemic According to Syriac Sources," in Little, ed., *The Plague and the End of Antiquity*, 59–86; and the important discussion in Whitby, "Recruitment in Roman Armies," 92–99. For magic and medicine, see G. Vikan, "Art, Medicine and Magic in Early Byzantium," *DOP* 38 (1984): 65–86; on sin and medicine, see V. Nutton, "From Galen to Alexander: Aspects of Medicine and Medical Practise in Late Antiquity," *DOP* 38 (1984): 7–9; for ascetics and physicians, see especially J. Duffy, "Byzantine Medicine in the Sixth and Seventh Centuries: Aspects of Teaching and Practice," *DOP* 38 (1984): 21–27; S. A. Harvey, "Physicians and Ascetics in John of Ephesus: An Expedient Alliance," *DOP* 38 (1984): 87–93.

21. Edict 7 praef. With Honoré, *Tribonian*: 63 generally, and 62–64 on his death; Procop. *Bell.* 2.22.10–11 (apparitions); 2.22.34 (recovery for no obvious cause); 2.23.5–10 (Theodore); Ps.-Dion. *Chron.* s.a. 543/4 p. 83 (town on the Egyptian border); p. 95 (death toll in Constantinople); p. 97 (death during transaction); pp. 100–101 (Theodore); p. 102 (house filled with the dead); pp. 108–109 (demons as monks). The description of the symptoms is from Evagr. *HE* 4.29; with P. Allen, *Evagrius Scholasticus the Church Historian* (Louvain, 1981): 190–194, on literary aspects of this and other plague narratives; for Theodore, see *PLRE* 3: 1248 (Theodorus 10).

22. H. Kennedy, "The Justinianic Plague in Syria and the Archaeological Evidence," in Little, ed., *Plague and the End of Antiquity*, 87–95; P. Sarris, "Bubonic Plague in Byzantium," in Little, ed., *Plague and the End of Antiquity*, 119–132; for the opposite case, see J. Durliat, "La peste du Vᵉ siècle: Pour un nouvel examen des sources byzantines," in V. Kravari, C. Morrison, and J. Lefort, eds., *Hommes et richesses dans l'empire byzantin* (Paris, 1989–91): 107–119.

23. Procop. *Bell.* 2.23.20; *Anecd.* 4.1 (Justinian's illness); Procop. *Bell.* 7.32.9; *Anecd.* 12.20; 13.28–30; 15.11–12 (stressing that he was readily accessible); see also *Anecd.* 13.1; Just. *Nov.* 8 *praef.; Anecd.* 1513–1515, inaccessibility of Theodora.

24. Procop. *Anecd.* 4.2–12; for Peter, see *PLRE* 2: 870–871 (Petrus 27); for John, see *PLRE* 3: 665–667 (Joannes 64).

Chapter 11

1. For the end of the consulship, see M. Meier, "Das Ende des Konsulats im Jahr 541/42 und seine Gründe: kritische Anmerkungen zur Vorstellung eines 'Zeitalters Justinians'," *ZPE* 138 (2002): 277–299 whose view is largely followed here; but see also Alan Cameron and D. Schauer, "The Last Consul: Basilus and his Diptych," *JRS* 72 (1982): 126–145, who stress the issues of cost and competition. On the significance of the plague for the Italian war, see E. Luttwak, *The Grand Strategy of the Byzantine Empire* (Cambridge, 2009): 85–92.

2. For John's reception, see Joh. Eph. *V. SS. Or.*, 155, 157–158; with Alan Cameron, "The House of Anastasius," *GRBS* 19 (1978): 272–273.

3. Joh. Eph. *V. SS. Or.*, 530–539; with W. H. C. Frend, *The Rise of the Monophysite Movement* (Cambridge, 1972): 287–288; see otherwise V. L. Menze, *Justinian and the Making of the Syrian Orthodox Church* (Oxford, 2008): 224–226.

4. G. Fisher, *Between Empires: Arabs, Romans and Sasanians in Late Antiquity* (Oxford, 2011): 56–58; Frend, *The Rise of the Monophysite Movement*, 285–286; for efforts to arrest Jacob, see Joh. Eph. *V. SS. Or.*, 493.

5. For John's ordination, see Joh. Eph. *V. SS. Or.*, 503; for his exploits, see Joh. Eph. *V. SS. Or.*, 479; *HE* 3.36–37 (pagans); Ps.-Dion. *Chron.* s.a. 861 p. 125 (Montanists), possibly reflected in Procop. *Anecd.* 11.23; with F. R. Trombley, "Paganism in the Greek World at the End of Antiquity: The Case of Rural Anatolia and Greece," *HTR* 78 (1985): 330–336; with caveats in S. Mitchell, *Anatolia: Land, Men and Gods in Anatolia* 2 (Oxford, 1993): 117–119; see also S. A. Harvey, *Asceticism and Society in Crisis: John of Ephesus and the* Lives of the Eastern Saints (Berkeley, 1990): 82, 99, 105–107; for the possibility of atrocities, see Procop. *Bell.* 11.23 describing a mass suicide; see also, for the end of the plague, Just. *Nov.* 122.

6. Procop. *Anecd.* 15.36; for the construction of the palace at Herion, see Procop. *Aed.* 1.11.16–17; for the whale, see Procop. *Bell.* 7.29.9–16; with J. R. Papadopoulos and D. Ruscillo, "A *Ketos* in early Athens: An Archaeology of Whales and Sea Monsters on the Greek World," *AJA* 106 (2003): 206.

7. Procop. *Anecd.* 5.8–10.

8. Procop. *Anecd.* 4.37; 5. 20–22 for Anastasius; for her other grandsons, see p. 54 n. 25; for the cause of death, see Malal. 18.104; Theoph. A.M. 6040; Procop. *Bell.* 3.30.4; Victor Tonn. s.a. 549: *Theodora Augusta Chalcedonensis synodi inimica canceris plaga corpore toto perfusa, vitam prodigiose finivit.*

Chapter 12

1. *Lib. Pont.* 60 (Silverius); Aimoin, *Libri V de gestis Francorum* 2.5; for the connection, see N. Alemanni, *Procopii Caesarensis VI ANEKΔOTA Aracana Historia, Qui est Liber Nonus Historicorum ex Bibliotheca Vaticana* (Lyons, 1623): 32.

2. Joh. Nik., 87 (relationship with Timothy); *History of the Patriarchs of the Coptic Church of Alexandria,* ed. Evetts, 195 (origin in Alexandria); Nicephorus Callistus, *HE* 17.28 (Cyprus); with J. A. Evans, *The Empress Theodora: Partner of Justinian* (Austin, 2002): 13; for the statue at the Chalke Gate, see *Par. Syn.* 80 (identified here as "Ariadne," but see the note in A. Cameron and J. Herrin, *Constantinople in the Early*

Eighth Century: the Parastaseis Syntomoi Chronikai [Leiden, 1984]: 271–2); *Patria* 3.93 (Paphlagonian origin); *Patria* 4.31 (Church of the Holy Apostles); *Patria* 3.50 (Bassus).

3. Michael Syrus, *Chron.* 9.20 (Manbij); from Daman, see Michael Syrus *Chron.* 11.5; *Chron. 1234* LV; and S. A. Harvey, "Theodora the 'Believing' Queen: A Study in Syriac Historiographical Tradition," *Hugoye: Journal of Syriac Studies* 4 (2001)[2010]: 214–217, 231–232.

4. For the encyclical letter of February 12, 2000, see Syrian Orthodox Resources: Lent Encyclical, February 12, 2000, retrieved from http://sor.cua.edu/Personage/PZakka1/20000212MYBurdconoTheodora.html. For St. Theodora the Empress in the Eastern Orthodox Church, see Orthodox Church in America: St. Theodora the Empress (commemorated November 14), retrieved from http://oca.org/saints/lives/2014/11/14/103302-st-theodora-the-empress (asserting that she abandoned her Monophysite ways when she became empress). See also G. B. Behnam, *Theodora*, tr. M. Moosa (Piscataway, 2007). Moosa translates the play written by Behnam, Bishop of the Syrian Orthodox Church in Iraq, based on Syriac sources, to demonstrate her piety.

5. Alemanni, *Procopii Caesarensis VI ANEKΔOTA*, 41; omitting *Anecd.* 9.10; 42 omitting 9.14 from ἀνακαγχάζειν to 9.25 ὅσοι δὲ. The passage concerning Theodora is on Alemanni, p. vi.

6. Montesquieu, *Considérations sur les causes de la grandeur des Romains et leur décadence* (Paris, 1900): 197; 194 (for the passage on Theodora quoted).

7. E. Gibbon, *The History of the Decline and Fall of the Roman Empire*, ed. D. Womersley (London, 1994) 2: 563 (the value of the *Secret History*); 565, for the passage on Theodora quoted in this text; and p. 565 n. 24 on the prelate. See also Averil Cameron, "Gibbon and Justinian," in R. McKitterick and R. Quinault, eds., *Edward Gibbon and Empire* (Cambridge, 1997): 38–45. For the text, see G. Ménage, *Menagiana; ou, Les bons mots et remarques critiques, historiques, morales & d'érudition*, 3rd ed. (Paris, 1715) 1: 347–352.

8. E. Renan, "L'histoire secrète de Procope," in E. Renan, *Essais de morale et de critique*, 4th ed. (Paris, 1889): 281–286.

9. Constant's *Empress Theodora* is in the National Museum of Fine Arts in Buenos Aires; *Theodora at the Colosseum* was most recently sold at auction by Schiller and Bodo in New York City; previously it was sold on November 8, 2007, for £42,500 at Christie's.

10. For an English translation of the play, see V. Sardou, *Theodora: A Drama in Five Acts and Eight Tableaux* (London, 1885); see also P. Cesaretti, *Theodora: Empress of Byzantium*, tr. R. M. Giammanco Frongia (New York, 2004): 20; 77–79.

11. C. Diehl, *Theodora*, tr. S. R. Rosenbaum (New York, 1972): 2.

12. *New York Times*, December 27, 1884, retrieved from "Sardou's Theodora," retrieved from http://query.nytimes.com/mem/archive-free/pdf?res=9901E2DE1F3BE033A25754C2A9649D94659FD7CF. For a review of the sort noted, see "Revue dramatique – Porte-Saint-Martin, Théodora de Victorien Sardou," retrieved from http://fr.wikisource.org/wiki/Revue_dramatique_-_Porte-Saint-Martin,_Th%C3%A9odora_de_Victorien_Sardou, concluding, "Restaurateur de Byzance, M. Sardou l'est sans doute, mais sans avoir ressuscité des âmes; il ne l'est pas comme l'auteur d'un drame, mais comme le poète d'une pantomime, le librettiste d'un ballet, ou l'inspirateur d'un panorama."

13. For Leroux's opera, see the review in *Musical Courier* 54 (1907), retrieved from https://books.google.com/books?id=W5xCAQAAMAAJ&pg=RA12-PA49&dq=Xavier+leroux+theodora&hl=en&sa=X&ei=TaylVKyKBI2GyATgmoGgAw&ved=0CC

gQ6AEwAA#v=onepage&q=Xavier%20leroux%20theodora&f=true; for the movie, see F. Carlà, "Prostitute, Saint, Pin-Up, Revolutionary: The Reception of Theodora in Twentieth-Century Italy," in S. Knippschild and M. Garcia Morcillo, eds., *Seduction and Power: Antiquity in the Visual and Performing Arts* (London, 2013): 244–245; the review mentioned in *New York Times,* October 15, 1921, retrieved from http://timesmachine.nytimes.com/timesmachine/1921/10/15/98753827.html.

14. Diehl, *Theodora,* 3–6; H.-G. Beck, *Kaiserin Theodora und Prokop: Der Historiker und sein Opfer* (Munich, 1986): 158.

Bibliography

Alemanni, N. 1623. *Procopii Caesarensis VI ANEKΔOTA Aracana Historia, Qui est Liber Nonus Historicorum ex Bibliotheca Vaticana.* Lyons.

Allen, P. 1981. *Evagrius Scholasticus the Church Historia.* Louvain.

Allen, P., and Hayward, C. T. R. 2004. *Severus of Antioch.* London.

Alpi, F. 2009. *La route royale: Sévère d'Antioche et les églises d'orient (512–518).* Beirut.

Andrade, N. 2009. "The Syriac Life of John of Tella and the Frontier Politeia." *Hugoye: Journal of Syriac Studies* 12: 199–234.

Angold, M. 1996. "Procopius' Portrait of Justinian." Pp. 21–54 in *ΦΙΛΕΛΛΗΝ, Studies in Honor of Robert Browning.* Venice.

Arjava, A. 1996. *Women and Law in Late Antiquity.* Oxford.

Bagnall, R. S. 1993. *Egypt in Late Antiquity.* Princeton.

Bagnall, R. S., and Cribiore, R. 2006. *Women's Letters from Ancient Egypt 300 BC–AD 800.* Ann Arbor.

Bagnall, R. S., and Frier, B. W. 1994. *The Demography of Roman Egypt.* Cambridge.

Baldwin, B. 1987. "Sexual Rhetoric in Procopius." *Mnemosyne* 40: 150–152.

Baldwin, B. 1992. "Three-Obol Girls in Procopius." *Hermes* 120: 255–257.

Banaji, J. 2001. *Agrarian Change in Late Antiquity: Gold, Labour, and Aristocratic Dominance.* Oxford.

Bardill, J. 1999. "The Great Palace of the Byzantine Emperors and the Walker Trust Excavations." *JRA* 12 (1999): 216–230.

Bardill, J. 2000. "The Church of Sts. Sergius and Bacchus in Constantinople and the Monophysite Refugees." *DOP* 54: 1–11.

Bardill, J. 2006. "Visualizing the Great Palace of the Byzantine Emperors at Constantinople: Archaeology, Text and Topography." Pp. 5–45 in F. A. Bauer, ed., *Visualisierung von Herrschaft frühmittelalterlicher Residenzen—Gestalt und Zeremoniell.* Istanbul.

Beck, H.-G. 1986. *Kaiserin Theodora und Prokop: Der Historiker und sein Opfer.* Munich.

Behnam, G. B. 2007. *Theodora,* tr. M. Moosa. Piscataway.

Bell, P. N. 2009. *Three Political Voices from the Age of Justinian*. Liverpool.

Bell, P. N. 2013. *Social Conflict in the Age of Justinian: Its Nature, Management, and Mediation*. Oxford.

Bjornlie, M. S. 2013. *Politics and Tradition between Rome, Ravenna and Constantinople: A Study of Cassiodorus and the* Variae. Cambridge.

Börm, H. 2007. *Prokop und die Perser: Untersuchungen zu den römisch-sasanidischen Kontakten in der ausgehenden Spätantike*. Stuttgart.

Börm, H. 2010. "Herrscher und Eliten in der Spätantike." Pp. 159–198 in H. Börm and J. Wiesehöfer, eds., *Commutatio und Contentio: Studies in the Late Roman, Sasanian and Early Islamic Near East in Memory of Zeev Rubin*. Düsseldorf.

Börm, H. 2013. "Justinians Triumph und Belisars Erniedrigung. Überlegungen zum Verhältnis zwischen Kaiser und Militär im späten Römischen Reich." *Chiron* 43: 66–75.

Börm, H. 2015. "Procopius, His Predecessors, and the Genesis of the *Anecdota*: Anti-monarchic Discourse in Late Antique Historiography." Pp. 1–32 in H. Börm, ed., *Antimonarchic Discourse in Antiquity*. Stüttgart.

Bowersock, G. W. 2006. *Mosaics as History: The Near East from Late Antiquity to Islam*. Cambridge, MA.

Bowersock, G. W. 2013. *The Throne of Adulis*. Oxford.

Brock, S. 1981. "The Conversations with the Syrian Orthodox under Justinian (532)." *Orientalia Christiana Periodica* 47: 87–121 (reprinted in S. Brock, *Studies in Syriac Christianity: History, Literature and Theology* [Brookfield, VT, 1992]).

Brock, S. 1985. "The Thrice Holy Hymn in the Liturgy." *Sobornost* 7.2: 24–34.

Brown, P. 1971. "The Rise and Function of the Holy Man in Late Antiquity." *JRS* 61: 80–100.

Brown, P. 1992. *Power and Persuasion in Late Antiquity: Towards a Christian Empire*. Madison.

Brown, P. 2002. *Poverty and Leadership in the Later Roman Empire*. Hanover.

Brown, P. 2012. *Through the Eye of a Needle: Wealth, the Fall of Rome, and the Making of Christianity in the West, 350–550 AD*. Princeton.

Brubacker, L. 2004. "Sex, Lies, and Intertextuality: The Secret History of Prokopios and the Rhetoric of Gender in Sixth Century Byzantium." Pp. 83–101 in L. Brubacker and J. M. H. Smith, *Gender in the Early Medieval World: East and West 300–900*. Cambridge.

Brubaker, L. 1997. "Memories of Helena: Patterns in Imperial Female Matronage in the Fourth and Fifth Centuries." Pp. 52–75 in L. James, ed., *Women, Men and Eunuchs: Gender in Byzantium*. London.

Brubaker, L. 2005. "The Age of Justinian: Gender and Society." Pp. 427–447 in M. Maas, *The Cambridge Companion to the Age of Justinian*. Cambridge.

Bury, J. B. 1897. "The Nika Revolt." *JHS* 17: 92–119.

Cameron, Alan. 1973. *Porphyrius the Charioteer*. Oxford.

Cameron, Alan. 1974. *Circus Factions*. Oxford.

Cameron, Alan. 1978. "The House of Anastasius." *GRBS* 19 (1978): 259–276.

Cameron, Alan, and Long, J., with a contribution by Sherry, L. 1993. *Barbarians and Politics at the Court of Arcadius.* Berkeley.

Cameron, Alan, and Schauer, D. 1982. "The Last Consul: Basilus and His Diptych." *JRS* 72: 126–145.

Cameron, Averil. 1969/1970. "Agathias on the Sassanians." *DOP* 23/24: 67–183.

Cameron, Averil. 1970. *Agathias.* Oxford.

Cameron, Averil. 1977. "Early Byzantine *Kaiserkritik:* Two Case Histories." *BMGS* 3: 1–17.

Cameron, Averil. 1978. "The Theotokos in Sixth-century Constantinople: A City Finds Its Symbol." *JTS* 29 (1978): 79–108.

Cameron, Averil. 1985. *Procopius and the Sixth Century.* London.

Cameron, Averil. 1987. "The Construction of Court Ritual: The Byzantine *Book of Ceremonies.*" Pp. 106–136 in D. Cannadine and S. Price, eds., *Rituals and Royalty: Power and Ceremonial in Traditional Societies.* Cambridge.

Cameron, Averil. 1997. "Gibbon and Justinian." Pp. 34–52 in R. McKitterick and R. Quinault, eds., *Edward Gibbon and Empire.* Cambridge.

Cameron, Averil, and Herrin, J. 1984. *Constantinople in the Eighth Century: The Parastaseis Syntomoi Chronikai.* Leiden.

Canepa, M. P. 2009. *The Two Eyes of the World: Art and Ritual Kingship between Rome and Sassanian Iran.* Berkeley.

Carlà, F. 2013. "Prostitute, Saint, Pin-Up, Revolutionary: The Reception of Theodora in Twentieth- Century Italy." Pp. 243–262 in S. Knippschild and M. Garcia Morcillo, eds., *Seduction and Power: Antiquity in the Visual and Performing Arts.* London.

Cesaretti, P. 2004. *Theodora: Empress of Byzantium.* Tr. R. M. Giammanco Frongia. New York.

Chastagnol, A. 1978. *L'Album municipal de Timgad.* Bonn.

Conrad, L. I. 2000. "Zeno the Epileptic Emperor: Historiography and Polemics as Sources of Realia." *BMGS* 24: 61–81.

Corcoran, S. 2009. "Anastasius, Justinian, and the Pagans: A Tale of Two Law Codes and a Papyrus." *JLA* 2: 183–208.

Croke, B. 1983. "Basiliscus the Boy-Emperor," *GRBS* 24: 81–91.

Croke, B. 1983. AD 476: The Manufacture of a Turning Point. *Chiron* 13: 81–119 (reprinted in B. Croke, *Christian Chronicles and Byzantine History, 5th-6th Centuries* [Aldershot, 1992] no. V).

Croke, B. 2001. *Count Marcellinus and His Chronicle.* Oxford.

Croke, B. 2005. "Justinian's Constantinople." Pp. 60–86 in M. Maas, *The Cambridge Companion to the Age of Justinian.* Cambridge.

Croke, B. 2005. "Procopius' *Secret History*: Rethinking the Date." *GRBS* 45: 405–431.

Croke, B. 2006. "Justinian, Theodora, and the Church of Sergius and Bacchus." *DOP* 60: 25–63.

Croke, B. 2007. "Justinian under Justin: Reconfiguring a Reign." *Byzantinische Zeitschrift* 100: 13–55.

Dagron, G. 1995. "Poissons, pêcheurs et poissonniers de Constantinople." Pp. 57–73 in C. Mango and G. Dagron, eds., *Constantinople and its Hinterland: Papers from the Twenty-seventh Spring Symposium for Byzantine Studies*. Oxford. April 1993. Aldershot.

Dagron, G. 2011. *L'hippodrome de Constantinople: jeux, peuple et politique*. Paris.

Dalby, A. 2003. *Flavours of Byzantium*. Totnes.

Dark, K. R., and Harris, L. R. 2008. "The Last Roman Forum: The Forum of Leo in Fifth-century Constantinople." *GRBS* 48: 57–69.

Daube, D. 1966–1967. "The Marriage of Justinian and Theodora. Legal and Theological Reflections." *Catholic University Law Review* 360: 380–399.

Declercq, G. 2002. "Dionysius Exiguus and the Introduction of the Christian Era." *Sacris Eruditi* 41: 165–246.

Deliyannis, D. 2010. *Ravenna in Late Antiquity*. Cambridge.

Detoraki, M., and Beaucamp, J. 2007. *Le martyre de saint Aréthas et de ses compagnons. BHG* 166. Centre National de la Recherche Scientifique. Centre de recherche d'histoire et civilisation de Byzance. Monographies no. 27. Paris.

Diehl, C. 1972. *Theodora: Empress of Byzantium*, tr. S. R. Rosenbaum. New York.

Dijkstra, J., and Greatrex, G. 2009. "Patriarchs and Politics in Constantinople in the Reign of Anastasius" (with a re-edition of "*O. Mon. Epiph.* 59." *Millennium* 6): 223–264.

Downey, G. 1961. *A History of Antioch in Syria from Seleucus to the Arab Conquest*. Princeton.

Duffy, J. 1984. "Byzantine Medicine in the Sixth and Seventh Centuries: Aspects of Teaching and Practice." *DOP* 38: 21–27.

Durliat, J. 1989–1991. "La peste du Vᵉ siècle: Pour un nouvel examen des sources byzantines." Pp. 107–119 in V. Kravari, C. Morrison, and J. Lefort, eds., *Hommes et richesses dans l'empire byzantine*. Paris.

Elton, H. 2000. "Illus and the Imperial Aristocracy under Zeno." *Byzantion* 70: 393–407.

Evans, J. A. S. 1971. "Christianity and Paganism in Procopius of Caesarea." *GRBS* 12 (1971): 81–100.

Evans, J. A. S. 1996. "The Dates of Procopius' Works: A Recapitulation of the Evidence." *GRBS* 37: 301–313.

Evans, J. A. S. 2002. *The Empress Theodora: Partner of Justinian*. Austin.

Evans, J. A. S. 2011. *The Power Game in Byzantium: Antonina and the Empress Theodora*. London.

Featherstone, J. M. 2006. "The Great Palace as Reflected in the *De Ceremoniis*." Pp. 47–61 in F. A. Bauer, ed., *Visualisierung von Herrschaft frühmittelalterlicher Residenzen—Gestalt und Zeremoniell*. Istanbul.

Fisher, E. A. 1978. "Theodora and Antonina in the *Historia Arcana*: History and/or Fiction." *Arethusa* 11: 253–257.

Fisher, G. 2011. *Between Empires: Arabs, Romans, and Sasanians in Late Antiquity*. Oxford.

Foss, C. 2002. "The Empress Theodora." *Byzantion* 72: 141–176.

Fowden, E. K. 1999. *The Barbarian Plain: Saint Sergius between Rome and Iran*. Berkeley.

French, D. R. 1998. "Maintaining Boundaries: The Status of Actresses in Early Christian Society." *Vigiliae Christianae* 52: 293–318.

Frend, W. H. C. 1972. *The Rise of the Monophysite Movement*. Cambridge.

Frier, B. W. 1983. "Roman Life Expectancy: The Pannonian Evidence." *Phoenix* 37: 328–344.

Gaddis, M. 2005. *There Is No Crime for Those Who Have Christ: Religious Violence in the Christian Roman Empire*. Berkeley.

Gardner, I., and Lieu, S. N. C. 2004. *Manichaean Texts from the Roman Empire*. Cambridge.

Garnsey, P. 1988. *Famine and Food Supply in the Graeco-Roman World*. Cambridge.

Gascou, J. 1976. "Les institutions de l'hippodrome en Égypte byzantine." *BIFAO* 76: 185–212.

Gascou, J. 1985. "Les grands domaines, la cité et l'état en Égypte byzantine: recherches d'histoire agraire, fiscale et administrative." *T&MByz* 9: 1–90.

Gibbon, E. 1994. *The History of the Decline and Fall of the Roman Empire*, ed. D. Womersley. London.

Glotz, A. 2009. "Die "Ende" des Weströmischen Reiches in der frühbyzantinischen syrischen Historiographie." Pp. 169–198 in A. Glotz, H. Leppin, and H. Schlange-Schoningen, eds., *Jensits der Grenzen: Beiträge zur spätantiken und frühmittelalterlichen Geschichtsschreibung*. Berlin.

Goodchild, R. G. 1976. "The 'Palace of the Dux'." Pp. 245–265 in R. G. Goodchild, J. G. Pedley, and D. White, *Apollonia: The Port of Cyrene: Excavations by the University of Michigan 1965–1968*. Supplements to *Libya Antiqua* IV. Spoleto.

Greatrex, G. 1996. "Flavius Hypatius: *Quem vidit validum Parthus sensitque timendum*. An Investigation into His Career." *Byzantion* 66: 120–142.

Greatrex, G. 1997. "The Nika Revolt—A Reappraisal." *JHS* 117: 60–86 (reprinted in Greatrex, G. 2003, "Recent Work on Procopius and the Composition of Wars VIII." *BMGS* 27: 45–67).

Greatrex, G. 2006. *Rome and Persia at War 502–532*, rev. ed. Cambridge.

Greatrex, G. 2007. "The Early Years of Justin I's Reign in the Sources." *Electrum* 12: 99–113.

Greatrex, G. 2014. "Perceptions of Procopius in Recent Scholarship." *Histos* 8: 76–121.

Greatrex, G., and Bardill, J. 1996. "Antiochus the 'Praepositus.' A Persian Eunuch at the Court of Theodosius II." *DOP* 50: 171–180.

Greatrex, G., and Lieu, S. N. C. 2002. *The Roman Eastern Frontiers and the Persian Wars, Part II: 365–630*. London.

Greatrex, G., ed., with Phenix, R. R., and Horn, C. B. (tr.). 2011. *The Chronicles of Pseudo-Zachariah Rhetor: Church and War in Late Antiquity.* Liverpool.

Grierson, P., Mango, C., and Sevcenko, I. 1962. "The Tombs and Obits of the Byzantine Emperors (337–1042); with an Additional Note." *DOP* 16: 1, 3–63.

Griffin, J. 1976. "Augustan Poetry and the Life of Luxury." *JRS* 66: 87–105.

Grimm, V. 2005. "On Food and the Body." Pp. 354–368 in D. S. Potter, ed., *A Companion to the Roman Empire.* Oxford.

Guilland, R. 1969. *Études de topographie de Constantinople byzantine. Berliner byzantinische Arbeiten.* Amsterdam.

Gwynn, D. M. 2007. *The Eusebians: The Polemic of Athanasius of Alexandria and the Construction of the "Arian Controversy."* Oxford.

Haarer, F. K. 2006. *Anastasius I: Politics and Empire in the Late Roman World.* Cambridge.

Harrison, M. 1989. *A Temple for Byzantium: The Discovery and Excavation of Anicia Juliana's Palace Church in Istanbul.* Austin.

Harvey, S. A. 1987. "Physicians and Ascetics in John of Ephesus: An Expedient Alliance." *DOP* 38: 87–93.

Harvey, S. A. 1990. *Asceticism and Crisis in Society: John of Ephesus and the Lives of the Eastern Saints.* Berkeley.

Harvey, S. A. 2001 (2010). "Theodora the 'Believing' Queen: A Study in Syriac Historiographical Tradition." *Hugoye: Journal of Syriac Studies* 4: 209–234.

Hatlie, P. 2006. "Monks and Circus Factions in Early Byzantine Political Life." Pp. 13–25 in M. Kaplan, ed., *Monastères, images, pouvoirs et société à Byzance.* Paris.

Hatlie, P. 2007. *The Monks and Monasteries of Constantinople ca. 350–850.* Cambridge.

Heather, P. 1986. "The Crossing of the Danube and the Gothic Conversion." *GRBS* 27: 289–319.

Hendy, M. 1985. *Studies in the Byzantine Monetary Economy c. 300–1450.* Cambridge.

Herrin, J. 2001. *Women in Purple: Rulers of Medieval Byzantium.* Princeton.

Herrin, J. 2013. *Unrivalled Influence: Women and Empire in Byzantium.* Princeton.

Hickey, T. 2012. *Wine, Wealth and the State in Late Antique Egypt.* Ann Arbor.

Holum, K. G. 1989. *Theodosian Empresses: Women and Imperial Dominion in Late Antiquity.* Berkeley.

Honoré, T. 1978. *Tribonian.* Ithaca.

Horden, P. 2005. "Mediterranean Plague in the Age of Justinian." Pp. 134–160 in M. Maas, ed., *The Cambridge Companion to the Age of Justinian.* Cambridge.

Humphrey, J. H. 1986. *Roman Circuses: Arenas for Chariot Racing.* Berkeley.

Jacoby, D. 1961. "La population de Byzance à l'époque byzantine: un problème de démographie urbaine." *BZ* 4: 81–109.

James, L. 2001. *Empresses and Power in Early Byzantium.* Leicester.

Jones, A. H. M. 1964. *The Later Roman Empire 284–602: A Social, Economic, and Administrative Survey.* Oxford.

Jones, C. P. 2014. *Between Pagan and Christian.* Cambridge, MA.

Kaldellis, A. 2004. *Procopius of Caesarea: Tyranny, History, and Philosophy at the End of Antiquity.* Philadelphia.

Kaldellis, A. 2009. "The Date and Structure of Procopius' *Secret History* and his Projected Work on Church History." *GRBS* 49: 585–616.

Kaldellis, A. 2010. *Procopios: The Secret History, with Related Texts.* Indianapolis.

Keenan, J. G. 1985. "Notes on Absentee Landlordism at Aphrodito." *BASP* 22: 137–169.

Kehoe, P. H. 1984. "The Adultery Mime Reconsidered." Pp. 89–106 in D. F. Bright and E. S. Ramage, eds., *Classical Texts and Their Traditions: Studies in Honor of C. R. Trahman.* Chico.

Kelly, C. 2004. *Ruling the Later Roman Empire.* Cambridge, MA.

Kennedy, H. 2007. "The Justinianic Plague in Syria and the Archaeological Evidence." Pp. 87–95 in Little, ed., *The Plague and the End of Antiquity.*

Kondoleon, C. 2001. *Antioch: The Lost City.* Princeton.

Kostenec, J. 2008. *Walking through Byzantium: Great Palace Region,* 2nd ed. Istanbul.

Lafferty, S. D. W. 2013. *Law and Society in the Age of Theoderic: A Study of the* Edictum Theoderici. Cambridge.

Laiou, A. 1981. "The Role of Women in Byzantine Society." *XVI. Internationaler Byzantinistenkongress.* Vienna. Akten I/1= *JÖB* 31: 233–260.

Lane Fox, R. J. 1994. "Literacy and Power in Early Christianity." Pp. 126–148 in A. Bowman and G. Woolf, eds., *Literacy and Power in the Ancient World.* Cambridge.

Lane Fox, R. J. 1997. "The Life of Daniel." Pp. 175–225 in M. J. Edwards and S. Swain, eds., *Portraits: Biographical Representation in the Greek and Latin Literature of the Roman Empire.* Oxford.

Lee, A. D. 2013. *From Rome to Byzantium AD 363–565: The Transformation of Ancient Rome.* Edinburgh.

Leppin, H. 2000. "Kaiserliche Kohabitation: Von der Normalität Theodoras." Pp. 75–85 in C. Kunst and U. Riemer, eds., *Grenzen der Macht: zur Rolle des römischen Kaiserfrauen.* Stuttgart.

Leppin, H. 2002. "Theodora und Iustinian." Pp. 437–481 in H. Temporini and G. Vitzthum, *Die Kaiserinnen Roms von Livia bis Theodora.* Munich.

Leppin, H. 2011 *Justinian: das christliche Experiment.* Stuttgart.

Liebeschuetz, J. H. G. W. 1990. *Barbarians and Bishops: Army, Church, and State in the Age of Arcadius and Chrysostom.* Oxford.

Liebeschuetz, J. H. G. W. 2001. *The Decline and Fall of the Roman City.* Oxford.

Little, L. K., ed., 2007. *The Plague and the End of Antiquity: The Pandemic of 541–750.* Cambridge.

Louth, A. 2009. "Why Did the Syrians Reject the Council of Chalcedon?" Pp. 107–116 in R. Price and M. Whitby, eds., *Chalcedon in Context: Church Councils 400–700.* Liverpool.

Luttwak, E. 2009. *The Grand Strategy of the Byzantine Empire.* Cambridge, MA.

Maas, M. 1986. "History and Ideology in Justinianic Reform Legislation." *DOP* 40: 17–32.

Maas, M. 1992. *John Lydus and the Roman Past: Antiquarianism and Politics in the Age of Justinian*. London.

Maas, M., ed., 2005. *The Cambridge Companion to the Age of Justinian*. Cambridge.

Macrides, R., and Magdalino, P. 1988. "The Architecture of Ekphrasis: Construction and Context of Paul the Silentiary's Poem on Hagia Sophia." *BMGS* 12: 47–82.

Mango, C. 2000. "The Triumphal Way of Constantinople and the Golden Gate." *DOP* 54: 173–188.

Maniatis, G. C., 2000. "The Organizational Setup and Functioning of the Fish Market in Tenth-Century Constantinople." *DOP* 54: 13–42.

Matthews, J. F. 2012. "The Notitia Urbis Constantinopolitanae." Pp. 81–115 in L. Grig and G. Kelly, eds., *Two Romes: Rome and Constantinople in Late Antiquity*. Oxford.

Mayer, W., and Allen, P. 2012. *The Churches of Syrian Antioch (300–638 AD)*. Leuven.

McCormick, M. 1986. *Eternal Victory: Triumphal Rulership in Late Antiquity, Byzantium and the Early Medieval West*. Cambridge.

McGinn, T. A. J. 1991. "Concubinage and the Lex Julia." *TAPA* 121: 335–375.

McGinn, T. A. J. 1997. "The Legal Definition of Prostitute in Late Antiquity." *Memoirs of the American Academy in Rome* 42: 73–116.

McGinn, T. A. J. 2004. *The Economy of Prostitution on the Roman World: A Study of Social History and the Brothel*. Ann Arbor.

McKinnon, C. A. 2011. "Trafficking, Prostitution and Inequality." *Harvard Civil-Rights Civil-Liberties Law Review* 46: 271–309.

Meier, M. 2002. "Das Ende des Konsulats im Jahr 541/42 und seine Gründe: kritische Anmerkungen zur Vorstellung eines 'Zeitalters Justinians.'" *ZPE* 138: 277–299.

Meier, M. 2003. *Das andere Zeitalter Justinians: Kontingenzerfahrung und kontingenz-bewältung im 6. Jahrhundert n. Chr.* Hypomnemata 147. Göttingen.

Meier, M. 2003. "Die Inszenierung einer Katastrophe: Justinian und der Nika-Aufstand." *ZPE* 142: 273–300.

Meier, M. 2004. "Zur Funktion der Theodora-Rede im Geschichtswerk Prokops (BP 1,24,33–37)." *RhM* 147: 88–104.

Meier, M. 2008. "Σταυρωθεὶς δι' ἡμᾶς: Der Aufstand gegen Anastasios im Jahr 512." *Millennium* 4: 157–238.

Meier, M. 2009. *Anastasios I. Die Entstehung des Byzantinischen Reiches*. Stuttgart.

Menze, V. L. 2008. *Justinian and the Making of the Syrian Orthodox Church*. Oxford.

Merrills, A., and Miles, R. 2010. *The Vandals*. Oxford.

Millar, F. 2006. *A Greek Roman Empire: Power and Belief under Theodosius II 408–450*. Berkeley.

Millar, F. 2008. "Rome, Constantinople and the Near Eastern Church under Justinian: Two Synods of CE 536." *JRS* 98: 62–82.

Mitchell, S. 1993. *Anatolia: Land, Men, and Gods in Anatolia*, 2 vols. Oxford.

Moberg, A. 1924. *The Book of the Himyarites*. Lund.

Modéran, Y. 2002. "L'établissement territorial des Vandales en Afrique." *An. Tard.* 10: 87–122.

Modéran, Y. 2003. "Une guerre de religion: les deux églises d'Afrique à l'époque vandale." *An. Tard.* 11: 21–44.

Montesquieu. 1900. *Considérations sur les causes de la grandeur des Romains et leur décadence.* Paris.

Moorhead, J. 1992. *Theodoric in Italy.* Oxford.

Moorhead, J. 1994. *Justinian.* New York.

Morony, M. G. 2007. "'For Whom Does the Writer Write?': The First Bubonic Plague Pandemic According to Syriac Sources." Pp. 59–86 in Little, ed., *The Plague and the End of Antiquity.*

Mueller, I. 2010. "Single Women in the Roman Funerary Inscriptions." *ZPE* 175: 295–303.

Müller, A. E. 1993. "Getreide für Konstantinopel. Überlegungen zu Justinians Edikt XIII als Grundlage für Aussagen zu Einwohnerzahl des Konstantinopels im 6. Jh." *JÖB* 43: 1–20.

Noethlichs, K. L. 2000. "'Quid possit antiquitatis nostris legibus abrogare?': Politische Propaganda und praktische Politik bei Justinian I im Lichte der kaiserlichen Gesetzgebung und der antiken Historiographie." *ZAC* 4 (2000): 116–132 (reprinted in M. Meier, ed., *Justinian: neue Wege der Forschung* [Darmstadt, 2011]).

Nutton, V. 1984. "From Galen to Alexander: Aspects of Medicine and Medical Practise in Late Antiquity." *DOP* 38: 1–14.

O'Donnell, J. J. 1979. *Cassiodorus.* Berkeley.

O'Donnell, J. J. 2008. *The Ruin of the Roman Empire.* New York.

Osborne, J. L. 1981. "Early Medieval Painting in San Clemente, Rome: The Madonna and Child in the Niche." *Gesta* 20: 299–310.

Papadopoulos, J. R., and Ruscillo, D. 2003. "A *Ketos* in Early Athens: An Archaeology of Whales and Sea Monsters on the Greek World." *AJA* 106 (2003): 187–227.

Parejko, K. 2003. "Pliny the Elder's Silphium: First Recorded Species Extinction." *Conservation Biology* 17: 925–927.

Patlagean, E. 1977. *Pauvreté économique et pauvreté sociale à Byzance 4ᵉ–7ᵉ siècles.* Paris.

Pazdernik, C. 1994. "'Our Most Pious Consort Given Us by God': Dissident Reactions to the Partnership of Justinian and Theodora, 525–548." *CA* 13: 256–281.

Pedley, J. G. 1976. "The History of the City." Pp. 11–28 in R. G. Goodchild, J. G. Pedley, and D. White, *Apollonia: The Port of Cyrene. Excavations by the University of Michigan 1965–1968.* Supplements to *Libya Antiqua* IV. Spoleto.

Potter, D. S. 2011. "Anatomies of Violence: Entertainment and Violence in the Eastern Roman Empire from Theodosius I to Heraclius." *Studia Patristica* 60: 61–72.

Potter, D. S. 2011. "Lot Oracles from Asia Minor." *JRA* 24: 764–772.

Potter, D. S. 2013. *Constantine the Emperor.* Oxford.

Potter, D. S. 2014. *The Roman Empire at Bay AD 180–395*, 2nd ed. London.

Pourshariati, P. 2008. *Decline and Fall of the Sasanian Empire: The Sasanian–Parthian Confederacy and the Arab Conquest of Iran.* London.

Pratsch, T. 2011. *Theodora von Byzanz: Kurtisane und Kaiserin.* Stuttgart.

Price, R. 2009. "The Council of Chalcedon (451): A Narrative." Pp. 70–91 in R. Price and Mary Whitby, eds., *Chalcedon in Context: Church Councils 400–700.* Liverpool.

Rey-Coquais, J. P. 2006. *Inscriptions grecques et latines de Tyre.* Beirut.

Reynolds, J. 1976. "The Inscriptions of Apollonia." Pp. 293–233 in R. G. Goodchild, J. G. Pedley, and D. White, *Apollonia: The Port of Cyrene. Excavations by the University of Michigan 1965–1968.* Supplements to *Libya Antiqua* IV. Spoleto.

Reynolds, R. W. 1946. "The Adultery Mime." *CQ* 40: 77–84.

Roueché, C. 1993. *Performers and Partisans at Aphrodisias in the Roman and Late Roman Periods. JRS* Monograph 6. London.

Roueché, C. 2007. "Spectacles in Late Antiquity: Some Observations." *An. Tard.* 15: 59–64.

Roussel, A. 1998. *Porneia: On Desire and the Body in Antiquity,* tr. F. Pheasant. Oxford.

Rubin, B. 1960. *Die Zeitalter Iustinians,* vol. 1. Berlin.

Rubin, B. 1995. *Das Zeitalter Iustinians,* vol. 2, ed. C. Capizzi. Berlin.

Rubin, Z. 1995. "The Reforms of Khusro Anushirwan." Pp. 227–297 in A. Cameron, ed., *The Byzantine and Early Islamic Near East,* vol. 3: *States, Resources and Armies.* Princeton.

Ruscu, D. 2008. "The Revolt of Vitalianus and the 'Scythian Controversy'." *BZ* 101: 773–785.

Sallares, R. 2007. "Ecology, Evolution, and the Epidemiology of Plague." Pp. 231–289 in Little, ed., *The Plague and the End of Antiquity.*

Sardou, V. 1885. *Theodora: A Drama in Five Acts and Eight Tableaux.* London.

Sarris, P. 2006. *Economy and Society in the Age of Justinian.* Cambridge.

Sarris, P. 2007. "Bubonic Plague in Byzantium." Pp. 119–132 in Little, ed., *The Plague and the End of Antiquity.*

Scarborough, J. 2013. "Theodora, Aëtius of Amida and Procopius: Some Possible Connections." *GRBS* 53: 742–762.

Scott, R. 1985. "Malalas, the *Secret History,* and Justinian's Propaganda." *DOP* 39: 99–109.

Shahîd, I. 1964. "Byzantino-Arabica: The Conference of Ramla AD 524." *JNES* 23: 115–131.

Shahîd, I. 1971. *The Martyrs of Najrân.* Subsidia Hagiographica 49. Brussels.

Sidebotham, H. 2011. *Berenike and the Ancient Maritime Spice Route.* Berkeley.

Soler, E. 2007. "L'état romain face au baptême et aux pénuries d'acteurs et d'actrices, dans l'antiquité tardive." *An. Tard.* 15: 47–58.

Stein, E. 1949. *Histoire du bas-empire,* vol. 2. Brussels.

Syme, R. 1972. The *Titulus Tibertinus.* Pp. 585–601 in *Akten des VI Internationalen Kongress für Griechische und Lateinische Epigraphik.* Munich (reprinted in R. Syme, *Roman Papers,* ed. A. Birley [Oxford, 1984]: 869–884).

Tate, G. 2004. *Justinien: l'épopée de l'Empire d'Orient.* Paris.

Tinnefeld, F. H. 1971. *Kategorien der Kaiserkritik in der byzantinischen Historiographie von Prokop bis Niketas Choniates.* Munich.

Treggiari, S. 1981. "*Concubinae.*" *PBSR* 49: 59–81.

Treggiari, S. 1991. *Roman Marriage:* Iusti Coniuges *from the Time of Cicero to the Time of Ulpian.* Oxford.

Trombley, F. R. 1985. "Paganism in the Greek World at the End of Antiquity: The Case of Rural Anatolia and Greece." *HTR* 78: 327–352.

Tsitsiridis, S. 2011. "Greek Mime in the Roman Empire (*P.Oxy.* 413: *Charition* and *Moicheutria*)." *Logeion* 1: 184–232.

Urbainczyk, T. 2002. *Theodoret of Cyrrhus: The Bishop and Holy Man.* Ann Arbor.

van Roey, A., and Allen, P. 1994. *Monophysite Texts of the Sixth Century. Orientalia Lovaniensia Analecta* 56. Leuven.

Vasiliev, A. A. 1950. *Justin the First.* Cambridge, MA.

Vesterinen, M. 2007. *Dancers and Professional Dancers in Roman Egypt.* Ph.D. thesis, University of Helsinki.

Vikan, G. 1984. "Art, Medicine and Magic in Early Byzantium." *DOP* 38: 65–86.

Walker, J. T. 2002. "The Limits of Late Antiquity." *AW* 33: 45–69.

Watts, E. J. 2004. "Justinian, Malalas, and the End of Athenian Philosophical Teaching in AD 529." *JRS* 94: 168–183.

Watts, E. J. 2006. *City and School in Late Antique Athens and Alexandria.* Berkeley.

Watts, E. J. 2010. *Riot in Alexandria: Tradition and Group Dynamics in Latin Antique Pagan and Christian Communities.* Berkeley.

Webb, R. 2008. *Demons and Dancers: Performance in Late Antiquity.* Cambridge, MA.

Weitzer, R. 2011. *Legalizing Prostitution: From Illicit Vice to Lawful Business.* New York.

Weitzmann, K., ed., 1979. *Age of Spirituality: Late Antique and Early Christian Art, Third to Seventh Century.* Catalogue of exhibition at the Metropolitan Museum of Art, November 11, 1977, through February 12, 1978. New York.

Whitby, Mary. 1985. "The Occasion of Paul the Silentiary's *Ekphrasis* of S. Sophia." *CQ* 35: 215–228.

Whitby, Mary. 2006. "The St. Polyeuktos Epigram (*AP* 10): A Literary Perspective." Pp. 159–188 in S. F. Fitzgerald, ed., *Greek Literature in Late Antiquity: Dynamism, Didacticism, Classicism.* Aldershot.

Whitby, Michael. 1995. "Recruitment in Roman Armies from Justinian to Heraclius (ca. 565–615)." Pp. 61–124 in A. Cameron, ed., *The Byzantine and Early Islamic Near East,* vol. 3: *States, Resources, Armies.* Princeton.

Whitby, Michael. 1998. "The Violence of the Circus Factions." Pp. 229–253 in K. Hopwood, ed., *Organized Crime in Antiquity.* Swansea.

Wickham, C. 2005. *Framing the Early Middle Ages: Europe and the Mediterranean 400–800.* Oxford.

Wiemken, H. 1972. *Der griechischer Mimus: Dokumente zur Geschichte des antiken Volkstheaters.* Bremen.

Wolfram, H. 1988. *History of the Goths*, tr. T. J. Dunlap. Berkeley.

Yasin, A. M. 2009. *Saints and Church Spaces in the Late Antique Mediterranean: Architecture, Cult and Community*. Cambridge.

Young, G. K. 2001. *Rome's Eastern Trade: International Commerce and Imperial Policy 31 BC–AD 305*. London.

Index